DATE DUE

VICTORIAN HERETIC

The Bookman (London), 1903

Mrs Humphry Ward

VICTORIAN HERETIC
Mrs Humphry Ward's *Robert Elsmere*

By
WILLIAM S. PETERSON

LEICESTER UNIVERSITY PRESS
1976

First published in 1976 by Leicester University Press
Distributed in North America by Humanities Press, Inc., New Jersey

Set in IBM Aldine Roman
Printed in Great Britain by Unwin Brothers Limited,
The Gresham Press, Old Woking, Surrey
Bound by Remploy Ltd (Bookbinding Division), Swansea

ISBN 0 7185 1147 6

To

FREDERIC E. FAVERTY

CONTENTS

Preface   *page* ix

Chapter 1   Mrs Ward and the Twentieth Century   1

Chapter 2   The Arnolds of Fox How   17

Chapter 3   Juvenilia   43

Chapter 4   Mrs Ward's Oxford   61

Chapter 5   The Novelist as Critic   85

Chapter 6   The Writing of *Robert Elsmere*   108

Chapter 7   *Robert Elsmere*: An Analysis   131

Chapter 8   *Robert Elsmere* and Its Readers   159

Chapter 9   Elsmere's Heirs   185

Epilogue   207

Appendix A   The *Robert Elsmere* Notebook   213

Appendix B   Sales of *Robert Elsmere*   221

Notes   223

Bibliography   237

Index   253

PREFACE

From the moment I began working on this book, I have enjoyed the generous cooperation of Mrs Mary Moorman, Mrs Ward's granddaughter and the owner of her literary rights. She has answered endless questions, made manuscript material available to me, and shown personal hospitality to me and my wife. For her many acts of kindness I am very grateful indeed.

I am also indebted to several persons who have read the book in typescript and offered useful suggestions. Professor Lawrence Evans of Northwestern University and my colleague Professor G. A. Cate have read the entire typescript; Professor John O. Waller of Andrews University provided stimulating criticisms of Chapter 2. My friend Norman W. Webster has shared with me his extensive knowledge of Mrs Ward's career. Mrs Enid Huws Jones gave me some helpful advice and allowed me to read her book on Mrs Ward while it was still in proofs.

I have received research grants from the following sources while writing this book: the American Council of Learned Societies, the Newberry Library (Chicago), and the University of Maryland General Research Board. The libraries that have given me permission to quote unpublished materials are indicated in my notes.

The following individuals have also assisted me in various ways: Mrs Georgina Battiscombe, Professor James Bertram, Professor James T. Covert, Arthur V. Coyne, Esq, the Revd C. S. Dessain (the Birmingham Oratory), Miss Ruth M. Hauser (the Honnold Library, Claremont University), Dr

Earle Hilgert, Dr Park Honan, Professor Walter Houghton, Professor P. A. Howell, W. L. Kitney, Esq (the Mary Ward Centre), Mr Robert C. Lester, Mrs Susan Martin, the Revd F. H. Maycock (Pusey House), Mrs Mary Jane Mitchell (the James White Library, Andrews University), Miss Winifred A. Myers, Dr N. A. Nilsson, Joseph W. Scott, Esq (the Library of University College, London), Dr Lola L. Szladits (the Berg Collection, the New York Public Library), Anthony Watkinson, Esq, Mr James Wells (the Newberry Library), Mr Arnold Whitridge, and Professor Basil Willey.

Part of Chapter 8 originally appeared in the *Review of English Studies* (November 1970) and is reprinted here by permission of Oxford University Press.

Finally, I must add that writing this book has left me two especially pleasant memories. Although I used many libraries, I did most of my research at the Newberry Library, an institution that provides a most congenial environment for scholars; on many gray autumn and winter days I found working in the Newberry so delightful that I entirely forgot the cold weather outside. I also remember a summer day in Longsleddale when I knocked unannounced at the door of what was once the vicarage (where Robert Elsmere was staying at the beginning of Mrs Ward's novel). Mr and Mrs John Kremer invited my wife and me in to tea, showed us around the valley, and displayed altogether remarkable courtesy to their unexpected visitors.

University of Maryland   W.S.P.
January 1976

VICTORIAN HERETIC

Chapter 1
MRS WARD AND THE TWENTIETH CENTURY

She was denying no old affection, deserting no ancient loyalty. Old and new:—she seemed to be the child of both—gathering them both into her breast.

—*Canadian Born* (p. 523)

I

On 28 March 1920, at the funeral of Mrs Humphry Ward, Dean Inge of St Paul's described her as 'perhaps the greatest Englishwoman of our time'.[1] The private thoughts which he recorded in his diary that evening, however, were both more cautious and more revealing:

It is difficult to predict how far her great reputation as a novelist will be lasting. The immense sale of *Robert Elsmere* was not due entirely to the merits of the book, and there is something soigné about her style which will not conduce to popularity. It may be that after a period of undeserved neglect her novels may be recognised as giving an accurate picture of the life of the upper and upper-middle class in the last generation of their prosperity.[2]

From the perspective of half a century later, we are able to see how really astute a prophet the Dean was. One of the most widely read novelists in England and America during her lifetime, Mrs Ward was already in 1920 quietly slipping into the ranks of forgotten authors (in that year Havelock Ellis, with only slight exaggeration, described her as 'probably unknown to the present generation'[3]), and, except for the obligatory biography by her daughter published in 1923 and a

1

more recent life by Mrs Huws Jones, remarkably little has been written about Mrs Ward since her death.

Yet even her severest critics acknowledge her virtues: she was intelligent, though immensely popular her fiction was rarely cheap or sensational, and her books were skilfully written in workmanlike fashion. 'How unjust it is that Mrs Humphry Ward, with her well-stored mind and her command of language, with her solid gifts, her conscientiousness and seriousness, should be so forgotten that even her name will be unknown to most readers today', wrote Somerset Maugham in 1952.[4] If Mrs Ward is now admired at all, it is—as Dean Inge foresaw—by the intellectual and ecclesiastical historians, who find in her novels the most complete literary record of late Victorian and Edwardian life. 'Trollope and Mrs. Ward', according to Sir Arthur Conan Doyle, 'have the whole Victorian civilization dissected and preserved.' It is all there in her novels, said Doyle—the late Victorian 'transition period, its mental unrest, its groping after new truths, its sharp contrasts between old conditions and new problems'.[5] As an observer of the social and intellectual life of late nineteenth-century England, Mrs Ward is clearly unsurpassed. But to claim no more for her is surely to damn with faint praise; no novelist wishes to think of himself or herself as merely the author of a series of valuable historical documents. We are still left wondering what happened to Mrs Ward's reputation as a literary artist, and why the sales of her books plummeted so dramatically during the last decade of her life. More importantly, we must ask ourselves whether the adverse judgment of Lytton Strachey's generation upon her work—which has not been seriously challenged to this day—is a just one.

It is not coincidental that Strachey's vitriolic portrait of Dr Arnold in *Eminent Victorians* (1918) was in part inspired by his personal hatred of the Doctor's granddaughter,[6] for Mrs Ward was perceived by the young men and women of that day as the living embodiment of Victorianism. (One unpublished essay which Strachey left behind at his death, incidentally, was an imaginary satiric dialogue between Mrs Ward and Cleopatra.[7]) Mrs Ward was born in 1851, the year of the Great Exhibition; she died two years after the holocaust of the Great War, and it is evident to anyone who reads her memoirs that the literary and cultural values of the new century seemed alien to one whose mind had been formed by Carlyle, Matthew Arnold, and Charlotte Mary Yonge. Not surprisingly, to the iconoclastic younger generation, Mrs Ward in her old age was an irresistible target for satire and ridicule. H. G. Wells' *Boon* (1915), for instance, solemnly offered this piece of information about her: 'Rumour that she is represented at the base of the Queen Victoria Memorial unfounded' (p. 155). Ezra Pound, in his poem 'Moeurs Contemporaines' (1915), satirized 'the Great Mary' as one who could be readily confused with the Virgin Mother. Rebecca West, in the most venomous attack of all, called Mrs Ward's literary career 'one long specialisation in the *mot injuste*' and ridiculed her 'assumptions of Papacy, her narrow political views and her limitless faith in the decency and respectability of reaction'.[8]

Was Mrs Ward, then, merely another victim of the rampant anti-Victorianism of the early decades of this century? It is a seductive theory, but in fact the complaints about the anachronistic quality of her novels can be traced well back into the nineteenth century. Already in 1892 George Gissing was observing that 'of course she has a mature mind, and wide knowledge; but artistically I believe she is at the very point I had reached, after study of George Eliot, some ten years ago'.[9] It should also be noticed that Mrs Ward's spectacular popular success was in itself a source of suspicion: Arnold Bennett declared in 1895 that though he had never read any of her novels, he felt instinctively that Mrs Ward was 'No Good', yet when he finally looked at the first instalment of *The Story of Bessie Costrell* he acknowledged, most unwillingly, that it was 'damn well done'. He found the writing 'without being great' nevertheless 'dignified and decent' and confessed that 'she is a real artist'. 'But', he added, 'one does not part easily or painlessly with the conviction of half a lifetime. I

have always said that Mrs. Humphry Ward never had done,
never could & never would do, anything decent.' (Bennett
later reverted to his original opinion—or rather prejudice—
and in 1908 offered the earnest wish that all of Mrs Ward's
heroines might be raped *en masse* by an invading army.)[10]

The fullest and most systematic effort ever made to diminish Mrs Ward's reputation during her lifetime was by a Yale
professor, William Lyon Phelps, who publicly announced in
1905 that 'it is high time somebody spoke out his mind about
Mrs. Humphry Ward. Her prodigious vogue', he declared, 'is
one of the most extraordinary literary phenomena of our
day.' Mrs Ward's books he found lacking in humour (a fact
that she herself admitted), in a sense of proportion, in charm,
and in freshness, spontaneity, and originality. That she was
not an entirely mediocre novelist, Phelps was ready to grant;
but neither was she very distinguished, and he insisted that
critics ought to stop writing of her as if she were the equal of
George Eliot or Tolstoy.[11]

It is at least arguable, however, that the primary grievance
of these disgruntled contemporaries was not the literary quality of Mrs Ward's novels but rather her formidable public
personality. She dined with bishops and prime ministers, pon-
tificated on political questions in lengthy letters to *The Times*,
and generally gave the impression of peering down serenely
(never 'storm-tossed', as Stopford Brooke said[12]) at modern
life from the Olympian heights of a complacent intellectual-
ism. Was there ever, it was asked, so thoroughly an Establishment figure as Mrs Ward? Bernard Shaw claimed that the
ultimate test of social respectability in London was whether
one could take Mrs Ward in to dinner—and Frank Harris, as
Shaw pointed out, could unfortunately not pass this test.[13]

Her private personality was of course another matter: those
who knew her well agreed that she was unpretentious, modest, and shy. In fact, if she had one conspicuous fault, it was
not egotism but an idolatrous devotion to work. Unlike most
readers of Trollope's *Autobiography*, she was not dismayed
by the revelation of his methodical, businesslike approach to

novel-writing;[14] she herself habitually rose at dawn and wrote energetically all morning, then devoted the rest of the day to an extraordinary range of public responsibilities. 'You do more real work, quantity and quality—than any woman I know', her publisher once told her.[15] She was, it appears, a representative product of the bourgeois ethic of industriousness, and her novel *David Grieve* is, from one point of view, merely Samuel Smiles' *Self-Help* writ large.

II

Mrs Ward was truly a Victorian—the youthful debunkers who mocked her were absolutely correct on that point—and this is particularly evident in her profound belief in an absolute, unchangeable moral law. Christian dogma she was quite willing, even eager, to discard, but (or should one say 'therefore'?) traditional ethical standards were completely sacred. We live, according to Mrs Ward, in 'a world at the heart of which broods a power austere and immutable; a power which man did not make, which, if he clash with it, grinds him to powder'.[16] In this statement one has very nearly the major theme of Mrs Ward's fiction—the immutability of Divine law (though the character of the Divinity behind it is a trifle obscure) and the futility of all human rebellion against it. 'What if after all the beaten roads are best?' she asks in one of her novels.[17] The answer, for her, is that the beaten roads are indeed best (except, of course, in theology). No orthodox Christian ever distrusted human passion more nor held a higher view of the sacredness of marriage than Mrs Ward who puts this speech into the mouth of David Grieve:

I have come to think the most disappointing and hopeless marriage, nobly borne, to be better worth having than what people call an "ideal passion,"—if the ideal passion must be enjoyed at the expense of one of those fundamental rules which human nature has worked out, with such infinite difficulty and pain, for the protection of its own weakness. (ii, 496)

Human laws share in this mysterious quality of awesomeness,

because they too are dykes holding back the surging tides of passion and instinct. Laws are the highest proof 'of some diviner power than our own will—our best clue to what that power may be!'[18]

All of this, needless to say, is a classic expression of conservatism, rather in the style of Burke, and it leaves one wondering how Mrs Ward could ever have been mistaken for a radical or even a liberal, as she frequently was during the early part of her career. By way of explanation, we should remind ourselves that her theological position, as outlined in *Robert Elsmere*, was genuinely 'advanced'. It is a curious fact that such a combination of attitudes—conservative morality and revolutionary theology—was not unusual among eminent Victorians.

Mrs Ward did also flirt with political liberalism for a time. In a letter to her mother, 3 March 1882, she remarked, 'Goldwin Smith came too and was very talkative & interesting. It did my Radical heart good to hear him discussing the various possible ways of abolishing the House of Lords.' However, in time events in Ireland drove her into the Tory camp. In 1880 she visited Dublin as the guest of her uncle William E. Forster, then Chief Secretary for Ireland, and walked with him through the Phoenix Park where slightly more than a year later Forster's successor was murdered by Irish patriots. Here were violence and social disorder viewed at close proximity, and like many other English observers at the time, Mrs Ward recoiled with horror. The Irish question so seized her imagination that 'night after night', as she later recalled, 'I would sit up half asleep to listen to the different phases of the story when in the early hours of the morning my husband came back from the *Times*, brimful of news, which he was as eager to tell as I to hear'.[19]

Mrs Ward's political conservatism, which increased with age, manifested itself in various ways in her novels. It led, for example, to a glorification of the English countryside, generally viewed through the window of a 'stately home', as in this typical passage in *The Marriage of William Ashe*:

The formal garden, the Georgian conservatory, the park, the river, the church—they breathed England, and the traditional English life. All that they implied, of custom and inheritance, of strength and narrowness, of cramping prejudice and stubborn force, was very familiar to Ashe, and on the whole very congenial. He was glad to be an Englishman and a member of an English government. (p. 71)

Mrs Ward built herself a country house near Haslemere with the royalties from *Robert Elsmere*, but its very newness seemed to her a serious drawback. Within a week after moving into it, she wrote her husband that she doubted 'whether I shall be content ultimately without an old house & old trees. If one may covet anything I think one may covet this kind of inheritance from the past to shelter one's own later life in. Life seems so short to make anything quite fresh in.'[20] Fulfilling this prophecy, the Wards two years later purchased Stocks, an estate near Tring which had been mentioned in Domesday Book and which nestled in a beautiful valley beneath the Chiltern hills. Mrs Ward, like her fictional heroines, found in a traditional country house the fullest expression of a desirable sense of continuity with the past. For one who was often publicly condemned for her liberal theology— and who shrank, as she said, 'from the violent contrasts of opinion her work calls forth'[21] —such a visible link with English history was a psychological necessity.

Another evidence of her growing conservatism was Mrs Ward's prolonged anti-suffrage campaign, which she carried on by means of public rallies, political manoeuvring (at which she became very adept), and propagandistic novels on the subject. Mrs Ward's anti-suffrage stance struck many observers as paradoxical, since she had been a leader in establishing women's colleges at Oxford, was probably England's best-known living woman writer, and was herself enormously active in political affairs (though as a rule discreetly behind the scenes). In fact, she campaigned so strenuously on behalf of her son Arnold for a parliamentary seat that, once elected, he became known as 'the Member for Mrs Humphry Ward'.

But Mrs Ward's inconsistency was only apparent. That the

highest moral act, especially for women, is submission rather than self-assertion is one of the dominant themes of her fiction; and it is this idea, derived ultimately from her childhood Evangelical training—and not the elaborate (and spurious) reasons which she offered in speeches and letters to newspapers—which really explains her opposition to suffrage. Duties, not 'rights': that was Mrs Ward's unheeded rallying-cry to the women of her day. The wife's responsibility was to be the Angel in the House, to provide a spiritual haven to which the husband, bruised and dusty after a day in the busy outside world, could retreat for solace in the evening. As one of her male characters (a Radical, no less) says: 'We've got somehow to push and harry and drive this beastly world into some sort of decency. But the women!—oughtn't they to be in the shrine—tending the mystic fire? What if the fire goes out—if the heart of the nation dies?'[22] A more perfect expression of the mid-Victorian view of woman's role could not be found, not even in Dickens or Trollope, though it is qualified by Mrs Ward's conviction that women should shape public events by working quietly in the background.

In the struggle for women's rights, Mrs Ward saw 'an element of fever, of madness, which poisons life'.[23] She tried to give expression to this vision of impending moral chaos in her novel *Delia Blanchflower* (1915), which culminates in a fanatical suffragette burning down Monk Lawrence, a country house of extraordinary beauty and historical importance. Monk Lawrence represents all of those hereditary, cherished values of English life which had filled the vacuum left in Mrs Ward's imagination by the disintegration of Christian orthodoxy; and Gertrude Marvell, the demented, self-destructive suffragette, was to Mrs Ward the embodiment of new, ominous forces at loose in the world which threatened the established social order.

III

Indeed, it might be argued that the central parable of Mrs Ward's novels (and life) is that of Tennyson's 'Palace of Art'.

In that poem, it will be recalled, the soul builds for herself 'a lordly pleasure-house', filled with exquisite statuary, paintings, 'long-sounding corridors', and cloistered courtyards, and well removed from the peasants in the valley below. Suddenly, however, from the dark corners of the palace 'uncertain shapes' and 'white-eyed phantasms' menacingly appear, and the soul flees to 'a cottage in the vale', where she vows to mourn and pray for four years to atone for her sin of selfish isolation. However, in the final stanza the soul offers this plea:

> Yet pull not down my palace towers, that are
> So lightly, beautifully built:
> Perchance I may return with others there
> When I have purged my guilt.

The equivocal conclusion is as characteristic of the age as the dilemma itself: how to preserve the beauty, art, and noble traditions of the past while at the same time extending their benefits to the unfortunate masses. It is a problem which troubled, even haunted, all sensitive Victorians. As late as 1886, in *The Princess Casamassima*, one can find Henry James, acutely responsive to the complexities of the situation, refashioning Tennyson's parable but, unlike the poet, offering no facile solution. His protagonist, caught hopelessly between the claims of the mellow old culture and the austere moral appeal of anarchism, can only put a gun to his own head.

In *Marcella* (1894), which bears a strikingly close resemblance to James' novel, Mrs Ward directly confronts the same problem, yet her answer, as one might expect, is closer to Tennyson's; she wants to open the gates of the Palace of Art so as to share it with the deserving poor. Marcella Boyce, her young heroine, who has been trained in the principles of socialism, unexpectedly finds herself installed on a fine estate and being wooed by a Tory gentleman. For a time Marcella so angrily and stridently asserts her liberal views that her lover is alienated, but at the end of the third volume they marry after all, and presumably in this union the warring

social philosophies are reconciled. Unlike the later suffragettes, Marcella declinés to burn down the house of culture in
the name of social justice. Instead she becomes the tolerant
and generous mistress of that house.

The Tennysonian parable also appears elsewhere in Mrs
Ward's fiction, as in the following dialogue in *Fenwick's
Career*:

'It [the Palace of Versailles] gives me a perfect hunger for fine
clothes, and jewels, and masquerades—and "fêtes de nuit"—and every
sort of theatricality and expense! Nature has sent us starvelings on the
scene a hundred years late. We are like children in the rain, flattening
our noses against a ballroom window.'
'There were plenty of them then,' said Eugenie. 'But they broke in
and sacked the ballroom.'
'Yes. What folly,' he said bitterly. 'We are still groping among the
ruins.'
'No, no! Build a new Palace of Beauty—and bring everybody in—out
of the rain.' (pp. 241-2)

Frequently Mrs Ward portrays a selfish inhabitant of the
Palace of Art who hoards up his wealth and artistic treasures
—Wendover in *Robert Elsmere*, Melrose in *The Mating of
Lydia*, and Mannering in *The War and Elizabeth* are the most
notable examples—and such an individual, one need hardly
point out, must be either reformed or suitably punished.
Melrose's case, in fact, offers the most direct parallel to 'The
Palace of Art': an eccentric connoisseur, he amasses a magnificent art collection at Threlfall Tower but neglects the cot-
tages on his estate to such an extent that a resentful peasant
creeps in through a window and murders him. After his death
the house and collection become a great museum open to all.

Even in one of her critical essays, Mrs Ward analyzes
Pater's novel *Marius the Epicurean* in frankly Tennysonian
terms:

One feels as though one were reading another *Palace of Art* with a
difference! Here, in Mr. Pater's system, the soul ceases to live solitary in
the midst of a dainty world of its own choice, not because it is over-
taken by any crushing conviction of sin and ruin in so doing, but be-

cause it learns to recognise that such a worship of beauty defeats its own ends, that by opening the windows of its palace to the outside light and air, and placing the life within under the common human law, it really increases its own chances of beautiful impressions, of "exquisite moments."[24]

Open the windows and doors—'and bring everybody in—out of the rain'. Mrs Ward disagreed with James' gloomy conclusion that social justice and culture were incompatible, and her own 'Palace of Art'—Stocks—was frequently filled on summer weekends with poor children from the streets of London.

IV

It is this same note of compromise and reconciliation which characterizes Mrs Ward's religious fiction. Since in matters of faith her heroes and heroines struggle to chart a course that avoids the Scylla and Charybdis of scepticism and superstition, it may seem at times to modern readers that Mrs Ward's 'middle way'—in religion as well as politics—is achieved by her characters too easily and recommended to her readers too complacently. This is especially true of the later novels, in which her own youthful religious conflicts have disappeared from view, to be replaced by a codified, authoritarian Theism more oppressively dogmatic than the Christianity it has supplanted. To read Mrs Ward's entire literary career in the light of her poorest books, however, is surely a mistake, for in her best novels—particularly *Robert Elsmere* and *Helbeck of Bannisdale*—she brilliantly captures the pain of spiritual loss so characteristic of the century.

If there is a common theme in Victorian confessional literature, it is the deep sense of isolation and sorrow which our forebears experienced when they found it necessary to renounce Christianity. The reason might be convinced of the need to reject it, but the emotions still clung to the discarded faith, associated as it was in the Victorian mind with all the highest ideals of home and childhood. Christianity, the innocence of youth, and remembered scenes of the parish church on Sunday morning were such potent emotional influences that they could overwhelm, and draw bitter tears from, the most sober Victorian unbeliever. Witness this impassioned paragraph from J. A. Froude's semi-autobiographical novel *The Nemesis of Faith* (1849):

When I go to church, the old church of my old child days, when I hear the old familiar bells, with their warm sweet heart music, and the young and the old troop by along the road in their best Sunday dress, old well-known faces, and young unknown ones, which by and by will grow to be so like them, when I hear the lessons, the old lessons, being read in the old way, and all the old associations come floating back upon me, telling me what I too once was, before I ever doubted things were what I was taught they were; oh, they sound so sad, so bitterly sad. The tears rise into my eyes; the church seems full of voices, whispering round me, Infidel, Infidel, Apostate; all those believing faces in their reverent attention glisten with reproaches, so calm, they look so dignified, so earnestly composed. I wish—I wish I had never been born. (pp. 24-5)

Tennyson too suffered from a divided will and repeatedly invokes these very same images of spiritual suffering in his poetry. 'How sweet to have a common faith!' he exclaims in 'Supposed Confessions of a Second-Rate Mind', and this leads (just as it does so often for Froude) in the following stanza to the wish that he might once again be 'the trustful infant on the knee!' Similarly, in 'The Two Voices' (originally entitled 'Thoughts of a Suicide'), one of the most chilling of all such Victorian internal dialogues, Tennyson's narrator is at last able to silence the voice of despair not with reasoned argument but only by throwing open a window and gazing upon a happy family walking to church amidst the peal of sweet bells. The poem's conclusion has often been condemned by modern critics as an instance of Tennyson's cloying domesticity, or as a genre painting in verse, but a fairer judgment upon it might be that although the metaphor does not speak very clearly to us today, it was doubtless to Tennyson's first readers an eloquent, familiar image of a fading yet cherished faith.

It is precisely this bittersweet quality of Victorian religious nostalgia which so thoroughly suffuses the fiction of Mrs Ward. She was conscious of wandering between two worlds, and like Tennyson and Froude (and of course her uncle Matthew Arnold), she felt all her life the tug of the religious associations of her youth. It was out of these personal tensions between old and new, between feeling and intellect, that Mrs Ward wrote her novels—often with her 'heart's blood', as she said of *Robert Elsmere*.[25] Her religious fiction was not merely polemical (which is the usual critical cliché about her work), for in her best moments Mrs Ward has left us a moving, vivid, human account of what it meant to go out into the wilderness of unbelief in the last century. Her lifelong preoccupation with theological questions, seen from this perspective, reflects Mrs Ward's desire to resolve, perhaps in part through the very act of writing, her own dialogue of the mind with itself. Lady Bell has left us an ironic and significant record of a conversation she had in 1885 with Mrs Ward, who outlined to her the story of *Robert Elsmere* that she was just then beginning to write.

> At the end she asked me what I thought [recalled Lady Bell]. I said I thought the story most interesting. But I was foolish enough and ignorant enough to add that I was not sure whether the main issue of the book, the question of believing and doubting, would interest the general public. She stood still in the moorland road and looked at me with astonishment,—and said with a fervour and conviction that I have remembered so often since, 'But surely, there is nothing else so interesting in this world!'[26]

Mrs Ward wrote 25 novels, of which five—*Robert Elsmere* (1888), *The History of David Grieve* (1892), *Helbeck of Bannisdale* (1898), *Eleanor* (1900), and *The Case of Richard Meynell* (1911)—deal directly with the conflict between Christianity and modern thought, though the issue is seldom entirely absent from any of the other books. Of the five, *Elsmere* and *Helbeck* are conspicuously superior by literary standards, yet in the case of *Robert Elsmere* the historical estimate (as Matthew Arnold called it) inevitably enters into our judgement, for it is both a finely written novel and one of very considerable importance in the history of nineteenth-century thought. As Lionel Trilling has observed, 'It is a sophisticated, civilized book, full of personal insight, often amusing, frequently imaginative. But its chief interest surely lay in the skill and completeness with which it recorded the movement of liberalized religion of its time.'[27]

'The book is eminently an offspring of the time', declared Gladstone in 1888.[28] Mrs Ward herself often spoke of her novel's symbolic relationship with its age. 'With all its many faults', she wrote some years later, ' "Robert Elsmere" had yet possessed a certain representative and pioneering character; and . . . to some extent at least the generation in which it appeared had spoken through it.'[29] If Carlyle's *Sartor Resartus* may be regarded as the most important spiritual autobiography (fictionalized and concealed, but autobiography nonetheless) of the early Victorian age, and Tennyson's *In Memoriam* and Newman's *Apologia* those of the mid-Victorian age, then certainly no literary work can lay stronger claim to that position in the century's closing decades than *Robert Elsmere*. Like its predecessors, it was a record of painful renunciation for the sake of intellectual honesty; it was a *cri de coeur* which large numbers of readers recognized as an expression of their own spiritual doubts and longings; and it attempted to reconstruct from the debris of orthodoxy a new faith for a faithless generation. Mrs Ward's novel was not only representative, it was seemingly inevitable: it is undoubtedly significant that Lord Acton, who was in Cannes when it was published and heard only fragmentary reports of it from friends, was nevertheless able to offer to Gladstone an amazingly accurate conjecture of what its plot must be.[30] If Robert Elsmere had not existed, it would have been necessary (for Acton, at least) to invent him.

V

It would seem, at this point in the twentieth century, that the time is finally ripe for a fresh look at *Robert Elsmere*, which has for too long been underrated—and virtually unread by any except specialists. Perhaps a modern critic's greatest temptation is to make the novel into something it is not:

a startling forerunner, for example, of the ideas of Bonhoeffer or Bishop Robinson. But *Robert Elsmere* is distinctly a product of its century, and to attempt to wrest it from that context would actually do violence to Mrs Ward's religious and literary achievement. Whereas Bonhoeffer has recommended to us a Christianity without 'religion' (in his special pejorative sense of that word), Mrs Ward espoused what was, in effect, religion with only the faintest tincture of Christianity; and we must keep such essential differences in mind as we read her. Nevertheless, there is no denying that the present religious situation—particularly in the Roman Catholic Church since the second Vatican Council—does often make *Robert Elsmere* seem eerily contemporary. A doubting, rebellious priest who renounces his orders yet continues to preach a gospel of Christian love is likely to be a familiar figure to any reader of today's newspapers.

Robert Elsmere, then, is the subject of this book, but, as I have already suggested, the story of the novel is inextricably connected with the story of Mrs Ward's life. I do not propose to write a biography; there are large periods and major interests in her career which I will pass over in silence. What I will attempt to do, however, is to describe those aspects of her intellectual and spiritual history, in roughly chronological order, which bear directly on *Robert Elsmere*, and to tell (in Mrs Ward's phrase) 'that inner history of the soul, which is the real history of each one of us'.[31] And though I will examine only *Robert Elsmere* in considerable detail, I will try to reveal that book in its relationship with all her other writings, both fictional and otherwise.

Robert Elsmere is, as we must remind ourselves, at once an historical document and a private confession. Though Mrs Ward professed to be describing the destructive effect of Biblical criticism upon Christian orthodoxy in the nineteenth century, she was also laying bare her own private religious anxieties. If the novel were merely a 'document', it would be as dull as some detractors have claimed it is. If it were merely a personal confession of loss of faith, it would be of interest only to Mrs Ward's biographers. But *Robert Elsmere* is the story of both an individual and an age, and therein lies its achievement.

In 1885, reviewing *Marius the Epicurean*, Mrs Ward observed:

As a nation we are not fond of direct 'confessions.' All our autobiographical literature, compared to the French or German, has a touch of dryness and reserve. It is in books like *Sartor Resartus*, or *The Nemesis of Faith*, *Alton Locke*, or *Marius*, rather than in the avowed specimens of self-revelation which the time has produced, that the future student of the nineteenth century will have to look for what is deepest, most intimate, and most real in its personal experience.[32]

Mrs Ward's comment is not only an astute analysis of the special value of Victorian confessional fiction but also a clue that points us towards her own novels as a means of understanding her inner life. Her memoirs, entitled *A Writer's Recollections* (1918), present the familiar public personality who wrote best-sellers and dined with the wealthy and powerful; but a careful reading of the novels, particularly *Robert Elsmere*, discloses a quite different human being, one who bore all her life the scars of an unhappy childhood and a wrenching religious struggle.

It will not do to claim too much for *Robert Elsmere*: it is not a *Sartor Resartus* or *In Memoriam*, but, despite its slightly more parochial and less resonant tone, it too is a deeply authentic account of that crisis of religious belief which shook the foundations of Western thought in the nineteenth century.

Chapter 2
THE ARNOLDS OF FOX HOW

[Mrs Ward] is much to be liked personally but is a fruit I think of what must be called Arnoldism.

—Gladstone[1]

I

The granddaughter of Dr Thomas Arnold of Rugby and the niece of Matthew Arnold, Mrs Ward never allowed either herself or others to forget these family connections. Nearly a third of her *A Writer's Recollections* is devoted to the Arnolds; she named her son Arnold Ward and urged him incessantly to live up to the family name; and her novels are conspicuously padded with quotations from her uncle and grandfather. Indeed, both publicly and privately she tended to interpret her own career as a writer very largely in terms of her family heritage, encouraging others to do so as well. As she once characteristically remarked to her publisher, 'The fact is that I was brought up with people in whom the strongest emotions of life were generally combined with some intellectual end, & I suppose this reflects itself in [my] books.'[2]

Mrs Ward's critics, following her example, have frequently emphasized her intellectual indebtedness to the two more famous Arnolds. During the height of the *Robert Elsmere* sensation in America, it was announced in the press that Mrs Ward was Matthew Arnold's niece, and there seems to have followed an almost audible sigh of relief, as if this piece of genealogical information 'explained' whatever was mysterious

17

about the novel. It was even rumoured in some American newspapers that Elsmere—or perhaps his Oxford tutor—was modelled upon 'Uncle Matt'.

Though Mrs Ward herself encouraged simplistic views of her relationship with the Arnolds, in reality that relationship was much more complex than she was willing to admit. Undoubtedly it is significant that nearly all of Mrs Ward's fictional protagonists are orphans (not even Dickens created more homeless waifs) or, if not orphans, deprived of their family inheritance by the recklessness of a parent or grandparent. This is a recurring pattern in Mrs Ward's novels, but the most dramatic, self-revelatory example is to be seen in the opening chapter of *Marcella*, in which her heroine, after years of poverty and parental neglect, suddenly finds herself and her parents restored to Mellor Park:

> Her great desire now was to put the past—the greater part of it at any rate—behind her altogether. Its shabby worries were surely done with, poor as she and her parents still were, relatively to their present position. At least she was no longer the self-conscious school-girl, paid for at a lower rate than her companions, stinted in dress, pocket-money, and education, and fiercely resentful at every turn of some real or fancied slur. . . . She was something altogether different. She was Marcella Boyce, a 'finished' and grown-up young woman of twenty-one, the only daughter and child of Mr. Boyce of Mellor Park, inheritress of one of the most ancient names in Midland England, and just entering on a life which to her own fancy and will, at any rate, promised the highest possible degree of interest and novelty. (i, 5-6)

Marcella's great-uncle, as we learn subsequently, had once been Speaker of the House of Commons, and her father also had begun a promising political career, which was ruined by a scandal involving gambling debts. Now, in old age, he finds himself once again the master of Mellor Park. Although his long-suffering wife regards this latest turn in their fortunes with her usual wary stoicism, Marcella rejoices to discover herself an heiress whose 'blot in the 'scutcheon' has been erased.

It does not require much ingenuity to see in this story a symbolic reflection of Mrs Ward's own youthful experiences:

a distinguished grandfather and uncle, active in public and literary life; a father who creates a scandal by becoming a Roman Catholic and thus renouncing his family's well-known religious traditions; a deeply embittered Protestant mother; an unhappy childhood spent at a series of boarding schools; and finally the exultation which Mary Arnold felt in 1865 when her father turned Anglican again, and she began to enjoy a life at Oxford which 'promised the highest possible degree of interest and novelty'. The great Arnold heritage was not simply transmitted to Mrs Ward by Apostolic Succession, as some Victorian wits suggested. It was a heritage of which she was partially deprived for many years by her father's religion and which had to be consciously re-acquired when she became a young adult. Moreover, as we shall see, there were three Arnolds, not two, who helped to shape her mind and spirit.

II

When Mary Arnold, five years old, arrived in 1856 at Fox How, the Arnold family home near Ambleside, her grandfather had been dead for 14 years, yet his presence could still be felt in an almost ghostly way. His books and papers and portraits were visible in the rooms of Fox How. His widow continued to speak of him in the present tense. Each year the anniversary of his death was solemnly observed by all his children, even though they were scattered round the world. Little wonder that in Mrs Ward's children's story, *Milly and Olly* (1881)—which is otherwise strictly autobiographical—when she refers to this period of her life, she tells us that 'grandpapa' was still alive then. For such a child, sensitive, intelligent, and enveloped by the peculiar atmosphere of Fox How, Dr Arnold must have seemed fully as alive as her own parents. In a diary kept when she was 16 years old, she noted her displeasure with the morning church service—'a very dogmatic party-spirited sermon, coming rather oddly from so young a man'—but added that she consoled herself in the evening by reading 'one of Grandpapa's sermons'.[3] Thomas

Arnold's voice, that eloquent voice which stirred so many young men from the pulpit of Rugby chapel, had not been silenced by his death.

Yet the religious legacy which Arnold left his granddaughter and others was, to say the least, ambiguous in meaning. R. H. Hutton, writing in 1892, observed that the four most eminent representatives of Arnold's ideas during the latter half of the century—Arthur P. Stanley, Matthew Arnold, Arthur Hugh Clough, and Mrs Ward—were busily engaged in destroying the very faith he had loved. 'It looks as if Dr. Arnold's intensity of moral purpose', said Hutton, 'contained implicit germs of a solvent for the Christian creed which he himself firmly held.'[4] According to this view of Arnold's work, in de-emphasizing the dogmatic basis of Christianity and appealing instead to the authority of moral conscience, his religion became (as Paul Elmer More said of Jowett's) 'a kind of reverberation from forces which have ceased to operate—like the prolonged intonation of a bell after the last stroke of a hammer'.[5] Jowett himself gave voice to this criticism in his famous assertion that 'Arnold's peculiar danger was not knowing . . . where his ideas would take other people and ought to take himself'.[6] Matthew Arnold, though he admired his father's efforts to liberalize English theology, was also conscious of this accusation. 'In papa's time the exploding of the old notions of literal inspiration in Scripture, and the introducing of a truer method of interpretation, were the changes for which, here in England, the moment had come', he wrote to his mother in 1869, 'and my dear old Methodist friend, Mr. Scott, used to say to the day of his death that papa and Coleridge might be excellent men, but that they had found and shown the rat-hole in the temple.'[7]

By the standards of our day, Dr Arnold's theological views appear quite conservative: though, like many intelligent young men of his generation, he agonized over the problem of subscription to the Thirty-nine Articles at Oxford in 1817, he later could express his belief in both the divinity and the resurrection of Jesus with the greatest fervour. 'I know of no

one fact in the history of mankind, which is proved by better
and fuller evidence of every sort to the understanding of a
fair inquirer', he declared in a Rugby sermon, 'than the great
sign which God has given us, that Christ died and rose again
from the dead.'[8] Nevertheless—and this distinction is vital—
Arnold supported such an assertion more by an appeal to the
'evidence of Christ's Spirit' than to the testimony of the gospels, even though he fully accepted the validity of the latter
evidence. Two generations later his granddaughter, in contrast, was willing to discard all alleged historical evidence in
favour of a total reliance upon the more subjective witness of
the conscience. What in Dr Arnold is an occasional faint distrust of the historicity of the Scriptures, especially of the Old
Testament, becomes in Mrs Ward the full rejection of Scriptural reliability in the accounts of Jesus' resurrection. She
argued, of course, that her position was merely a logical development of his: once elevate the role of the inward witness,
and it must then become the only possible arbiter of religious
systems in an age when the entire fabric of the Bible is under
attack. The possibility of such an extension (or distortion, if
one prefers) of Dr Arnold's premises was part of what Newman had in mind when he complained that 'there is so little
consistency in his intellectual basis'[9] and that liberals like
Arnold always feared to explore the full implications of their
own ideas. In Arnold's case, however, he had a granddaughter
who was more than willing to push his ideas to their final
limit.

Arnold did not believe that he was undermining the Christian faith by introducing the distinction between the religious
spirit and the various historically conditioned manifestations
of that spirit. Unlike most of his contemporaries, he kept
abreast of German Biblical scholarship and regarded his own
'mediating' position as the only defence of orthodoxy against
the more destructive and rationalistic critics on the Continent. 'In fact, if we would hope to restrain that wildness of
criticism on theological topics which is too prevalent in Germany, we must learn to tolerate amongst ourselves a sober

freedom of honest and humble inquiry', he declared.[10] Though to other Englishmen it sometimes seemed that he was recklessly throwing overboard the fundamental beliefs of Christianity, Dr Arnold believed that he was merely lightening the ship so that it might survive the storms of modern scepticism. If it was necessary to acknowledge that the language and narratives of the Old Testament represented a Divine accommodation to man's imperfect understanding, then Arnold was willing to make that concession for the sake of preserving more essential doctrines. The chief paradox of his theological writings—and this was to be true of the writings of Matthew Arnold and Mrs Ward as well—is that he was impelled by genuinely conservative motives to employ a liberal method of Scriptural interpretation. In *Robert Elsmere* one can perceive this same renunciation of certain dogmas, coupled with the most profound religious feeling—a contrast which led R. H. Hutton to complain of Mrs Ward's 'curious Arnoldian intensity of resolve to make people at once believe more than they did before, and reject more than they rejected before'.[11]

Another indication of Dr Arnold's fundamental conservatism was his conviction that an officially established form of Christianity was necessary for the moral health of the nation. In the 1830s there was much talk of disestablishment, mainly because of the growing size of the Dissenting sects; a state Church, admirable as it might be in theory, was beginning to seem a rather hollow institution if it could claim the allegiance of only a minority of Englishmen. The solution which Dr Arnold proposed was startling in its simplicty: welcome back the Protestant Dissenters into the Church of England with no conditions attached. 'The *"Idea"* of my life, to which I think every thought of my mind more or less tends, is the perfecting the "idea" of the Edward the Sixth Reformers', he wrote to one of his closest friends in 1835—'the constructing a truly national and Christian Church, and a truly national and Christian system of education.'[12]

Two years earlier Arnold had explained this private vision of a national Church in a pamphlet entitled *Principles of Church Reform*. In a prose style characterized by his usual

vigour and clarity, Arnold spelled out the alternatives as he
saw them:

These principles I believe to be irrefragable; that a Church Establishment is essential to the well-being of the nation; that the existence of
Dissent impairs the usefulness of an Establishment always, and now,
from peculiar circumstances, threatens its destruction; and that to extinguish Dissent by persecution being both wicked and impossible, there
remains the true, but hitherto untried way, to extinguish it by compre-
hension.[13]

To Arnold this logic seemed inescapable, but to Evangelicals
and High Churchmen alike it appeared that he was merely
ignoring the enormous theological and liturgical differences
which had historically separated Church and Dissent in England. Some readers of the pamphlet were especially amused
by his proposal that two or more services be scheduled in each
parish church on Sunday, these to be conducted in various
ways to satisfy the needs of different categories of worshippers. Newman's satirical observation, in a letter to a friend,
was that if some of the sects (and of course the Jews) could
use the church on Saturday, and the Mohammedans on Friday, then Arnold's scheme would be even more efficient.[14]
    Between Arnold and Newman there grew up during this
decade a public antagonism which was the inevitable result of
their symbolic leadership of two large, rival factions within
the Church of England: the liberal Protestants and the Anglo-
Catholics. Arnold, who generally emphasized morality rather
than dogma in his preaching and writing, held a remarkably
'low' view of the Eucharist, Apostolic Succession, and the
other doctrines so important to the men of the Oxford Movement. References to 'Newmanism' and 'Newmanites' began
to appear after 1833 in his correspondence, and that frankness of expression which was his outstanding literary gift
gradually became an unpleasantly bitter, polemical tone
when he turned to this subject, as in this letter written
shortly before his death:

... my feelings towards [a Roman Catholic] are quite different from
my feelings towards [a Newmanite], because I think the one a fair

enemy, the other a treacherous one. The one is the Frenchman in his own uniform, and within his own praesidia; the other is the Frenchman disguised in a red coat, and holding a post within our praesidia, for the purpose of betraying it. I should honour the first, and hang the second.[15]

In 1836, in an *Edinburgh Review* article entitled (by the editor) 'The Oxford Malignants and Dr Hampden',[16] Arnold openly attacked what he regarded as 'the fanaticism of mere foolery' of 'the Oxford conspirators'. Comparing the High Church party to the Judaizers of the early church, he accused Newman and his followers of not only '*intellectual* error' but also '*moral wickedness*' in their opposition to Hampden's appointment as Reguius Professor of Divinity. Newman, for his part, was said to have wondered whether Arnold could even be regarded as a Christian. Newman regretted the wide circulation given this casual remark of his ('those few words are dragged forth, and I have to answer for them, in spite of my very great moderation and charity as touching him', he complained to Hurrell Froude[17]), and in the *Apologia* he attempted to soften it by supplying the context of the conversation which had occasioned the outburst; yet despite his subsequent explanations, there can be no doubt that when Newman asked 'But is Arnold a Christian?' he was expressing his honest reaction to Anglican liberalism. Shortly after Newman's conversion to Roman Catholicism in 1845, George Grove heard him deliver a lecture in London on 'Anglicans under Difficulties'.

I do not remember the exact subject of the lecture [Grove wrote later], but the part which much interested me was his reference to men who were certainly good men, and yet were quite in error in their attitude towards the Church—for instance 'What are we to say with respect to such people as Bunyan or Wesley, or to that man who doubted the efficacy of sacramental grace at night and'—in the most solemn tone—'died in the morning,' evidently referring to Arnold and his conversation with Lake reported in Stanley's *Life* [of Arnold], then only recently published.... It produced an indescribable effect on his audience.[18]

It seems sad in retrospect that Arnold and Newman, both

decent and honourable men, were driven by their theological differences to use such reckless language about one another. Yet their conceptions of the Church were so radically distinct —Newman saw the Church as a Divine institution deriving its authority ultimately from Christ, whereas Arnold saw it as a national institution designed for the moral and spiritual benefit of Englishmen—that their quarrel was more than an unpleasant disagreement between two strong-willed personalities. It was an expression of .a basic division within the Church at large. And a generation later, in the strange, tortured soul of Dr Arnold's second son, Mrs Ward's father, this dialectic was to work itself out in a highly dramatic fashion.

Dr Arnold's most distinctive trait was not a mere 'earnestness', the word usually associated with his name, but rather an intense, consuming passion for truth (as he understood it); hence his attacks upon Newman and other High Churchmen were made with an almost martial zeal. In 1886, at the dedication of a bust of Arnold in Westminster Abbey, E. W. Benson was disappointed by the meekness of its expression. 'It represents him, I think, just after closing a sermon in a moment of reposeful spirit', remarked Benson. 'It was generally said [by those present at the dedication ceremony], "Not fierce enough." No one ever ceased to be afraid of him.'[19] Even his children were awed by him (above all they feared the frown that gathered on his brow after some wrongdoing), but to his family and intimate friends Arnold generally revealed a gentler, more relaxed side of his nature which strangers never saw. As the reforming headmaster of Rugby, Arnold drew down upon himself the abuse of Tory newspapers such as *John Bull* and the *Northampton Herald*; and as an outspoken liberal in religious and political matters, he was a focus of controversy during most of his waking hours. He therefore sought to escape these pressures of public life by taking his wife and nine children away from Rugby on lengthy holidays and enjoying their company in the relative seclusion of distant lodgings. 'As my family grow up, we are so large and companionable a party, that we need no society out of ourselves', he explained.[20]

In the summer of 1831, returning from Scotland, the Arnolds stopped for a few days in Westmorland, where at Rydal they visited the Wordsworths and decided to spend their holidays thereafter in this lovely, remote valley of the Rotha. In old age Mrs Ward's father could still vividly remember those twice-yearly migrations to Westmorland, involving a three-day journey by coach over old turnpike roads and through quiet little villages. As Dr Arnold often said, the Lakes satisfied his almost physical craving for beauty and serenity. At Rydal he found a small band of select spirits, most notably Crabb Robinson and the Wordsworths, in a setting of incomparable natural beauty. With Wordsworth he took daily walks, cheerfully arguing as they tramped over the fells about the Reform Bill and the crisis in the Church. The poet, by now a staunch Tory, professed to be shocked by his companion's liberalism (Arnold 'is a good man, an admirable schoolmaster, but he would make a desperate bad bishop', he told Robinson[21]), yet despite their divergent views an abiding intimacy sprang up between the two men and their families.

During his Westmorland holidays Arnold's notorious sternness disappeared, and he plunged enthusiastically into long excursions—one of which is described in Matthew Arnold's poem 'Resignation'—with his children. Almost every day, whatever the weather, was spent clambering up Loughrigg or Nab Scar or exploring the delights of their tarns, always with the Doctor in the lead and a small battalion of children straggling along behind him. For several seasons the Arnolds stayed in temporary lodgings—Brathay Hall, Allan Bank, and a lodging house near Rydal Mount—but as early as 1832 Dr Arnold announced that 'we are thinking of buying or renting a place at Grasmere or Rydal, to spend our holidays at constantly'.[22] In that year, following the advice of Wordsworth, he purchased for £800 a small estate called Fox How, between Rydal and Ambleside, on the bank of the Rotha. On this site Arnold built a house in the old-fashioned Westmorland style under the close supervision of Wordsworth ('not the least of a modern appearance', Mrs Wordsworth noted

with satisfaction when it was completed[23]) which he intended
to serve as both a holiday retreat and a home for his eventual
retirement. Surrounded by mountains on all sides and snugly
planted at the foot of Loughrigg, Fox How was, as Matthew
Arnold's son called it, a 'house of paradise'.[24] Even casual
visitors testified to its extraordinary charm. Charlotte Brontë,
approaching it at twilight in 1850, observed that 'the house
looked like a nest half buried in flowers and creepers; and,
dark as it was, I could *feel* that the valley and the hills round
were beautiful as imagination could dream'.[25]

At Fox How Dr Arnold achieved that tranquillity of spirit
and intimacy with his children for which he longed in vain at
Rugby. In fact, he worried at times that the seductive charms
of Westmorland might tempt him to abandon the 'great experiment' of the Rugby headmastership. When it became
known in 1835 that a bishopric could not be offered to him
because of a change in the government, Arnold openly re-
joiced that he would not have to leave Fox How. It is impossible to understand the distinctive ethos of the Arnold family
—its spiritual intensity, its close personal relationships, its
feeling for the English landscape—without recognizing the
role that Fox How, and all that it represented, played in the
creation of their values. For four generations, from 1834
until the death of Dr Arnold's youngest daughter, Frances
('Aunt Fan'), in 1923, Fox How was the Mecca of Arnold
family life. During the 1840s and 1850s, young Tom Arnold
wandered about New Zealand and Van Diemen's Land, day-
dreaming all the while of Fox How; meanwhile his brother
William in India was also constantly turning his thoughts
towards home (indeed he died trying to come back to it);
Matthew admitted to his sister in 1859 that 'not a day passes
without my thinking five or six times of you, dear Fan, and
Fox How'.[26]

In his memoirs Tom Arnold recalled that

the Fox How portion of our life was a time of unspeakable pleasure to
us all. Loughrigg, the mountain at whose foot we dwelt, was bountiful
to us of joy. In the winter there were the frozen tarns, which would

bear [skaters] for several days before Rydal Lake was safe, the deliciously pure and bracing air, the slides, the little streams, each forcing its way down its own obstructed gully through a succession of lovely ice grottoes, which wrapped round and hushed its noisy little waterfalls.[27]

One summer day Dora Wordsworth, the poet's daughter, gave a tea party for the Arnold children on the large island in Rydal Water. In a spot 'embowered with trees, and floored with fresh moss', the children drank their tea while Wordsworth stretched out upon the grass and Mrs Wordsworth read aloud some of his manuscript poems.[28] In 'Memorial Verses' (1850) an older and sadder Matthew Arnold evoked these memories when he eulogized Wordsworth:

> He laid us as we lay at birth
> On the cool flowery lap of earth,
> Smiles broke from us and we had ease;
> The hills were round us, and the breeze
> Went o'er the sun-lit fields again;
> Our foreheads felt the sun and rain.
> Our youth returned; for there was shed
> On spirits that had long been dead,
> The freshness of the early world.

'It is not for nothing that one has been brought up in the veneration of a man so truly worthy of homage; that one has seen him and heard him, lived in his neighbourhood and been familiar with his country', he declared on another occasion.[29]

By 1840 Dr Arnold was telling friends that he hoped to retire permanently to Fox How as soon as 'Matt and Tom have gone through the University'.[30] However, early on the morning of 11 June 1842, intending to leave Rugby for the summer within a few days, he suffered an attack of angina pectoris. Mrs Arnold read to him from the Bible and the Prayer Book, and Tom said, 'I wish, dear Papa, we had you at Fox How'. He died a few hours later. W. C. Lake, who was staying with the Arnolds at the time, journeyed quickly up to Fox How to give the news to Matthew and two of his sisters.

Matthew recalled the events of that Sunday morning in a later tribute to his father, 'Rugby Chapel':

> *Fifteen years have gone round*
> *Since thou arosest to tread,*
> *In the summer-morning, the road*
> *Of death, at a call unforeseen,*
> *Sudden. For fifteen years,*
> *We who till then in thy shade*
> *Rested as under the boughs*
> *Of a mighty oak, have endured*
> *Sunshine and rain, as we might,*
> *Bare, unshaded, alone,*
> *Lacking the shelter of thee.*

John Kenyon, visiting the Wordsworths shortly thereafter, 'met Mrs. Arnold and her children crossing a field by a country pathway in their deep mourning, and . . . it impressed him like a village funeral'.[31] The Arnold children, 'Bare, unshaded, alone', would now have to face the intellectual and spiritual crises of the Victorian age with only their own resources. It was a traumatic blow, the consequences of which were to be felt in the life of Dr Arnold's most celebrated granddaughter.

III

From India, William Delafield Arnold wrote his mother in 1850:

I sometimes think . . . I should have been a more useful active Man had I never known the Truth as Papa taught it to us. But . . . the Talent of Knowledge of Good and Evil has been given to me and I must double it or hide it in the Earth at the Peril of my Soul.[32]

It was a sentiment which was echoed by Matthew Arnold, who recognized that his father's high-minded commitment to Truth, with an implied disregard for any theological consequences, inevitably meant a lonely and arduous journey through life—'With frowning foreheads, with lips / Sternly compressed', as he wrote in 'Rugby Chapel'. And when at last we reach 'the lonely inn 'mid the rocks' at nightfall, we are compelled to admit to 'the gaunt and taciturn host':

> *We bring*
> *Only ourselves! we lost*
> *Sight of the rest in the storm.*
> *Hardly ourselves we fought through,*
> *Stripped, without friends, as we are.*
> *Friends, companions, and train,*
> *The avalanche swept from our side.*

If, as Jowett claimed, Dr Arnold's danger was not knowing where his ideas might take other poeple, then his children at least were to discover the hidden potential for private maladies of the soul in those ideas. His eldest daughter, Jane ('the best German scholar of the rising generation', according to Crabb Robinson[33]), was portrayed by Matthew in 'Resignation' as 'Fausta', a female Faust restlessly searching for new impressions and new experiences; very much the same mood of anxious, sincere confusion is attributed by Mrs Ward to her heroine Marcella Boyce (in *Marcella*), who is in part a portrait of her aunt. ('I wonder whether you remember my Aunt Forster?' she asked George Smith on 6 October 1896—'there are all sorts of impressions from her, as a younger woman, in Marcella.') Similarly Jane's sister Mary Twining, widowed in her twenties, plunged into the London maelstrom as an eager disciple of liberal reformers like Charles Kingsley and F. D. Maurice. 'The fact is, it was in London that I first seemed to live—no words can say what Mr. Maurice's lectures and sermons were to me', she wrote to her brother Tom in 1850.[34]

Two such strong-willed and intelligent aunts, both caught up in the swirling time-stream of the nineteenth century, must have made a profound impression upon young Mary Arnold. It was, however, above all 'Uncle Matt', always gay and ironical in person yet elegaic in his poetry, who most directly influenced Mrs Ward's intellectual development. 'It must have been about 1868 that I first read "Essays in Criticism" ', she declared. 'It is not too much to say that the book set for me the currents of life; its effect heightened, no doubt, by the sense of kinship.'[35] Matthew Arnold was to her 'a voice of inspiration, discipline, and delight'.[36] In the copy of *Robert Elsmere* which she presented to him, Mrs Ward wrote the following inscription: 'To my dear Uncle Matthew Arnold—a small acknowledgement of all I owe to his books & his influence. M.A.W.'[37] Indeed, Uncle Matt even made a brief appearance in the book itself, for one of Squire Wendover's visitors is a man described as 'the most accomplished of English critics' (i, 499).

Oscar Wilde allegedly complained that *Robert Elsmere* was *Literature and Dogma* without the Literature, and certainly the similarities between the religious perspectives of uncle and niece are extremely obvious in the novel. Both are eager to find a new religion which will retain the best aspects of Christianity yet liberate men and women of the nineteenth century from the tyranny of superstition. As Matthew Arnold wrote in the preface to the Popular Edition (1883) of *Literature and Dogma*:

> The object of *Literature and Dogma* is to re-assure those who feel attachment to Christianity, to the Bible, but who recognise the growing discredit befalling miracles and the supernatural. Such persons are to be re-assured, not by disguising or extenuating the discredit which has befallen miracles and the supernatural, but by insisting on the natural truth of Christianity.[38]

'The natural truth of Christianity', like Dr Arnold's appeal to the inward witness of the Spirit, represents an attempt to discover in psychology rather than history a verification of the Christian faith. Though Matthew Arnold was less enthusiastic about German Biblical criticism than his niece was, he fully recognized that the traditional bases of Christianity were under attack in the modern age; nevertheless (and this habit of his can be annoying at times) he asserted repeatedly that we can know beyond any doubt that Jesus' life reflects the moral order of the universe—a moral order which was self-evident to Arnold (if not to everyone else) and which, because it was assumed by Arnold, did not have to be demonstrated. For uncle and niece alike, a radical system of theology was mysteriously reconciled with a traditional system of ethics.

Given these parallels—which are so conspicuous that it is probably unnecessary to belabour them—it is not surprising that Mrs Ward was even mistakenly supposed to be Matthew Arnold's daughter. This story was given considerable circulation in America in 1888, and as late as 13 September 1893, George Smith, writing from Germany, offered Mrs Ward this version of it:

> You may be amused to hear that an Englishman who sat beside me yesterday, said apropos of a remark that was made about Matthew Arnold 'one of his daughters has taken to literature.' I said that I did not think so. He replied "oh yes she wrote a book called 'Robert Elsmere'—have you not heard of it?"

It is tempting to believe that Mrs Ward must have secretly wished she were in fact Uncle Matt's daughter. Though their personal relationship was comparatively casual, she felt closer to him intellectually than she ever did to her own father.

However, it should be added that Matthew Arnold had grave reservations about his niece's abilities as a novelist. Following the publication of *Miss Bretherton*, her first serious fictional effort, in 1884, Arnold jokingly remarked to George Smith: 'She cannot write a novel. No Arnold could write one; otherwise I should have done it myself!'[39] Frank Harris, admittedly an unreliable witness, quotes Arnold as saying about *Robert Elsmere*, 'She's very serious. I wonder why women are so much more serious than men?'[40]

Arnold was unable to finish reading *Robert Elsmere*, as he died a few weeks after its appearance. He told Mrs Ward that he liked the first volume, but she acknowledged that the latter two-thirds of the book would not have appealed to him:

> My uncle was a Modernist long before the time. In 'Literature and Dogma,' he threw out in detail much of the argument suggested in 'Robert Elsmere,' but to the end of his life he was a contented member of the Anglican Church, so far as attendances at her services was con-

cerned, and belief in her mission of 'edification' to the English people. He had little sympathy with people who 'went out.' Like Mr. Jowett, he would have liked to see the Church slowly reformed and 'modernised' from within. So that with the main theme of my book—that a priest who doubts must depart—he could never have had full sympathy.[41]

Arnold, though he would have sympathized with Robert Elsmere's dilemma as keenly as Mrs Ward did, believed that heretics were wrong in voluntarily separating from the Church because of differences in opinion; only a low moral standard in the Church, he said, could be regarded as a sufficient justification for such a separation.

It is amusing to speculate, too, what Arnold's response would have been to the 'New Brotherhood of Christ' which Elsmere eventually founds in the East End of London. Arnold was suspicious of any form of Dissent, especially when its cultural impoverishment and narrowness were concealed by 'the grand name without the grand thing'. Arnold's remarks on the 'British College of Health' (a pretentious institution which had little more than an impressive title) in 'The Function of Criticism' reveal his bias against makeshift religions outside the structure of the Established Church:

Everyone knows the British College of Health; it is that building with the lion and the statue of the Goddess Hygeia before it. . . . In England, where we hate public interference and love individual enterprise, we have a whole crop of places like the British College of Health; the grand name without the grand thing. Unluckily, creditable to individual enterprise as they are, they tend to impair our taste by making us forget what more grandiose, noble, or beautiful character properly belongs to a public institution. The same may be said of the religions of the future of Miss Cobbe and others. Creditable, like the British College of Health, to the resources of their authors, they yet tend to make us forget what more grandiose, noble, or beautiful character properly belongs to religious constructions. The historic religions, with all their faults, have had this; it certainly belongs to the religious sentiment, when it truly flowers, to have this; and we impoverish our spirit if we allow a religion of the future without it.[42]

Matthew Arnold would have felt acutely uncomfortable in

the dreary, bare rooms on Elgood Street where Elsmere's 'New Brotherhood' regularly met.

Despite her intellectual resemblance to him, Mrs Ward differed from Arnold in the strain of radical, unyielding Puritanism which lay concealed beneath her veneer of cultural sophistication. As Arnold himself might have said, she had too much Hebraism, and not enough Hellenism, in her personality. Mrs Ward, who wished to see herself as a faithful disciple of her uncle (and hoped others would also regard her in this light), really absorbed only those ideas from him which were congenial to her own temperament, so that the Arnoldian logic which appears in her novels is often slightly conventionalized, attenuated, and at times distorted. Mrs Ward's mind was deeply coloured by her uncle's books, but it was the product also of other forces, other personalities—one of the most important of which was her father, Thomas Arnold the Younger.

IV

Tom Arnold's 'wandering life', as he himself called it, his vacillating course that wavered perpetually between Anglicanism and Roman Catholicism, may at first glance appear faintly absurd to the twentieth-century reader. Rose Macaulay, in her novel *Told by an Idiot* (1923), has offered an amusing parody of his odd career in the story of Mr Garden, who periodically loses his faith and becomes at various times an Anglican clergyman, a Unitarian minister, a Roman Catholic layman, 'some strange kind of dissenter', and an agnostic. Yet though there is undeniably an element of unconscious humour in Tom Arnold's frequent conversions, he was also an honest man of great integrity and generosity, a quintessential example of the Victorian dialogue of the mind with itself whose very confusion compels our admiration.

Tom's years at Oxford were bounded by two deeply unsettling events: in 1842 his father died, and in 1845 Newman left the English Church. As Arthur Stanley wrote at the time, 'To any one who has been accustomed to look upon Arnold and Newman as *the* two great men of the Church of England, the death of one and the secession of the other cannot but look ominous, like the rattling of departing chariots that was heard on the eve of the downfall of the Temple of Jerusalem.'[43] Tom later remembered this period as 'the unhappiest of my life',[44] but outwardly he appeared to be a cheerful member of the 'Clougho-Matthean set'—a group that included his brother Matthew (two years older than Tom), Arthur Hugh Clough, and Theodore Walrond—who roamed the Cumnor hills on Sundays and shared the same literary enthusiasms, especially for George Sand and Emerson. All the while that painful disintegration of faith which is recorded so eloquently in Matthew Arnold's poems was also being experienced by Tom, who by the spring of 1845 was spending much time alone in his room overlooking the High Street, shivering over a small fire as a north-east wind rattled the large oriel window, and sinking ever deeper into the Everlasting No. 'A universal doubt shook every prop and pillar on which his moral Being had hitherto reposed', he afterwards recalled.[45]

Having taken his First Class degree at University College, Tom went to London and found employment for a time in the Colonial Office. In London he sympathetically observed the degradation and restlessness of the lower classes (for there were signs of impending revolution all over the Continent); he also witnessed the increasing secularization of Victorian urban life which seemed to mirror his private loss of faith. Suddenly in 1847 he sailed for New Zealand, where he evidently hoped to participate in the building of a new and just society and, like Browning's Gigadibs (in 'Bishop Blougram's Apology'), to find spiritual convalescence behind a plough. Dr Arnold had often talked of emigrating and had actually before his death purchased a plot of land near Wellington, which Tom now proposed to cultivate. Needless to say, he was a complete failure as a farmer, and within a year he began a small school near Nelson. By 1850 he was appointed inspector of schools in Tasmania (then called Van Diemen's Land).

On 13 June of that year (his father's birthday) Tom Ar-

nold married Julia Sorrell, the beautiful, temperamental
granddaughter of a former Lieutenant-Governor of the col-
ony, and a year later their first child, Mary, was born. Nevertheless, at the very moment when his professional career and
family life were flourishing, Tom was becoming ever more
spiritually disturbed. Though his letters from New Zealand
and Tasmania to Fox How were filled with contemptuous
references to Roman Catholicism, his old scepticism was
undergoing a strange transformation.

One Sunday in October 1854 a passage from the First Epis-
tle of Peter floated up from his memory, and Tom was
moved to ask himself: 'Who was this Peter? What was his
general teaching? Who were his helpers and successors?'
These questions in turn brought to mind the famous 'Newmanite' *Tracts for the Times*, since they dealt with this very
problem, and Tom began to read them. Shortly afterwards, in
a country inn where he was spending the night, he happened
upon a copy of Butler's *Lives of the Saints* and read, more or
less at random, an account of St Brigit of Sweden, which had
a powerful effect upon him. The scales fell off his eyes, he
said, and he knew that he must become a Roman Catholic.[46]
Early in 1855 he wrote to—of all people—Newman, declaring,
'I ardently long for the hour for making my formal submission to the Catholic Church.' Newman's reaction, when he
received this curious letter, was one of astonishment: 'How
strange it seems! What a world this is! I knew your father a
little, and I really think I never had an unkind feeling towards
him.'[47] That Tom Arnold should have turned for guidance to
his father's arch-enemy continued to amaze Mrs Ward in her
later years. 'He was never able to explain it afterwards, even
to me, who knew him best of all his children', she said. 'I
doubt whether he ever understood it himself. But he who had
only once crossed the High Street [of Oxford] to hear Newman preach, and felt no interest in the sermon, now, on the
other side of the world, surrendered to Newman's influence.'[48]

The tragedy of Tom Arnold's life was that he was caught

helplessly between the forces represented by Newman and Dr Arnold, and, in good Arnoldian fashion, he hoped always to reconcile their opposing viewpoints rather than to make a choice between them. In 1891, when Newman's early correspondence was published, Tom wrote:

I had myself noted the passages where my father is mentioned, and had seen with pleasure, that, except for the outrageous utterance about him at Rome ['But is Arnold a Christian?'], (which there was really nothing to justify,) Newman seems on the whole to have thought and spoken kindly of my father,—at least, rather kindly than the reverse. . . . For me, who owe so much—so incalculably much,—to both men, the multiplied proofs, afforded by these early letters, of Newman's veracity and sincerity, which ensured to his great dialectical powers its true logical fruit and outcome, were the cause of great joy and satisfaction. On the other hand, of course I know my father to have been as sincere and truthful with himself as ever man was. He was not the man to stand still, when Conscience beckoned onward, any more than Newman was.[49]

Both, then, were 'sincere and truthful'—but where did that leave Dr Arnold's son?

Yet this divided allegiance of Tom's heart was a minor problem in 1855 compared with the fury which his decision inspired in Julia Arnold. She threatened to leave him, she begged him not to take the fateful step until he consulted with his mother, and on the day in January 1856 when he was finally received into the Catholic Church in Hobart Town, she hurled a brick through the church window.[50] The following July he, Julia, and their three children sailed in a small, rat-infested ship for England, arriving there in October. For a time they stayed at Fox How, where Julia, always a restless and rebellious spirit, chafed under the discipline of Arnold family life, until Tom took an underpaid position as Professor of English Literature at Newman's Catholic University in Dublin. Then in 1862 he followed Newman to Edgbaston as a master in the Oratory school, which Newman was attempting to raise to the academic level of the older English public schools.

During these years Julia's violent hatred and fear of Catholicism were transmitted to Mary, who occasionally saw 'the great and to me mysterious figure of Newman haunting the streets of Edgbaston' and who shrank from him 'in a dumb childish resentment as from someone whom I understood to be the author of our family misfortunes'.[51] At Edgbaston Julia, according to Newman's account, 'used to nag, nag, nag [Tom], till he almost lost his senses'. Newman regarded Dr Arnold's son as a considerable asset to the school, 'a very good amiable fellow, but weak and henpecked'.[52]

Feeling this domestic pressure and increasingly unhappy with the repressive political policies of Pius IX, Tom began to entertain doubts again. In April 1865 Ambrose St John, the headmaster, wrote to him reporting that Julia was telling her friends that 'you have quite given up Catholicism';[53] he sent the letter, however, to Newman, who forwarded it to Tom and requested a denial. He was still a Catholic, Tom replied, but 'I cannot guarantee where, or in what form of opinions, the course of thought may eventually land me'.[54] That summer Tom sadly severed his connexion with the Oratory school and moved to Oxford, unable to believe any longer, he said, in an infallible Church. Mary, now 14, heard the news at her boarding school in Clifton:

Mother I have indeed seen the paragraphs [in the newspaper] about Papa. The Lancasters showed them to me on Saturday, thinking I might know something about who put them in. You can imagine the excitement I was in on Saturday night not knowing whether it was true or not. Miss May [one of her teachers] has seen it too. Your letter confirmed it this morning and Miss May seeing I suppose that I looked rather faint, sent me on a pretended errand for her note books to escape the breakfast table. My darling mother how thankful you must be. One feels as if one could do nothing but thank Him.[55]

Newman's response to Tom's decision was prophetic: Arnold, he said, was not now a Protestant. 'He is a non-practising Catholic, if he is anything.'[56]

From 1865 to 1876 Tom was nominally an Anglican, privately tutoring students at Oxford and enjoying greater financial security than he had ever before experienced, though Julia sensed that her husband's allegiance to the Church of

England was extremely tenuous. 'On one occasion', according to her grandson, 'she had gone to London, but returned earlier than expected, to find her husband entertaining two priests at dinner. Legend has it that she flew into a great tantrum, and the party broke up under a shower of plates.'[57]

Without warning, Tom Arnold left one morning in February 1876 for London, where he attended mass and conferred with two Catholic friends, Canon Frederick Oakley and Monsignor Thomas J. Capel, about his wish to change his religious allegiance once again. Julia followed him by train but went instead to see his brother-in-law, William Forster, who joined with Mrs Ward (by this time married but still living in Oxford) and Julia in attempting to dissuade Tom.[58] For a few days Tom remained in London, still hesitating. On 16 February Mrs Ward wrote to him from Oxford:

With regard to my mother your letter did I think bring her some little relief, but she is very unhappy mainly I think from the remembrance of your last interview in London. She bids me say that she deeply regrets the bitter things she said and she promises that for the future she will do her very best to abstain from saying wounding or bitter words. She was in a state of frenzy from the feeling of loneliness and lovelessness and hardly knew what she said. And she also bids me say that if when the children are a little older and your prospects are more assured you decide to become a Roman Catholic she will feel it 'her bounden duty not to oppose you.'

Tom came back to his family at Oxford, and until that autumn life seemed to go on as usual for the Arnolds.

Tom's reputation as a tutor and scholar had grown so greatly that it was generally supposed he would be elected to the new Chair of Anglo-Saxon in October. The night before the election, however, he again secretly fled Oxford and sent round letters to several individuals announcing that 'any member of Congregation, who thinks of voting for me at the election to the chair of Anglo-Saxon, should know that I intend, as soon as may be, to join, or rather to return to, the communion of the Catholic & Roman Church'.[59] Naturally the Chair went to another candidate. Why had Tom Arnold quixotically chosen the eve of his probable election to make his move? He wrote lengthy letters of explanation to both Mrs Ward and her husband, telling them that election to the Chair would have meant 'my being tied to Protestantis... for a term of years'. Rather than shut himself out from the presence of Christ so long by accepting the office, he had decided to declare openly what he had privately believed for some time. 'You or Mary will probably show this letter to my wife', he declared to Humphry Ward; 'it is better than that I should write.'[60] There was a series of angry interviews between husband and wife, at one of which Mrs Ward suffered what she described as a 'break-down' as a result of trying to mediate between them.[61]

Julia and Tom Arnold were never to live together again. She remained in Oxford, bitter and debt-ridden; Tom returned to Dublin. There were occasional visits, but these generally ended in fierce quarrels. Julia, meanwhile, was discovered to have a malignant tumour, and expensive operations followed. Little wonder that when Matthew Arnold met Newman for the first time in 1880, they talked mainly about 'Tom and his troubles'.[62] Matthew, however, was also capable of taking a more light-hearted view of his brother's turbulent career. One anecdote which has survived was recorded by Mrs Ward in 1881: 'The servant cuts her finger at dinner & a drop of blood falls on the tablecloth. So says Uncle Matt sauntering airily into the dining room after dinner, ["]My dear Tom, did not that gory spot remind [you] of the blood of all those martyrs your beastly church has shed?" '[63]

What is fascinating about Mrs Ward's state of mind throughout all these family tribulations is that even though she abhorred Catholicism as much as her mother did, she was also strongly attracted to her father's variety of unworldly mysticism. 'Whatever happens you and I are more one in heart than we know', she wrote to him at the time of his second conversion;[64] and this tone of personal sympathy—blended of course with theological disagreement—runs through her many letters to her father. 'I am afraid we differ as to first principles dearest!' she confessed to him on 5 March 1884. Nevertheless, it is typical of Mrs Ward that she always minimized their differences and stressed instead the points in common between her Theism and his Catholicism. Writing to him from Italy on Good Friday, 1896, she reflected:

> How differently we think, my dearest, you and I! Yet I feel no antagonism, either as I think of your Good Friday, or as I hear the bells of these little churches that fringe the lake. Each of us must approach the Eternal as he may & can, & 'righteousness' remains still as in Isaiah's day the one thing needful.

If Mrs Ward's theological views came primarily from her grandfather and uncle, then it is equally clear that her essentially religious temperament—which was a constant factor in her personality despite her departure from orthodoxy—came primarily from her father.

The greatest test of this generous relationship between father and daughter was Mrs Ward's decision to write *Helbeck of Bannisdale*. 'Would you mind my dearest, if I chose a certain *Catholic* background for my next story?' she asked him on 15 November 1896. 'I won't do it if you dislike it, but though of course my point of view is anything but Catholic, I should certainly do what I had thought of doing, with sympathy, & probably in such a way as to make the big English public understand more of Catholicism than they do now.' As usual, Mrs Ward immersed herself in 'background reading' while writing the novel during 1897, and at one point the Catholic books she was examining led her to exclaim (though not to her father): 'Oh! how strange this Catholic world is! Alluring indeed, if only consciously or unconsciously, you "hate history, reason & freedom." ' Catholicism had an enormous attraction for her, she admitted—'yet I could no more be a Catholic than a Mahometan'.[65]

In *Helbeck of Bannisdale*, published the following year, Mrs Ward skilfully captured this response of mingled fascination and revulsion in the character of her heroine, Laura Fountain, a charming young agnostic who falls in love with the Catholic gentleman Helbeck. Laura (who strongly resembles Julia Arnold) at last agrees to marry him, but before the ceremony takes place she commits suicide because she has found his spiritual world so tyrannical and suffocating. Mrs Ward sensed uneasily that she was drawing upon some of her most intensely private memories and those of her father in writing this novel, and consequently she suffered more anxiety than usual while reading proofs. During the spring of 1898 the *Helbeck* proofs followed her all over Italy on what was supposed to be a holiday as she made numerous small revisions and then sent on the proofs to her father in Ireland for his approval in each instance. 'Well, I have written it with my heart', she told him on Easter Monday. 'I have alternately felt with Helbeck & with Laura, and have loved them both.'

Tom Arnold once confessed that 'my brother and my daughter cause me perplexing thoughts',[66] but Mrs Ward did not have to fear his disapproval, for as he had written some years earlier: 'My own dearest Polly (let me call you for once what I often called you when a child), God made you what you are, and those who love you will be content to leave you to Him.'[67] Two years after *Helbeck* appeared, her father became seriously ill, and as death approached Mrs Ward 'asked him . . . if he loved me & forgave me everything, & he made a little motion as though to put up his hand to my cheek, with a sweet faint smile'.[68] He died on 12 November 1900 and was buried in the University church, Stephen's Green, Dublin. A medallion portrait was placed on the same wall as the bust of Cardinal Newman, the only other monument in the church; a cast of the medallion was also made for the sitting room at Stocks where Mrs Ward did all her literary work.

A year and a half later, she reported having 'a vivid dream of Papa. . . . I kissed him & laid my cheek against his—"Dearest Papa do you love me?"—"Yes—always." '[69] In this dream and in the deathbed scene, which reveal so plainly Mrs Ward's feelings of guilt and anxiety about their relationship, one can detect the roots of her life-long effort, particularly in *Robert Elsmere*, to persuade us that all who feel a hunger for God, whatever their creed, worship the same Deity.

Chapter 3
JUVENILIA

The writing [in *Robert Elsmere*] is exactly like Charlotte Yonge, only better.

—Walter Besant (1888)[1]

I

One of the reasons why Mrs Ward has been frequently ignored by literary critics in this century is that she appears to have done their work for them already. She was an extremely gifted critic, and when she turned her attention to her own novels in *A Writer's Recollections* and in the Introductions to the Westmoreland Edition of her works, she candidly analyzed both the strengths and weaknesses of her books, discussed her indebtedness to other writers, and in general created the illusion of having said the final word on all such matters. The few critics who have written about her since 1920 have depended heavily upon the perspective and information supplied by Mrs Ward herself. Nevertheless, despite her astuteness and essential honesty, she is not entirely to be trusted as a critic of her own novels, for she habitually ignored (or perhaps could not recognize) the true emotional background of her writings and placed the entire emphasis instead upon intellectually respectable influences such as Matthew Arnold, T. H. Green, and the German Biblical critics.

One means of shedding the blinkers placed upon us by Mrs Ward's criticism—and of seeing *Robert Elsmere* and her other mature novels in a new light—is to examine a series of short stories and a novella, all but one unpublished, which she wrote as an adolescent. These stories, which have been preserved in a group of her literary notebooks recently acquired by the Honnold Library, Claremont University, constitute an exceptionally full record of Mary Arnold's imaginative world between the ages of 13 and 18, an important period in her life about which little is otherwise known. The stories also serve to remind us that Mrs Ward had, in a manner of speaking, two separate careers as a writer of fiction, as she herself hinted in her Introduction to *Miss Bretherton*:

'Miss Bretherton' [1884] was my first serious attempt at a novel. After much scribbling of tales in my childhood and school-days, after a long story in three volumes, written at the age of seventeen, and of no merit whatever, after the publication in, I think, 1869 [actually 1870], of 'A Westmoreland Story' in *The Churchman's Magazine* [actually *The Churchman's Companion*], and a later and much more ambitious effort called 'Vittoria,' a novel of Oxford life, which was never finished, I had come despondently to the conclusion that fiction was not for me. In the years between 1869 and 1880, so far as writing was concerned, I turned entirely to history and criticism. (p. 221)

However, in these youthful stories, which Mrs Ward said made her 'laugh and blush when I compare them to-day [1917] with similar efforts of my own grandchildren',[2] there are numerous fascinating clues which make comprehensible many of the attitudes displayed in her later fiction. Despite the decade-long hiatus which separates the juvenilia from her published novels, the two groups of stories interpenetrate and interlock at times in startling fashion.

II

Mary Arnold's arrival with her family at Fox How in 1856 must have seemed a homecoming to her, for since infancy she had been taught by her father in Tasmania to lisp the names of 'Aunt Thuthy', 'Aunt Dane', and 'Grand-dada'. Even after Tom Arnold accepted the professorship in Dublin, she remained at Fox How under the care of 'Grandmamma' and Aunt Fan. In *Milly and Olly* Mrs Ward recalled the large hall, with all kinds of corners in it, just made for playing hide-and-seek in; and the drawing room was full of the most delightful things. There were stuffed birds in cases, and little ivory chessmen riding upon ivory elephants. There were picture-books, and there were mysterious drawers full of cards and puzzles, and glass marbles and old-fashioned toys, that the children's mother and aunts and uncles and their great-aunts and uncles before that, had loved and played with years ago. (p. 72)

Mary's ungovernable temper soon became a legend in the Arnold household. While still in Tasmania, Tom Arnold had written to his mother that 'I have seen and had to deal with a good many children, but such self will as Mary's I never met with in my life'.[3] And in *Milly and Olly* Mrs Ward confessed: 'I'm afraid I was often very naughty, Milly. I used to get into great rages and scream, till everybody was quite tired out' (p. 64). Her aunt and grandmother, however, patiently tried to subdue her, and Mrs Ward admitted that 'it always did naughty children good to live in the same house with . . . grandmamma, and so after a while I got better'.

Yet the tantrums persisted even after Mary became in the autumn of 1858 a boarder at Miss Anne Clough's school on the outskirts of Ambleside. Years later, while visiting the old school, Mrs Ward pointed to a door and remarked: 'Look! You can still see the damaged panel which I bashed in with my fists in my fury when I was locked into the cloakroom for punishment.'[4] It was probably also at Eller How that Mary, on one memorable occasion, ran 'up to the top of a flight of stairs with a large plate full of bread-and-butter and flung slice after slice smack in the face of the governess standing at the foot, finally hurling the plate after'.[5]

Lonely and rebellious, Mary found at least a few compensations at Eller How. She was close enough to spend the weekends at Fox How, where her grandmother told fascinating stories that 'went on for years and years till all the children in it—and the little children who listened to it—were almost grown up'.[6] There were long walks to Rydal Mount (where she once met Mrs Wordsworth), to the Sweden Bridge, and to Rydal Water. Above all, there were quiet evenings at Eller How when she could read Scott and pretend that Windermere, visible in the distance, was really Loch Katrine.[7] On a visit to Woodhouse, the new home of her Aunt Mary in Leicestershire, she 'rushed through many of the Waverleys—I can still remember vividly the joy of the Talisman'. Wandering alone by a pond at Woodhouse, she turned 'every tree and summerhouse into the furnishings of a dream'.[8]

In a world of imaginary heroes and heroines, whether her own or Scott's, Mary Arnold found the surest defence against the unhappiness that sometimes overwhelmed her. Separated most of the time from her brothers, sisters, and parents, she became a voracious reader and an expert spinner of tales to the other girls at Eller How. Yet at the same time that these fantasies provided solace, they also inspired guilt, for the strict piety of Fox How and Eller How left little room for the free play of the young imagination. Dr Arnold had once been alarmed to discover that his boys were reading such frivolous novels as *The Pickwick Papers* and *Nicholas Nickleby*. 'These completely satisfy all the intellectitle appetitite of a boy, which is rarely very voracious', he complained, 'and leave him totally palled, not only for his regular work, . . . but for good literature of all sorts, even for History and for Poetry.'[9] It is useful to keep in mind that it was in such a moral atmosphere, pervaded by a distrust of 'light' fiction, that Mary Arnold spent her childhood.

Robert Elsmere's wife is described by Mrs Ward, in a cancelled passage of the novel's manuscript, as 'one of those persons who regard art except as used for missionary purposes or for the sake of earning bread & butter, as a more or less culpable waste of time'.[10] It is tempting to dismiss this viewpoint as merely another instance of Catherine Elsmere's religious fanaticism, but an examination of the novelists who figure as characters in Mrs Ward's published stories suggests that her own attitude towards the art of fiction was not so far removed from Catherine's as one might suppose. Without exception, every novelist-character who appears in Mrs Ward's fiction is portrayed as either morally or intellectually deficient. Mrs Darcy, in *Robert Elsmere*, is a senile old woman verging on madness whose literary aspirations are treated entirely from a comic perspective. Captain Warkworth, who has written a 'military novel' in *Lady Rose's Daughter*, is an irresponsible, Byronic adventurer. Lady Kitty, in *The Marriage of William Ashe*, composes a novel with '*real* people—*real* things that happened—with just the names altered' (p. 330), but in so doing she carelessly destroys her husband's parliamentary career.

In a speech which Mrs Ward delivered at the opening of a public library in 1897, she said:

Vast numbers of novels are read through the free libraries. Perhaps you will hardly expect me to object! You will rather expect me to hold that a man or woman who does not read novels cannot possibly be a healthy human being, just as in Charles Lamb's language "A man cannot have a pure mind who refuses apple-dumplings." But, on the contrary, I have a good deal of sympathy with the attack upon wholesale novel-reading. Highly as I respect my own craft, if free libraries were to exist always and only for the provision of novels and newspapers, I at least should not feel towards them as I do. For, after all, the best of novels, though it may be and often is, an education, yet if it will perversely try to be a discipline, why, then, we are wroth with it, and throw it away. But in this, as in other things, happiness is best got by aiming at something different—by aiming at knowledge, let us say, and putting yourself to toil to it. Then in the end, like Charles Lamb's Oxford friend, you will be "as happy and good on the Muses' hill as one of the shepherds on the Delectable Mountains," but it will be because you have tempered your novels with the harder things of literature and not been merely lazy and languid in your courting of books.[11]

As an adult, Mrs Ward clearly retained some of the traditional Evangelical fear of fiction.

But such a moralistic view is scarcely in evidence in her earliest surviving literary effort. At the age of nine and a half she was enrolled at the 'Rock Terrace School for Young Ladies' in Shifnal, Shropshire, where—as she tells us in an autobiographical chapter in *Marcella*—her most 'precious volumes' were Bulwer-Lytton's *Rienzi* (1835), Miss Porter's *Scottish Chiefs* (1810), and Scott's *Marmion* (1808). 'The parts which it bored her to read she easily invented for herself, but the scenes and passages which thrilled her she knew by heart; she had no gift for verse-making but she laboriously wrote a long poem on the death of Rienzi' (i, 13)—a poem which, incidentally, is in a notebook of hers dated 1864. This same notebook also contains her first extant story, entitled 'A Tale of the Moors', a piece of historical fiction reminiscent of both Bulwer-Lytton and Scott in its colourful, dramatic style. Though the subject may have been inspired by Bulwer-Lytton's *Leila; or the Siege of Granada* (1838), the historical details and descriptions of the story appear to have been drawn largely from Washington Irving's *Chronicle of the Conquest of Granada* (1829). The tale describes the adventures of Inez, a 'girl beautiful to excess', who is compelled by conscience to tell others that her father is a traitor to the Moors. When he retaliates by publicly revealing that she is actually the daughter of a Spanish nobleman, she is sentenced to die; but just as she is about to be executed, Inez is rescued by the invading Spaniards, who take her to the royal court at Cordova. There she finds her real father, marries the daring young cavalier who saved her from death, and emerges at the end of the story 'purified and refined', having come forth from these trying experiences 'brighter and purer from the furnace of affliction'.

There are two things about this story that should be observed. First, Mrs Ward's later absorption in Spanish history and literature is prefigured in it. Second, except for the unconvincing moral tacked on the last paragraph, 'A Tale of the Moors' reflects the cheerful, extroverted, robust tone of Scott's fiction. However, in her next surviving story, 'Lansdale Manor', dated 6-23 August 1866 (Mary by then having moved to a boarding school near Clifton), we are transported from the lusty, passionate world of the historical romance to the mild piety and quiet domesticity of mid-Victorian religious fiction. Clearly something had happened to Mary Arnold during these two years. The rebellious behaviour—'the sulks, quarrels and revolts'—that she had displayed at Eller How and Shifnal had disappeared, and now, at Clifton, Scott and Bulwer-Lytton were supplanted by Charlotte Mary Yonge, whose popular and morally earnest stories for children even Dr Arnold might have endorsed.

This transformation was partly brought about by the influence of Mrs Cunliffe, the saintly Evangelical wife of the vicar of Shifnal, to whom Mary addressed some ardently religious poems in her 1864 notebook. But a more potent force was the fiction of Miss Yonge, who held sway over so many Victorian nurseries and schoolrooms. From 1859 to 1874, as 'Mother Goose', she reigned with special power over a select group of her young admirers who produced a manuscript magazine called the *Barnacle* under her direction and submitted monthly questions and riddles to her and each other by post. The 'goslings' included Sir J. T. Coleridge's daughters, Mrs Henry Wood, author of *East Lynne* (1861), and, for a short time, Mary Arnold, who contributed to the *Barnacle* under the pseudonym 'Windermere'.[12] Through these years the influence of Miss Yonge's fiction upon Mary's adolescent stories was profound and pervasive. Curiously, it is an influence which Mrs Ward never publicly acknowledged; perhaps she was embarrassed by the fact that Miss Yonge, near the end of the century, was increasingly regarded by most readers as a mid-Victorian curiosity, a literary figure who could no longer be taken seriously.

Miss Yonge, however, shaped Mary Arnold's literary tastes at a very deep level, and to understand this is to understand, at least in part, one of the most puzzling aspects of Mrs Ward's novels. Repeatedly her most intelligent and aggressive heroines are brought to a state of humility and self-understanding by their trials; the lesson they invariably must learn is that a woman's role, no matter how brilliant she may be, is one of submission and dependence upon her husband and God. It is a viewpoint which Mrs Ward appears to have absorbed chiefly from Miss Yonge, though of course it was a widely held cultural attitude in nineteenth-century England. As Margaret Maison has pointed out, 'Instances . . . could be quoted from all [Miss Yonge's] stories of the punishment of those who fail to be serious and submissive in Church and family life. Uncontrolled female intellects or emotions are particularly heavily penalized.'[13] Though this theme of feminine self-abnegation runs through so many of Miss Yonge's stories, it finds its fullest expression in *The Clever Woman of the Family* (1865), a book which Mary Arnold apparently read with care, since echoes of it can be heard in several of her early stories. The word 'clever' in the title is strongly pejorative; the heroine, intellectual and imaginative, is forced to confess the sinfulness of her professional ambitions, and by the end of the story she is subdued and properly married.

In a letter written to her mother on 30 December 1885, Mrs Ward declared:

I am *so* sorry my dearest for your own suffering. This is a weary world, —but there is good behind it, 'a holy will' as Amiel says, 'at the root of nature & destiny', and submission brings peace because in submission the heart finds God & in God its rest. There is no truth I believe in more profoundly.

Notwithstanding the attribution, it was a truth she had learned from Miss Yonge long before she ever read Amiel.

Mary's 'Lansdale Manor: A Children's Story' (1866) reflects this new quality of moral strenuousness which she had adopted. It is described on the title page as the first volume of *Alford Rectory* (though the succeeding volumes either were not completed or have not survived) and bears this dedication: 'To dearest Grandmamma this early literary attempt of her eldest grandchild is affectionately inscribed.' Edith Lansdale, the heroine, might have stepped directly out of one of Miss Yonge's novels: she most closely resembles Ethel May in *The Daisy Chain* (1856). The eldest child in the large family of a Devonshire clergyman, 14-year-old Edith is bookish and distant from her brothers and sister; as the story opens, in fact, she is sitting on the opposite side of the room from them, hunched over a book, with hands over her ears to shut out their voices. Edith, who writes stories incessantly and dreams of becoming a famous authoress, receives a forceful lesson in the importance of domestic duties when, on a picnic, her neglect (while reading) allows her brother Percy to fall over a cliff and suffer a skull concussion. Chastened by this experience, Edith resolves to 'put books comparatively aside' so that she can devote most of her time to family responsibilities.

Mary Arnold offers this comment:

Our readers must not misunderstand us. No one can say that to improve or cultivate the talents God has given us—to turn them to account in every possible way so far as is compatible with other duties—could ever be an action worthy of censure. Far from it—what *is* blameable, what *is* worthy of censure is the reckless indulgence of any one taste or inclination be it intellectual or otherwise, to the utter oblivion of those obligations and responsibilities to the rest of the human race which no member of it can escape from. Each is bound to each in this world with such indissoluble ties of connection & responsibility, that none can ever stand alone, or voluntarily loose those ties which God has ordained without incurring fearful risk if not here at least hereafter.

In the latter part of 'Lansdale Manor' Edith's cousin Margaret, who is pretty, wealthy, and sophisticated, pays a visit and tempts Edith once again to study Italian at the expense of her family responsibilities. However, eventually Margaret too discovers 'that intellect in this world, as an influence is as nothing beside unselfishness and love'. Beyond this point the notebook draft of the story becomes fragmentary and confused, and it is not clear how 'Lansdale Manor' concludes, except that Margaret's discovery of intellectual and social humility is meant to be merely a variation upon Edith's earlier experience.

The story is obviously, to some degree, confessional in nature. Edith's personality—her secret literary ambitions, her sense of isolation—reminds one immediately of what we know of Mary Arnold at this age. Edith's feelings of guilt about her relationship with her brother are paralleled in a diary entry by Mary dated 14 January [?1865]:

Oh how bitterly bitterly have I failed this holiday with regard to my brothers. If in one thing the struggle is successful in another it is as weak as ever if not more so. I am writing in miserable pain & expect to be awake half the night. What if reason should go altogether some day.[14]

Edith Lansdale, with her morbidly over-developed conscience, is perhaps a self-portrait as well as an utterly typical Charlotte Yonge heroine.

'Lansdale Manor' is also significant for its relentless, didactic emphasis upon the 'fearful risk' of intellectual pride—a theme which Mrs Ward was to explore more fully (and more maturely) in the character of Squire Wendover in *Robert Elsmere*. Mrs Ward knew that the life of the mind had its rewards—she was, paradoxically, one of the most scholarly English novelists of the nineteenth century—yet, in both her juvenilia and her published fiction, she expressed a profound distrust of the intellect that is not controlled by moral purpose. No matter what heterodoxy Mrs Ward may have been formally espousing by the 1880s, Squire Wendover and Edith Lansdale alike are the creations of a novelist imbued with the old-fashioned orthodox Christian attitudes towards the mind.

The next group of extant stories by Mary Arnold dates from 1869, when she was 18 years old and, finally liberated from the dreary boarding schools, was now living with her parents at Oxford. Though these stories are more sophisticated in plot and characterization than her earlier efforts, the theme remains (to quote again Mrs Maison's phrase about Charlotte Yonge's fiction) the punishment of 'uncontrolled female intellects or emotions'.

In 'A Gay Life', for example, we are introduced to Lena Warenne, another 'clever', ambitious young woman who has become engaged to Edward Woolley solely because his annual income is £5,000. Yet when a better prospect arrives on the scene—in the person of Sir Arthur Elsnore (a foreshadowing of Elsmere's name?), with £12,000 a year—she also becomes secretly engaged to him. That very evening Woolley falls over a cliff and dies; Lena is stricken with guilt; and a friend consoles her by saying, 'It was God's doing Miss Warenne not yours.' Precisely why Woolley must be punished for Lena's unfaithfulness is not explained, but, in any event, Lena repents and later marries a relatively poor man.

Mary submitted this story for publication in Miss Yonge's magazine the *Monthly Packet*, but Miss Yonge declined it saying, 'I am afraid it is too novelish for the Monthly Packet. I do not go on the principle of no love at all, and letting nobody marry, but I do not think it will do to have it the whole subject and interest of the story.'[15]

In 'Believed Too Late' (the locale of which is based on her observations during a visit to Glasgow in 1867), the erring woman is Maggie Phemister, an orphan who has been raised by her aunt and is now about to marry Hamish Graham. These happy plans are ruined by the arrival of Maggie's cousin Robin, who provokes jealousy and quarrels between the engaged couple. Robin is a significant character, because he represents the first appearance in Mary's fiction of a religious sceptic. He is, in fact, a prototype of Edward Langham, the Oxford don in *Robert Elsmere*, and his relationship with Maggie is very much like that of Langham and Rose Leyburn. But whereas in the novel Mrs Ward was able to portray sympathetically the sterile personality of Langham, in this story Robin is seen only in the most unpleasant light and from the outside. The psychology of unbelief—which later virtually became Mrs Ward's specialty as a novelist—is never examined by her in this story.

Maggie, a 'stout little Presbyterian', feels strangely drawn to Robin, for we are told that

nothing interests a woman so much as a suspicion of mental trouble or unhappiness in a man with whom she may be thrown in contact. Her clear quick sense of religious truth condemns him, but her tender woman's heart pities and excuses him, and between the two influences the delinquent is sure to obtain a large amount of sympathy & attention from her.

When Robin finds Maggie reading a hymnal on Sunday afternoon, he says with 'a melancholy sarcastic smile': 'You are very happy in your innocent childlike faith. I held the same once and was happy too. Bring back that time to me little cousin.' Maggie mildly suggests that there may be some remedy for his doubts, but Robin replies:

Remedy! . . . I know of none. I have read, I have travelled, I have conversed with some of the deepest intellectuals of the day and here I am, still uncertain about, still doubting the central truths of existence. Remedy little cousin! There is none.

Assuming that she is now in love with Robin, Hamish abandons Maggie in a fit of anger, and though they are reconciled at the end, it is only so that the heart-broken Maggie may die in his arms. Robin, in the meantime, has eloped with an heiress, but we are informed that he 'never lost that melancholy way of his. To the last day of his life he could never resist the temptation of reposing sentimental confidences in pretty women; or help laying himself out to win their compassion and approval.'

Of another story which doubtless would have borne traces of Charlotte Yonge's influence had it been completed, a mere one-sentence fragment seems to have survived. Entitled 'A Woman of Genius', it begins: 'All her life she had been told she was a genius and by this time she believed it.' (It may not be coincidental that, three decades later, Mrs Ward's original title for *Lady Rose's Daughter* [1903] was *A Woman of Talent*.[16])

Mary's first attempt to use a Westmorland setting in her stories can be seen in an untitled fragment which opens with a description of a valley—perhaps the valley of the Rotha—in which a house resembling Fox How 'stands on a rising tongue of land, . . . fronting a great curving hollow of hill'. The fragment abruptly ends with the complaint that the valley's church has a tall spire which 'carries with it an air of competition[,] of rivalry' with the surrounding hills. (This seems to be a paraphrase of a similar remark which Harriet Martineau had made about the new Ambleside church in her *Complete Guide to the English Lakes*.[17]) Since this valley in some of its features also resembles the 'Long Whindale' of *Robert Els-*

mere, it is at least conceivable that the fragment represents her first groping attempt to use the setting that she was later to adopt in the novel; but that would be a conjecture based on very slender evidence.

Mary Arnold's most ambitious literary undertaking of these years, a novella entitled *Ailie* (1869), reveals her still under the sway of Miss Yonge, though by now she has also discovered Hawthorne. To William D. Howells, in 1907, she confessed that 'my first book—happily unprinted!—was a sort of imitation of *Transformation* [the British title of *The Marble Faun* (1860)]'.[18] In an essay on Hawthorne published in 1904 she explained the nature of his fascination for her:

When I look back to the books which most strongly influenced my own youth, I am aware of a love for certain writings of Hawthorne, a love most ardent, and tenacious, which succeeded a passion of the same kind for certain writings of Mr. Ruskin. In both cases the devotion was hardly rational; it did not spring from any reasoned or critical appreciation of the books, for it dates from years when I was quite incapable of anything of the kind. It was the result, I think, of a vague, inarticulate sense of an appealing beauty, and a beauty so closely mingled with magic and mystery that it haunted memory 'like a passion.' Some scenes from 'The Scarlet Letter,' and some pages from 'The Stones of Venice,' haunted me in this way. And I can still remember how much this early impression depended upon Hawthorne's *austerity*, upon his deep-rooted Puritanism, upon what has often been pointed to as 'the sense of sin' in him.[19]

Her sense of affinity is not surprising: like Hawthorne, Mrs Ward devoted much of her career as a novelist to an exploration, characterised by intense but ambivalent emotion, of her Puritan heritage.

However, it must be acknowledged that the reminders of *Transformation* in *Ailie* are relatively superficial: an Italian setting, a walk through the Villa Borghese, a broken statue of a faun, and characters with mysterious pasts. The plot itself, like that of 'Believed Too Late', hinges upon a misunderstanding between two lovers that is finally resolved. The story is complicated, slightly melodramatic, and filled with declamatory speeches. Again the moral is one of submission:

'My darling it was God's will and we have no right to say the burdens he lays upon us are too heavy or too hard. He knows best.' Once the full story of Colonel Musborough's heroism in India during the Mutiny has been told so as to lay to rest certain rumours about his conduct, he and Ailie are able to marry, though two other figures in the story, because of their selfishness and shallowness, are permitted by the author to die.

Ailie was submitted in 1869 to Smith, Elder, who later became the publishers of Mrs Ward's books from *Robert Elsmere* onwards, but they expressed no interest in it. Mary Arnold promptly wrote to them: ' "Ailie" is a juvenile production and I am not sorry you decline to publish it. Had it appeared in print I should probably have been ashamed of it by and by.'[20]

Mary finally succeeded in breaking into print through the assistance of Felicia Skene, a very pious Anglo-Catholic novelist then living in Oxford—significantly, in a magazine to which Miss Yonge herself frequently contributed. Mrs Ward offered this recollection of the experience:

My friendship with dear Miss Skene must have begun very early, though I cannot exactly remember how or when. But it was she who encouraged me to print my first published story, 'A Westmoreland Story,' which I wrote when I was seventeen or eighteen, and published by her help in the *Churchman's Magazine* [sic].

I remember getting a few pounds for it. How proud I was, and how pleased she was to have been able to help me![21]

'A Westmoreland Story' begins with this paean to Loughrigg Fell, which towers above Fox How:

A long upward-trending stretch of ferny mountain-side, spreading itself out green and sunny and undulating as far as the eye can see; overhead a dappled June sky, clear and deep and dome-like, and immediately beneath at the mountain's foot, a river-threaded valley, mapped out in alternating patches of sheeny cornfield and sheep-dotted pasture, and bounded, and shut in from all the world by hills blue in colouring and sweeping and harmonious in outline—such is the scene which meets the eye when breathless, but with a sense of victory, the successful climber stands upon a summer's day on the bold and rocky brow of Loughrigg

Fell, and looks around rejoicing in the range and breadth of vision his
high position allows. (pp. 45-6)

The assured rhythm and subtle texture of this passage suggest
that Mrs Ward's talent for landscape description, nourished
by her reading of Ruskin, developed very early. The human
beings in 'A Westmoreland Story', unfortunately, are a good
deal less impressive and interesting than the fells. Dorothy
Morden, who is beautiful but thoughtless, trifles with the
affections of a manly young farmer, Amyas Sternforth. Because of her flirtation with Mr Paton, a clergyman, Sternforth
stalks off into the mountains, where he loses his way in the
dark and dies by stumbling over a cliff. Dorothy (like several
of Mrs Ward's later heroines, including Marcella Boyce) tries
to ease her conscience by nursing cholera victims. Inevitably
she becomes ill and is converted on her deathbed by Mr
Paton. Paton, incidentally, resembles Robert Elsmere in physical appearance and temperament: he is tall and thin, with
small hands, and has a nervous disposition. However, though
he speaks much of the historical context of scriptural texts in
a sermon (which, unfortunately, is reported verbatim), there
is no hint of heresy in his religious views.

Of Mary Arnold's final attempt at fiction during this
period, the novel of Oxford life entitled *Vittoria*, only a
scrap remains, and it tells nothing of the story's tone or plot.

III

The inescapable conclusion to be drawn from these stories
is that Mrs Ward's rebellious heroines, who appear in so many
of her novels, can trace their ancestry directly to the mid-Victorian didactic fiction which she read and wrote as an adolescent. Hence there is much justice to the charge often made
by her contemporaries that Mrs Ward's novels are very old-
fashioned in conception and execution. But of course the flirtatious and restless young women of the early stories are not
transplanted directly into the novels; when they reappear
after 1884, they have become, like their author, infinitely

more subtle and intellectually sophisticated. Underneath, however, they are recognizably the same persons.

Rose Leyburn (in *Robert Elsmere*), with her ardent pursuit of the 'aesthetic' life, Marcella Boyce (in *Marcella*), with her noble political ideals, and Julie Le Breton (in *Lady Rose's Daughter*), with her social ambitions, have been regarded by some critics as interesting variations upon the 'New Woman' of the late Victorian period, yet in fact they are really descendants of those heroines of Miss Yonge's who sinfully reject the customary submissive role of woman. To the extent that Mrs Ward is able to describe convincingly the inner life of women in revolt against Victorian feminine stereotypes, it is fair to say that she has partially liberated herself from the grip of Miss Yonge upon her literary imagination; but to the extent that Mrs Ward displays her desire to punish and tame these same women, it is also fair to say that she never fully escaped the influence of Miss Yonge.

Torn between the modern and mid-Victorian views of woman, Mrs Ward was never quite certain to what fate she ought to assign her obstreperous heroines. Her frequent solution was to allow the heroine to be jilted (the supreme Victorian punishment) or to suffer in some other way for a time, then to reward her in the third volume with a rich husband. In Mrs Ward's introduction to *Lady Rose's Daughter*, the artistic and moral tension produced by such a confused set of values is most evident:

I foresaw indeed a tragedy; the natural result of Julie's character and temperament, from which no Delafield would avail to save her. Undoubtedly, it seems to me now, the book ought to have closed in storm and darkness. The Julie of the story has in truth little to do with a happy ending and ducal honours. (pp. ix-x)

In other words, Mrs Ward regretted not having killed Julie. All that prevented such a denouement was that she 'no longer had the nervous energy wherewith to do it'. But the final chapters of Mrs Ward's other novels are strewn with the wrecked lives (and sometimes the dead bodies) of young women whose credo is summed up by Lady Kitty Ashe: 'My nature is hunger and storm.'[22]

As Edward Hallin says in *Marcella*: 'There is one clue, one only—*goodness—the surrendered will*. Everything is there—all faith—all religion—all hope for rich or poor' (ii, 343). The moral climax in each of Mrs Ward's novels arrives when her heroine, through personal suffering, finally learns this lesson and is thereby transformed. The face of Marcella, for example, after she has undergone such an experience, is described as filled with 'something new—something sad and yet benignant, informed with all the pathos and the pain of growth' (ii, 71). Of the heroine of *Lady Connie* we learn that 'some heat of feeling or of sympathy had fused in her the elements of being; so that a more human richness and warmth, and deeper and tenderer charm breathed from her whole aspect' (pp. 342-3). Rose Leyburn 'had suffered' and 'some searching thrill of experience had gone through the whole nature' (ii, 301). The lesson that each of these chastened heroines has learned is described in *Lady Connie* as 'the old spiritual paradox—that there is a yielding which is victory, and a surrender which is Power' (p. 393).

Though the pattern of self-renunciation remains constant in Mrs Ward's fiction, the specific behaviour of her heroines gradually changes. In the early books they are infatuated with Paterian aestheticism or socialism; in the later novels they have become suffragettes or simply 'flappers'. It is a sign of Mrs Ward's progressive deterioration as a novelist that in the stories written during the final decade of her life, she was no longer capable of maintaining that delicate balance between sympathy and condemnation of her aggressive heroines. Alarmed by the behaviour of women in the twentieth century, Mrs Ward tended more and more to fall back upon the stereotypes she had learned from Miss Yonge. Lady Connie—to cite only one example—is, in effect, a twin sister of Edith Lansdale's wicked cousin. She has expensive tastes, she flirts, she eats breakfast in bed, she smokes as she reads *The Times*, and (in another distinct echo of 'Lansdale Manor') she tempts her cousin Nora to neglect family obligations by offering to teach her Italian. Mrs Ward was retreating into the moral certitudes of children's fiction, and she was too intelligent a woman not to be aware of what she was doing. When in *Lady Connie* Radowitz and Falloden, bitter enemies, are brought together in a melodramatic scene, Falloden reflects: 'What a nursery tale!—how simple!—how crude! Could not the gods have devised a subtler retribution?' (p. 309).

Mrs Ward spoke often in later life of the need for achieving greater 'simplicity' in her novels, but it is evident that this simplicity was achieved by abandoning the moral complexity of her best fiction. It meant returning to the circumscribed world of Miss Yonge. Yet the important fact about Mrs Ward's fiction is that during her best years—between, let us say, 1888 and 1906—the novels were able to reflect simultaneously the narrow piety of Miss Yonge and the more informed, more cosmopolitan spirit which Mrs Ward acquired at Oxford under the tutelage of Mark Pattison. The naive, simplistic stories of her adolescence and old age reveal, as it were, the crude substratum upon which her greater achievements were built.

If one were asked to describe in a single sentence the unique quality of Mrs Ward's novels (though of course all such brief formulations are unsatisfactory), one would have to say that she displays the conservative moral sensibility of a Charlotte Mary Yonge overlaid with the incisive, uncompromising intellect of a Mark Pattison. It sounds like an impossible combination: little wonder that her books sometimes seem baffling to us. But the drama of Mrs Ward's life and fiction alike lies in her unending struggle to reconcile these strangely contrasting demands of head and heart, and it is a drama that holds a good deal of fascination even today.

Chapter 4

MRS WARD'S OXFORD

The air seemed to be full of bells—a murmurous voice—the voice of
Oxford; as though the dead generations were perpetually whispering to
the living.

—*Lady Connie* (p. 115)

I

After a childhood which she described as 'very miscellaneous
& often out-at-elbows'[1] and a boarding-school education
which seemed to her wretchedly inadequate, Mary Arnold,
with unconcealed delight, joined her family in 1867 for a
new life in Oxford. 'We are happier there than we have ever
been before I think', she had written to Mrs Cunliffe.[2]
Though painfully shy and always conscious of her poverty,
Mary, in her unostentatious way, set out to conquer Oxford,
and by the time she moved to London in 1881, she had indeed made her mark upon the university. She came to Oxford an unformed, untrained schoolgirl; she left one of the
most promising scholars of her generation. And Oxford made
its imprint upon her. It gave shape to her developing religious
convictions, and it implanted itself in her imagination as a
permanent symbol of all that was desirable in the intellectual
life.

The Oxford which Mary Arnold first saw in the 1860s was
as yet unspoilt by industrialism and the automobile. The
cobblestone streets were nearly empty, and the city's boundaries extended only to St Giles' church on the north and to

the bridges in the other directions. Yet, tranquil as it seemed
on the surface, Oxford was undergoing vast theological and
academic upheavals of which Mary was to become quickly
aware. During the Tractarian period (1833-45), when, according to Mark Pattison, 'our promising young men spent the
time which ought to have been devoted to study in endeav-
ouring to find the true Church',[3] there had been little concern for scholarship or academic reform. It was a highly in-
trospective time given over to soul-searching and theological
controversies, but the spell was finally broken by Newman's
conversion to Catholicism in 1845, an event that Pattison
later called 'a deliverance from the nightmare which had
oppressed Oxford for fifteen years'.[4] By then the pressure for
long-deferred academic renewal was irresistible. The desire
for change became so feverish that Mandell Creighton said
life in Oxford was like 'life in a house which always has the
workmen about it'.[5]

Likewise the departure of Newman from the scene (and
the attendant collapse of the Oxford Movement) produced a
new climate of rationalism and anti-clericalism in the university. The methods and conclusions of Biblical criticism were
belatedly introduced to English readers through such books
as *Essays and Reviews* (1860), which stank of heresy in the
nostrils of the orthodox. Naturally there were frequent and
lively clashes between the liberal and conservative forces
during these years. A. H. Sayce, who came to Oxford in the
spring of 1865, spent his first Sunday attending both the
morning and afternoon university sermons at St Mary's. In
the morning he heard Pattison end his sermon by declaring:
'It will be an ill day for the Church of England when dogma
and authority gain the upper hand and reason is denied its
rightful place as the corner-stone of all religion.' In the afternoon Sayce heard Liddon open his sermon with these words:
'Dogma and authority, authority and dogma—these two form
the keystone in the arch of our holy faith.'[6]

Had Mary Arnold lived at Cambridge—which Kingsley said
lay 'in magnificent repose'[7]—rather than Oxford, her religious

thought would probably have developed in a different direction, for at Cambridge theological inquiries were overshadowed by the enlightened yet orthodox exegetical studies of Westcott, Hort, and Lightfoot. At Oxford, however, it was more difficult to find a middle ground, as liberal and orthodox opinions tended to be sharply divided.

To Mrs Ward, looking back upon her early years of marriage, it seemed that strong intellectual winds eddied and swirled through Oxford as she and her husband quietly studied in the evenings. The theological antagonisms were symbolized, she thought, by three colleges which offered varying responses to the new learning of the nineteenth century. Christ Church was the bulwark of the High Church party, which by and large rejected modern Biblical criticism; Lincoln, avowedly rationalistic, embraced that very criticism and denounced an obscurantist orthodoxy; Balliol, uncomfortable in the presence of both Anglo-Catholicism and rationalism, charted a course that might be described as roughly Broad Church. For Mrs Ward, the names of these colleges became shorthand symbols for the dialectic of denial and assent which she saw being enacted at Oxford and in her own life.

What she had learned during her schooldays, she wrote, 'was learnt from personalities',[8] and the same can be said of her years at Oxford: in later life, whenever she called up memories of the university, her imagination dwelt upon the men of Christ Church, Lincoln, and Balliol and the system of theology that each represented. Though Mrs Ward was a 'novelist of ideas', as is often said, she was primarily responsive to ideas embodied in human flesh. At Oxford she was able to clarify her very mixed responses to modern unbelief by observing at first hand the personalities of eminent men whose reactions mirrored, in varying degrees, the conflicts within her own mind.

Mrs Ward seems not to have been personally acquainted with H. P. Liddon, Canon of St Paul's and Dean Ireland Professor of Exegesis at Oxford. In *A Writer's Recollections* she

paid tribute to his pulpit eloquence, and in *Lady Connie* she
described how 'at Christ Church and in St. Mary's the beautiful presence, and the wonderful gift of Liddon kept the old
fires burning in pious hearts' (p. 396). Primarily, however,
she regarded Liddon as a convenient symbol of Anglo-Catholic orthodoxy and as the heir of Newman and Pusey.

Though her subsequent remarks upon him were surprisingly generous, it is evident that Liddon was to Mrs Ward a
vaguely sinister and threatening figure at Oxford. Just as she
had shrunk in terror from encounters with Newman as a child
in Edgbaston, so she regarded Liddon with silent alarm and
saw him as a more potent force than he really was. Despite
her obvious powers of intelligent observation, Mrs Ward was
very slow in grasping the fact that it was actually the traditionalists, not the liberals, who were losing the important bat-
tles at Oxford. With a naïveté resulting from the peculiar circumstances of her childhood, Mrs Ward trembled before the
supposed power of the orthodox.

Liddon perceived the situation at Oxford quite differently
—and no doubt more realistically. In 1881 he wrote in the
Church Quarterly Review:

The days are gone when those who knew the real state of the case could
talk of Oxford as one of the 'eyes' of the Church. . . . The plain truth is
that henceforth Oxford will belong to the Church of England just as
much and just as little as does the House of Commons. It is still a centre
of social and intellectual interests; but as a centre of religious force it is
no longer what it was, and is unlikely in its future to be what it still is.[9]

At about the same time he referred sadly to the 'men like
myself' who linger 'about their ancient homes, but', he
added, 'death will soon do its work'.[10] The signs of these impending changes had been visible to High Churchmen for
many years. In 1869, when Liddon was offered a canonry at
St Paul's, he nearly declined it because Pusey feared that Liddon's partial absence from Oxford would allow the Theological School to fall into the hands of the rationalists. Pusey
'became very pathetic and emphatic' on the subject, Liddon
recorded in his diary.[11]

Conservatives like Liddon were not entirely helpless at Oxford, of course. They were capable of making life distinctly uncomfortable for Benjamin Jowett by withholding his salary as Professor of Greek, and they could still denounce from the pulpit the atheistic tendencies of modern thought. But they were losing their grip on Oxford, which was no longer the small, self-contained, clerical society that it had been at mid-century. The character of the university was increasingly being shaped by those winds of change that Mrs Ward heard blowing outside her study window on Bradmore Road.

II

In a letter written to Louise Creighton in 1916, Mrs Ward observed: 'In my "Recollections" lately I have been describing the old Oxford life, especially the Pattisons & the Paters. I have been almost startled to find how intimate I was with the Pattisons just before my marriage.'[12] And in *A Writer's Recollections* she explained that

I was much at Lincoln in the years before I married, and derived an impression from the life lived there that has never left me. . . . From 1868 to 1872, the Rector, learned, critical, bitter, fastidious, and 'Mrs. Pat,' with her gaiety, her picturesqueness, her impatience of the Oxford solemnities and decorums, her sharp restless wit, her determination *not* to be academic, to hold on to the greater world of affairs outside—mattered more to me perhaps than anybody else. (p. 103)

It was the Pattisons, as this passage suggests, who skilfully brought Mary Arnold out of her adolescent 'evangelical phase' and made her into a culturally and intellectually polished young woman.

Emilia Frances Pattison, who struck Mary at first sight as 'a perfect model of grace and vivacity',[13] was a woman of extraordinary beauty who charmed Oxford undergraduates yet at the same time was writing excellent articles on Renaissance art for the *Westminster Review* and other journals. Her learning, her irreverent wit, and her stylish dresses would have set her apart as an unusual figure in Oxford, even had she not been the wife of the Rector of Lincoln College. Mary

Arnold must have felt a shock of recognition when she met her, for Mrs Pattison was in fact a living embodiment of all those qualities in a woman which Charlotte Mary Yonge abhorred. Far from being properly submissive, she pursued her own career as an art critic, took separate holidays from her husband (ostensibly because of her health), and treated men as equals by sharing her French cigarettes with them under the starlight in cosy têtes-à-tête. With what mingled fascination and horror Mary must have watched her! Mrs Pattison, for her part, was undoubtedly amused by this intelligent but excessively sober girl who sat quietly at her suppers, dressed in a high woollen frock because it was Sunday. Shortly after Mrs Ward's marriage Mrs Pattison wryly observed in a letter to a friend that 'she is decidedly improved steadied & more thoughtful, & less angular'.[14]

Bertha Johnson, who belonged to the same circle of intellectual young Oxford women, felt that 'there was a sense of strain in [Mrs Pattison's] talk at one time and a provoking frivolity at another, often when you specially wanted her to be serious and helpful'.[15] There is no doubt that her witty manner concealed numerous hidden anxieties, particularly of a religious nature. During her childhood she had claimed to have repeated visions of angels. As a young student at the Art School in Kensington, she alarmed her more conventional friends by advocating drawing from the nude and, with characteristic inconsistency, by lying for hours on a bare floor to do penance for some real or imagined fault. Her marriage to Pattison dispelled all traces of Puseyism, and for a while she turned to Comtism; by the early 1880s, however, she developed a mystical, undogmatic religion, seldom communicated to others except in some of her short stories, which satisfied her sense of the supernatural.

But during the period that Mary Arnold knew her best, Mrs Pattison, notwithstanding her brilliant social and professional success, was inwardly struggling against a feeling of despairing scepticism. In one of her stories written at this time she spoke of 'the emptiness of life at Oxford',[16] and afterwards she looked back upon Oxford with contempt as 'that hole'.[17] What inspired such hatred was the memory not only of her spiritual turmoil there but also the failure of her marriage. Mrs Pattison was nearly 30 years younger than her husband, and although they shared certain intellectual interests, she was at last moved to confess to him in 1876 that she found him sexually repellent.[18] This frank admission was the final blow to an already weak relationship, and thereafter they rarely shared the same roof. Mrs Pattison fled to the Continent; her husband retired to his books.

Though Mary Arnold was dazzled by Emilia Pattison and envied her easy social grace, it was Pattison himself who fully captured her imagination. She spent uncounted hours in his library, which contained the largest private collection in Oxford, as he and Ingram Bywater, fellow and tutor of Exeter College, discussed the important topics of the day:

To listen to these two friends as they talked of foreign scholars in Paris, or Germany, of Renan, or Ranke, or Curtius; as they poured scorn on Oxford scholarship, or the lack of it, and on the ideals of Balliol, which aimed at turning out public officials, as compared with the researching ideals of the German universities, which seemed to the Rector the only ideals worth calling academic; or as they flung jibes at Christ Church whence Pusey and Liddon still directed the powerful Church party of the University:—was to watch the doors of new worlds gradually opening before a girl's questioning intelligence.[19]

Mary's name is first mentioned in Pattison's engagement diary on 31 December 1867, only a few months after she had settled there, and for the next three or four years she was one of his most frequent visitors.[20]

In *Lady Connie* Pattison appears in slightly disguised form as Mr Wenlock, Master of Beaumont College, of whom Mrs Ward says that

he had married a cousin of his own, much younger than himself; and after five years they had separated, for reasons undeclared. She was now dead [not literally true, of course, but the Pattison marriage at least was dead], and in his troubled blue eyes there were buried secrets no one would ever know. But under what appeared to a stranger to be a harsh, pedantic exterior the Master carried a very soft heart and an invincible liking for the society of young women. (p. 50)

Pattison's fondness for pretty faces was notorious. He was a lonely man desperately in need of the sympathy his wife could not give him, and so he gathered round himself a coterie of intelligent young female disciples, of whom Mary Arnold was one. Though he preferred that they be attractive, Pattison sought especially in such women that 'intellectual freemasonry', as he described it, 'by which liberal minds recognise each other, however widely separated they may be by station in life, by age, by acquirements, by extent of information'.[21]

On winter evenings Mary and Pattison would sit in his library, a cheerful fire and the Rector's cat between them, and he would open his mind to her 'with a frankness he showed much more readily to women than to men, and to the young rather than to his own contemporaries'.[22] What she especially absorbed from him was a rigorous intellectual standard and an appreciation of the delights of a literary life. Pattison's *Memoirs* (1885) began with the remarkable assertion that 'I have really no history but a mental history'. All his energy, he wrote, had been directed to one end—'to improve myself, to form my own mind, to sound things thoroughly, to free myself from the bondages of unreason, and the traditional prejudices' (pp. 1-2). Pattison's dedication to a life of the mind was revealed even in the manner of his death, for during his final illness he would say, 'Ah! I am to leave my books. . . . They have been more to me than my friends.' Then he would ask that more books be brought to his bed, until they at last covered him almost to his shoulders and were strewn about the floor next to him.[23]

It is surprising that Pattison, with his critical, sarcastic outlook, had been a disciple of Newman during the Oxford Movement. Pattison spent some time at Newman's 'monastery' in Littlemore, and it was rumoured that on one occasion he would have become a Roman Catholic had he not missed a train. Yet even during this Tractarian phase he attended and enjoyed Dr Arnold's inaugural address as Regius Professor of Modern History in 1841. Clearly anyone who could describe Arnold's views on the difficulty of miracles as 'admirable' was not a typical Newmanite.[24]

As Newman moved toward Roman Catholicism, Pattison moved toward an agnosticism disguised as liberal Anglicanism. To the end of his life, however, Pattison spoke generously of Newman, whose picture always rested on the mantelpiece of his study. They occasionally corresponded, and on 30 October 1877 Pattison recorded in his diary an 'affecting' interview with Newman at Edgbaston in which they 'talked of old times' and Newman 'gave me his blessing when I left'.[25] Mrs Ward was conscious of this odd but profound relationship between the two men, for she had noticed that 'in that sceptical and agnostic talk which never spared the Anglican ecclesiastics of the moment, or such a later Catholic convert as Manning, I cannot remember that I ever heard him mention the great name of John Henry Newman with the slightest touch of disrespect'.[26]

The closest that Newman and Pattison ever came to a rupture of their friendship was in 1861, following the publication of Pattison's essay 'Tendencies of Religious Thought in England, 1688-1750' in *Essays and Reviews*.[27] Newman's initial response was that 'Pattison professes no more than a survey or history—and so far is less to blame than Temple, who puts forth a theory',[28] but this was not an accurate assessment, and Newman came to realize that it was not. Though Pattison's essay appeared to be an innocuous historical account, it was actually subversive of Victorian orthodoxy in that it revealed trends in eighteenth-century theology to be as transient as tastes in literature, and it emphasized that theological systems were a product and expression of the intellectual forces of their age.

Pattison, in an earlier but less well-known essay, had described in vivid terms the impermanence of religious 'truth'. 'The dogma', he wrote, 'consecrated by the blood of martyrs, becomes in lapse of time a tyrant over reason; and from having been the bulwark of faith, settles into its chief impediment.' Hence in time it is necessary for religious men to initiate a new revolution 'to displace the charter which the old had inaugurated'.[29] History, to Pattison, was a record of this perpetual unravelling and reweaving of systems of truth—religious or otherwise—in which each generation was required to re-examine the past from its own unique perspective.

It is this view of historical scholarship that pervades a pamphlet entitled *A Morning in the Bodleian* which Mary Arnold wrote in 1871 when she was much under the Pattisonian spell. She describes the shelves of the Bodleian as being laden with forgotten, exotic books and manuscripts, and, like Pattison, she finds in this sight an occasion for sad reflections upon the transience of literary fame:

> Who can pass out of such a building without a feeling of profound melancholy? The thought is almost too obvious to be dwelt upon; but it is overpowering and inevitable. These shelves of mighty folios, these cases of laboured manuscripts, these illuminated volumes of which each may represent a life—the first, dominant impression which they make cannot fail to be like that which a burial-ground leaves—a Hamlet-like sense of 'the pity of it.' Which is the sadder image, the dust of Alexander stopping a bunghole, or the brain and lifeblood of a hundred monks cumbering the shelves of the Bodleian? (p. 13)

But Mrs Ward had also learned from Pattison to find solace in the 'perfect flower', the occasional great book, which emerges in this scene of literary waste. Pattison had taught her that the great goal of the scholar's life is to sift through this debris of the past, to give it shape with the aid of the best critical perceptions of one's age, and then to go to the grave with the awareness that one's own books will in all likelihood join that great dust-heap in the future. It is an austere vision, one which accounts perhaps for the mood of gloomy renunciation which characterizes so many of Pattison's intellectual endeavours.

Pattison was so enraged by the uproar which greeted *Essays and Reviews* that he decided to wash his hands of theology and church history because there was no 'proper public' for such work in England.[30] He resolved instead to write a history of learning from the Renaissance to the present. When it became evident that this task was too ambitious even for a scholar of Pattison's erudition, in time he limited himself to the French school of philology. During the final decades of his life he devoted nearly all of his time and energy to this undertaking, but he was increasingly haunted by the possibility that his plans would be frustrated by death. In *Robert Elsmere* Mrs Ward quotes an 'Oxford scholar' as saying '*a propos* of the death of a young man of extraordinary promise, "*What learning has perished with him! How vain seems all toil to acquire!*" ' (ii, 377). This was doubtless an authentic Pattisonian remark, for in old age he was continually preyed upon by such fears. While he was writing a book on Isaac Casaubon, which was to serve as a sort of prolegomenon to the larger survey of French philologists, he recorded these feelings in his diary on 10 October 1873:

My devouring anxiety now is grown to be to live to complete my book. It is the only thing which now really interests me. But a despair comes over me when I find myself this day 60, and still face to face with a chaos of materials to which my feeble memory affords the only clue!

Pattison was so fascinated by Joseph Scaliger, the sixteenth-century classical scholar, that eventually he narrowed down even further the subject of his magnum opus to be a life of Scaliger, in whom he found a distinguished but forgotten forerunner of modern Biblical critics. Because he preferred truth to convenience and would not recant his heresies, Scaliger, according to Pattison, was wickedly slandered by Roman Catholic controversialists of his time, especially the Jesuits.

Mrs Ward, while completing the final chapters of *Helbeck of Bannisdale* in the winter of 1898, read the portion of Pattison's life of Scaliger that was published posthumously, and it persuaded her to treat Catholicism more harshly in her novel than she would have otherwise. To her son Arnold, on 7 March 1898, she explained:

Look at the whole story of Scaliger's struggle with the Jesuits, they in defence of such things as the False Decretals, & the historicity of Dionysius the Areopagite, he speaking the truth & soberness of criticism. Now all the world, Jesuits included, knows where the truth lay, but then no weapon was too foul to use. It has made me feel rather sternly as to the end of Helbeck.

For Pattison, too, Scaliger's career had an immediate and personal relevance. Though purporting to be an objective historical study, Pattison's biography of Scaliger was really his answer to those ecclesiastical forces which had attempted to silence the contributors to *Essays and Reviews*. Pattison (perhaps unconsciously) saw himself as the persecuted Scaliger and the High Church party as the Jesuits.

This deep vein of bitterness in Pattison was not fully apparent even to Mrs Ward, who remarked that when his *Memoirs* were published posthumously, they revealed much about him that she had not known before.[31] To only a few close acquaintances did Pattison reveal the full extent of his personal frustration and religious scepticism. 'I doubt very much the truth of the proposition that Priests believe in the Gods they worship', he observed acidly to one such friend, his wife's niece, in 1881.[32] In the autumn of 1883 his recurrent nightmare became a reality: having spent nearly 30 years of his life gathering materials for his vindication of Scaliger, he suddenly suffered a terminal illness just as he was about to begin writing the book. 'I cannot conceal from myself that I am dying, & that I shall never see you again', he wrote to Mrs William Hertz on 30 November. 'My regret at leaving the world touches many points, one is the vast variety of schemes left incomplete or not even begun, the thoughts I shall carry away with me without ever having had the opportunity of communicating them.'[33] A few days before the end he dictated a confession of his religious agnosticism which his widow later decided not to publish as an appendix to his *Memoirs*. Pattison died in August 1884, nursed by his estranged wife, who was horrified by his last hours—'the always uncontrollable temper, the rage, the pathos, the abject fits of terror, the immense vitality'.[34]

Mrs Ward had caught her final glimpse of him a few months earlier, when she found him 'lying a white and dying man on his sofa in London' with 'sad haunting eyes'.[35] She never forgot that moment. A year later, when she began to write *Robert Elsmere*, Mrs Ward was to pay a subtle tribute to this great but troubled man who had been her mentor at Oxford.

III

Despite her great affection for Pattison, Mrs Ward could not ignore the fact that his negations had produced little but personal unhappiness. Christ Church might represent reactionary superstition, but it was equally obvious that Lincoln represented only barren scepticism. The *via media* (not in the usual Anglican sense, of course) which she was seeking could be found only at Balliol, where Mrs Ward discovered in both Benjamin Jowett and T. H. Green an admirable juxtaposition of intellectual freedom and personal piety. Though Pattison was instrumental in forming her mind, Jowett and Green spoke directly to her deeply-rooted religious instincts.

Jowett had more real claim to be a liberal martyr than did Pattison, for his unorthodox theological opinions brought upon him a good deal of harassment from his enemies at Oxford. Mrs Ward, in *Lady Connie*, described the Master of Balliol as 'a chubby-faced, quiet-eyed man, with very white hair, round whom the storms of orthodoxy had once beaten, like the surges on a lighthouse' (p. 396). Yet Jowett, unlike Pattison, did not relish the role of martyr, nor did he secretly nurse a hatred of the Church. Whatever his private theological opinions might be, he was willing to conform cheerfully in outward matters and to avoid pursuing his logic to the point of confrontation. During the Voysey heresy trial, Jowett's cryptic comment was that 'Voysey looked too far over the hedge'.[36] He agreed with Matthew Arnold that the Church of England was too valuable an institution to allow it to be endangered by petty quarrels over doctrine.

Nevertheless, Jowett was conscious of his own ambiguous

status in the Church, and he often asked himself whether it would continue to be possible to retain his footing as a liberal Anglican clergyman. His conclusion was that 'although we are in a false position in the church, we should be in a still more false position out of the church'.[37] To a Catholic priest who was thinking of becoming either an Anglican or Unitarian, Jowett wrote in 1889:

> I should not myself have advised you to leave the Roman Catholic Church when life is half over. All churches in the present age of criticism & of physical science have their difficulties but probably in none of them is it impossible to live a life like Christ's or to do his work. Of course one must be loyal to his church:—he must not speak or write against it: or take part with its assailants. But I do not see how any ecclesiastical Superior can find fault with one for preaching *only* the best parts of one's religion—the elements in which all the best men of all religions are agreed.

He acknowledged that the liberal clergyman might sometimes feel himself to be in a difficult, isolated position, but he cautioned against any separation from one's Church in a moment of excitement. 'I have been lately trying to urge the same view on a Protestant who wants to become a Catholic', Jowett concluded. 'For the short time which we have to live, either church is enough.'[38]

Mrs Ward could not accept this argument, and in *Robert Elsmere*, she said, she tried to show 'a man in revolt against the doctrines and services of the English Church, and seeing no way—he being a minister of the Church—to maintain a personal honesty, other than the way of voluntary secession'.[39] Though Mrs Ward later defended Jowett's decision to remain within the Church as 'a mistaken *hopefulness*',[40] she continued to believe, in the words of her Richard Meynell, that 'Jowett . . . ought to have gone'—i.e., gone out (p. 14). Meynell himself decides to fight the battle inside the Church, but his defiant declaration of war against orthodoxy is more reminiscent of the spirit of Pattison than of Jowett. It is noteworthy that Mrs Ward eventually came round to Jowett's view that the Church of England must be reformed from within, while she still retained Pattison's mood of militant, aggressive hostility towards the Church. In fact, both strains of thought are incongruously mixed in *The Case of Richard Meynell*.

Jowett was not unaware that in subscribing to the Creeds and Articles in a private sense he lay himself open to the charge of dishonesty. In one of his notebooks he listed the 'disadvantages of a liberal theology in practical life':

Isolation & hostility
Nothing definite to teach . . .
Unsettlement in self leading to unsettlement in others.
Self criticism causing impotence for action
Feebleness

However, among advantages he noted that the liberal is 'always going forward—though separated from the clergy [he] partake[s] of the deeper & wider movement of the age'.[41]

Jowett's contribution to *Essays and Reviews*, 'On the Interpretation of Scripture', has often been summarized as advocating that the Bible must be interpreted like any other book. But what Jowett actually said was more carefully qualified than that:

No one who has a Christian feeling would place classical on a level with sacred literature . . . yet in what may be termed the externals of interpretation, that is to say, the meaning of words, the connexion of sentences, the settlement of the text, the evidence of the facts, the same rules apply to the Old and New Testaments as to other books. (p. 337)

Jowett, like the Arnolds, was certain that the essential moral qualities of Scripture could be retained even though critical investigation might call into doubt particular dogmas or particular received readings of the text. 'On the Interpretation of Scripture' ended on a curiously autobiographical note, as Jowett was moved to ask himself whether the liberal theologian, always incurring the disfavour of the traditionalists, had a legitimate role in the Church. 'He may depart hence before the natural term, worn out with intellectual toil; regarded with suspicion by many of his contemporaries; yet not without a sure hope that the love of truth, which men of saintly lives often seem to slight, is, nevertheless, accepted before God' (p. 433).

Jowett regarded modern Biblical criticism as a logical extension of the fundamental principles of the Protestant Reformation, and he also looked forward to a creedless, nonmiraculous 'new Christianity' of the future. For him, the essence of the Christian faith was to be found in moral action, not a set of theological propositions. Whereas Pattison in his deathbed confession had declared that 'the true slavery is that of the "doers" to the free idle philosopher who lives not to do, or enjoy, but to know',[42] Jowett insisted that learning ought not to be pursued for its own sake. Mrs Ward, who had earlier learned from Miss Yonge the 'fearful risk' of unrestrained intellectual development, did not hesitate in casting her lot with Jowett. 'There is a great difference between us, Squire', Robert Elsmere says at one point to Wendover (who is clearly to be identified with Pattison). 'You look upon knowledge as an end in itself. It may be so. But to me knowledge has always been valuable first and foremost for its bearing on life' (ii, 379).

At Balliol Mrs Ward also became acquainted with another man who, as she said in *Robert Elsmere*, 'had never shirked action in the name of thought, for whom conduct had been from beginning to end the first reality' (ii, 431). Thomas Hill Green, Balliol tutor and Professor of Moral Philosophy, was exactly the sort of thinker who would naturally appeal to Mrs Ward: a 'philosophical Puritan'[43] who had renounced the dogmatic basis of Christianity but clung tenaciously to Christian morality. Pattison, on the other hand (in language which Mrs Ward quoted in *Robert Elsmere*), was alarmed by the 'fresh invasion of sacerdotalism' which he thought was resulting from Green's Hegelian metaphysic, and claimed that only Green's 'puzzle-headedness' prevented him from seeing that the Tories would 'carry off his honey to their hive'.[44] There was, in fact, a studied ambiguity about Green's theological pronouncements which enabled Evangelicals, Anglo-Catholics, and Theists alike to claim him as their own. Green's importance for many of his disciples lay not in the technical details of his philosophical writings (which few understood) but in his apparent success in making religion once again intellectually respectable at Oxford. He was a godly man—*Gottbetrunken*, as Mrs Ward liked to say—whose sympathetic treatment of Christianity, even though an involuted prose style sometimes obscured his precise meaning, was symbolically important at a university that had been dominated for several decades by rationalistic philosophical systems.

Despite his unorthodox ideas, the impression which Green conveyed to Mrs Ward and others was one of strength, solidity, and imperturbability. Though his personal religious views were close to a 'modified unitarianism',[45] he was extremely cautious in expressing them, for he wished to avoid a 'revolutionary notoriety'.[46] He considered it essential to phrase his disagreement with orthodox Christianity in moderate, conciliatory language. 'Though I admire and agree with the leaders of the unorthodox', he said, 'I do not like the tone and spirit of their following.'[47] It was primarily Green's example, we may surmise, that revealed to Mrs Ward the importance of espousing heterodox opinions in a sober, discreet manner.

Unlike most Victorian heretics, Green had experienced no sudden, cataclysmic loss of faith, but the departure from the Church had been painful nevertheless. 'The parting with the Christian mythology is the rending asunder of bones & marrow', he once told Mrs Ward (who attributed these words to Mr Grey in *Robert Elsmere*). 'A long intellectual travail had convinced him that the miraculous Xtianity was untenable', she declared; 'but speculatively he gave it up with grief and difficulty, & practically, to his last hour, he clung to all the forms & associations of the old belief with a wonderful affection.'[48] Mrs Ward believed that the mainspring of Green's life was a search for God, 'the absorbing desire to find ever firmer & firmer bases in the sphere of reason for that faith which governed his every action & affection'.[49] (To which Gladstone's amused response was that Green's substitution of philosophy for theology suggested 'a farmer under the agricultural difficulty who has to migrate from England and plants himself in the middle of the Sahara'.[50])

Green's catholicity (or perhaps confusion) of outlook was such that he could applaud both apostates and those young men who, presumably under his influence, decided to take orders. Henry Sidgwick, on the one hand, recalled that Green 'did not sympathize intellectually with the views which led me to leave the Church of England, but I think he sympathized with the spirit that prompted some resolute and definite action—something more than mere critical talk—on the part of persons holding these views'.[51] Henry Scott Holland, on the other hand, received a lengthy, hearty letter of congratulation from Green when he was ordained:

> There can be no greater satisfaction to me [wrote Green] than to think that I helped to lay the intellectual platform of your religious life; and that, not merely out of my personal regard to you, but because if I were only a breeder of heretics I should suspect my philosophy. If it is sound, it ought to supply intellectual formulae for the religious life whether lived by an "orthodox" clergyman or (let us say) a follower of Mazzini.[52]

Robert Elsmere, too, was to meet just such an oddly mixed response in his various encounters with Mr Grey.

In *Robert Elsmere* Mrs Ward gives an evocative description of one of Green's two lay sermons[53] at Oxford (delivered in 1870 and 1877) that summarize the basic religious ideas to which she gave expression in her novel. In the first of them, entitled 'The Witness of God', which develops a line of thought almost identical to that of Matthew Arnold's *St Paul and Protestantism* (1860), Green argued that the faith of the early Church had been undogmatic and based on personal experience, the archetypical example of which was Paul's conversion on the road to Damascus. Our task today is to penetrate the language of dogmatic theology which separates us from the true moral wisdom of Jesus.

We do [Christianity] wrong in making it depend on a past event [i.e., the Resurrection], and in identifying it with the creed of a certain age, or with a visible society established at a certain time. What we thus seem to gain in definiteness, we lose in permanence of conviction; for importunate inquiry will show us that the event can only be expressed through a series of fluctuating interpretations of it, behind which its original nature cannot be clearly ascertained; that the 'visible church' of one age is never essentially the same as that of the next; that it is only in word, or to the intellectually dead, that the creed of the present is the same as the creed of the past.

Like Matthew Arnold and Jowett, Green disparaged separation from the Church, for he saw in the Eucharist an emblem of Christian unity which transcended all credal differences. 'We cannot afford to individualise ourselves even in respect of outward symbols', he said. 'We do wrong to ourselves and them, if we allow any intellectual vexation at the mode in which they may be presented to us to prevent us from their due use.' Not until late in her life, however, did Mrs Ward learn to accept this particular tenet of Green's. 'With regards to conformity to church usage & repression of individual opinion he & I disagreed a good deal', she wrote in 1888.[54]

'Faith', the second lay sermon, was merely an exposition and further development of these same ideas, although Mrs Ward felt that it 'expresses his thought more clearly'.[55] Green insisted that to strip faith of dogmas—i.e., the vulnerable scientific and historical statements in the Creeds—is to restore Christianity to its original form. Propositions concerning matters of facts (e.g., supposedly miraculous occurrences) must be judged by the ordinary canons of reason and probability. Hence the Creeds, which can no longer bear up under the scrutiny of impartial inquiry, have outlived their usefulness. 'It is not the reality of God or the ideal law of conduct that is in question, but the adequacy of our modes of expressing them.' Green acknowledged that many individuals would experience personal anxieties in a transitional period when the old beliefs were translated into new language, but he looked with hope to the future. 'Faith in God and duty will survive much doubt and difficulty and distress, and perhaps attain to some nobler mode of itself under their influence.'

It is not at all fanciful to see in this last sentence the germ of *Robert Elsmere*.

IV

Mrs Ward was not a merely passive receptacle of various 'influences' at Oxford, though *A Writer's Recollections* distinctly creates that impression. Her memoirs, in their almost exclusive emphasis upon Oxford personalities and ideas, tell us little about Mrs Ward herself during this period of her life. For a novelist, she was remarkably non-introspective; she habitually abstracted and flattened her past into a series of intellectual 'stages'. To see her as a living human being at Oxford rather than an embodiment of various ideologies, therefore, we must turn to other documents and records.

It is useful to learn, for example, that Tom Arnold's daughter came to Oxford with an already fully developed interest in religious controversies. In the autumn of 1867, Lord Wyfold, a pupil and boarder with Arnold, returned to the house one day to announce that he had just matriculated at Worcester. 'I wonder if you will join the High Church party or the Low Church party', Mary, then 16, asked him immediately. 'This remark I have always remembered', Wyfold said, 'because it showed the bent of her mind. I did not know what High Church or Low Church meant.'[56]

A diary which she kept in June and July of 1869 also reveals hers strong moral predilections. 'A day frittered away in croquet and idleness', she wrote disapprovingly on 22 June. 'Some end must come to this idle self-indulgent life. I feel too ashamed of myself to go on longer with croquet at 11 in the morning.' She repeatedly reproaches herself for indolence, records her reading (Carlyle's *On Heroes and Hero-Worship*, Huxley's article on 'Scientific Aspects of Positivism'), and reflects unhappily upon her inability to please young men.

When not playing croquet, Mary was participating in an active family life with seven younger brothers and sisters, revelling in the libraries of Oxford, and reading Hawthorne, Ruskin, *Ecce Homo*, 'Uncle Matt', and of course Carlyle. In *Eltham House* Caroline Wing describes (in a passage which had a private significance for Mrs Ward) how at the age of 17 'she had learnt pages of [*Sartor Resartus*] by heart, slept with it under her pillow, declaimed "The Everlasting Yea," and generally behaved, as her grandmother might have behaved a century before, when Carlyle was the fashion!' (p. 255). During a holiday visit to her family at Oxford in 1865, Mary had recorded in her diary that she was reading *Sartor* and declared that the 'Everlasting No' made one 'feel the mystery of life & the dignity and thank God that we are such glorious things as living souls'.

But Mark Pattison would not allow her to drift along in this adolescent stage of desultory reading. 'Get to the bottom of something', he said; 'choose a subject and know *everything* about it'.[57] Mary, who had written 'A Tale of the Moors' at Shifnal, obeyed this injunction by plunging impetuously into the depths of the Bodleian and making herself, within a few years, one of England's leading authorities on early Spanish literature and history. It was an astonishing achievement for a girl in her early twenties. In the solitude of the Bodleian's 'Spanish room', surrounded by ancient volumes in sheepskin and vellum, the silence broken only by the voices of Oxford's many bells, Mary patiently pored over the records of the past. 'With much undisciplined wandering from shelf to shelf and subject to subject, there yet sank deep into me the sense of history, and of that vast ocean of the recorded past, from which the generations rise, and into which they fall back', she recalled. 'And that in itself was a great boon—almost, one might say, a training, of a kind.'[58] By 1871 even J. R. Green in Cannes had heard of her 'great fame for learning'.[59]

This experience gave Mrs Ward that keen insight into the vagaries of the scholarly temperament which she was to reveal in her treatment of Squire Wendover and Edward Langham in *Robert Elsmere*. The scholar, she realized, could become a mere parasite whose reading offered him an escape from life;

Mrs Ward, as we have seen in her early stories, was convinced that the pursuit of knowledge without reference to moral considerations was ultimately self-destructive. In *A Morning in the Bodleian* she described such a pedant:

That old man in the study that you are passing, with his face buried in a folio of Plotinus, has learning enough to make even Dr. Grausam stare. Perhaps, if the paradox be allowed, he is too literally a student; too much bent on study, too little on realising study for the world's benefit. . . . He has settled down to a life of mere luxury, not of the table but of the library, not of wines but of books. (p. 4)

Similarly, in a cancelled passage of *Robert Elsmere*, Mrs Ward pictured

a strange & scanty university race,—men of whom all Oxford knew the names and nothing more, who might be seen occasionally in the Bodleian or met in a daily constitutional round the Parks[,] the bats of learning living in retreats unknown of man, pale Avatars of mysterious forces. . . . Such men are not producers of books; no nation in its senses would endow their research; the scholar's venerable crown is not for them. They feed on literature as the parasite on the oak-leaf and batten on other's [*sic*] men's thoughts and feelings, while their own die out.[60]

Mrs Ward may have been strongly influenced by the Pattisonian ideal of scholarship, but she certainly did not accept his view that learning was its own end. Jowett and Miss Yonge had convinced her otherwise.

Oxford was of course not all libraries and books, even for a studious girl like Mary Arnold. Taine, who met her in 1871, found that she wore her learning lightly—'a most intellectual lady, but yet a simple, charming girl'.[61] She often managed to go to balls, though she was so poor that once Miss Skene had to buy a ticket for her,[62] and Thomas Humphry Ward, a young fellow and tutor of Brasenose, wrote in his diary after such an evening: 'The Chambers' dance: very spirited. M.[ary] A.[rnold] shows her gayer side, being arrayed (externally) in *black*.'[63] On 16 February 1871 he recorded: 'M.A. by reason of being overtired takes up certain serious points & rather shocks me by being shocked. If poor Comte had foreseen how even the elect wd. shudder at his name—he would have changed it!—' (From other sources we know that Mrs Ward was much fascinated by Comtism; obviously she 'shuddered' at his ethical practices rather than his theory.) Humphry hesitated to propose to a penniless girl, but a new regulation at about this time permitted Brasenose fellows to marry, and so on 16 June they became engaged, with Humphry confiding to his diary: 'What worries broken down! What mists dispelled!' In the following weeks they were photographed by Charles Dodgson (who had an affectionate regard for Mary's younger sisters), took Communion together, visited the Matthew Arnolds at Harrow, and clambered up Loughrigg. 'It is a true "holy day" for us', wrote Humphry about the latter event. 'She is never so delicious as when she is showing me her treasures—& Loughrigg is one of the chiefest of them.' On 6 April 1872 they were married by Arthur Stanley.

Humphry Ward, whom James Knowles thought very priggish and Pattison (perhaps slightly jealous) described as 'somehow unpleasant',[64] was a quiet, unassuming man, destined always to be overshadowed by his more famous wife. (There were in fact rumours that in later years he occasionally wearied of his role as husband of Mrs Humphry Ward.) The deepest friendship of his life was with Pater, also a Brasenose tutor, who lived directly across Bradmore Road from the Wards' house in the new tract of redbrick villas then springing up north of St Giles' church.

Mrs Ward spent her mornings in the Bodleian, wrote for journals and newspapers, helped in the founding of Somerville College, and bore three children by 1879. In their home, tastefully decorated in the latest aesthetic style ('not amiss though it falls somewhat short of rather ambitious intention', Mrs Pattison airily announced[65]), the Wards entertained a circle of intimate friends that included the Mandell Creightons, the Arthur Johnsons, Pater and his two sisters, and the James Thursfields. It was, in short, a comfortable little society of earnest young dons and their wives.

The most intriguing question about these Oxford years— and one that cannot be answered with any precision—is when

Mrs Ward formally renounced Christianity. While painting her portrait in July 1876, Mrs Johnson discovered that Mrs Ward's religious opinions were already quite unconventional:

I was surprised at the full extent of her vague religion. Jowett is her great admiration and Matt Arnold her guide for some things. She is great on the rising Dutch and French and German school of religious thought, very free criticism of the Bible, entire denial of miracle, our Lord only a great teacher.[66]

Between 1879 and 1881 when she was doing her 'sheer, hard, brain-stretching work'[67] for the *Dictionary of Christian Biography* (of which more later), this amorphous liberalism was gradually transformed into a settled disbelief in orthodox Christianity. The reading, the historical research, the evenings spent in Pattison's study—all had combined to drive her out of the Church.

Receiving an invitation to write for *The Times* in 1880, Humphry moved to London with the understanding that his wife and children would follow him within a year. On 19 July 1881 Mrs Ward wrote to him from Oxford:

I have been sitting in the Parks to-night, thinking of *historical* religion, and of the basis history affords for faith in God and a spiritual life. It is borne in upon me more & more that there lies our only or our main "ground of certainty"[,] there and in conscience. Conscience is surely God's revelation to each one of us, and the interpretations of conscience do not practically matter. . . . Conscience within, knowledge without, God's inner & outer laws, these are the guides of the future. And behind and above all the Power who hath brought us thus far, and into whose bosom we yield ourselves at death.

By the eve of her departure from Oxford, she had thus formulated her reverent, quasi-Christian Theism. London and the larger world were to teach her much of men and manners ('one never dreamt of all this at Oxford', she remarked after lecturing to large audiences of working men in 1892[68]), but her religious and literary education was essentially completed in 1881. In an intellectual sense, as *Robert Elsmere* indicates, Mrs Ward never left Oxford.

Chapter 5
THE NOVELIST AS CRITIC

This morning I got on with the first chapter [of *Helbeck of Bannisdale*], & felt a glow of pleasure in it—something like "This is my work after all and I am glad I can do it." So often I don't see clearly what I ought to do—I want to be at Biblical criticism or something quite different—and then there are moments again when the gift for fiction seems quite clear.

—Mrs Ward (1897)[1]

I

The self-doubts which Mrs Ward occasionally experienced as a novelist—whether, as she put it in 1890, 'I may believe in my métier and give myself up to it without qualms'[2]—grew directly out of the advice which reviewers and friends alike offered her. Was her literary gift primarily critical rather than creative? Many thought so, including Mandell Creighton, who sent her this counsel following the publication of *Miss Bretherton* in 1884:

It seems to me that a novelist must have seen much, must lay himself out to be conversant with many sides of life, must have no line of his own, but must lend himself to the life of those around him. This is the direct opposite of the critic. I wonder if the two trades can be combined. . . . You are a critic in your novel. . . . You threw into the form of a story many critical judgements, & gave an excellent sketch of the possible worth of criticism in an unregenerate world. This was worth doing once: but if you are going on with novels you must throw criticism to the winds & let yourself go as partner of common joys, common sorrows & common perplexities.[3]

The same view was expressed by Jowett about *Robert Elsmere*. 'Shall I tell you my real opinion?' he wrote to Mrs Ward in 1888. 'The form of it does not seem to me perfectly suited either to its subject or to you: my feeling is that you have the ability & knowledge which could make a great authoress but in the realm of serious writing rather than of fiction.'[4] E. A. Freeman, who had hoped Mrs Ward would pursue her historical studies, lamented: 'I have been reading *Robert Elsmere*. What a fool he was! . . . And for this kind of thing the West-Gothic kings are left undone.'[5]

Mrs Ward was almost inclined to agree with such admonitions. Between 1871 and 1883 she wrote little fiction, devoting her time instead to literary journalism and scholarship. Even after the stunning success of *Robert Elsmere* in 1888, there were various abortive attempts on her part to return to non-fictional writing, and at one point she and her husband seriously considered purchasing the *Saturday Review*. Since Mrs Ward's fame as a novelist has overshadowed her substantial achievements as a critic, this aspect of her career is worth describing in some detail, especially as the themes of her criticism and fiction are often so similar and mutually illuminating. If we expect to grasp the significance of *Robert Elsmere* and Mrs Ward's other novels, we must view them in the context of her prodigious number of essays, reviews, prefaces, pamphlets, and speeches, all of which, frequently in unexpected ways, bear important relationships with her fiction.

Mrs Ward's first articles, published during the 1870s in *Macmillan's Magazine*, the *Saturday Review*, and the *Fortnightly Review*, grew directly out of her Spanish research in the Bodleian. 'Everyone writes or lectures here', she explained casually to Taine in 1871, 'and one must follow the fashion. Besides it passes the time, and the library is so fine and convenient.'[6] J. R. Green, Creighton, Stubbs, and Freeman were all impressed by her knowledge of Spanish history. 'There is nobody but Stubbs doing such work in Oxford now', Creighton declared,[7] and as early as 1871 (when she was only 20 years old), Freeman asked her to write a book on Spain for a historical series which he was editing.

However, after their marriage in 1872, Mrs Ward and her husband had to write articles (rather than books) prolifically in order to supplement his modest income as a tutor. In 1879, for example, Humphry found it necessary to ask his uncle to introduce him to the editor of the *British Quarterly Review* as a potential contributor,[8] even though he was already writing for other journals and lecturing at a furious pace. When an offer came from *The Times* in 1880, therefore, the Wards abandoned Oxford with regrets but with a sense of expanding literary and financial opportunities before them. Mrs Ward wrote book reviews for the *Oxford Chronicle*, contributed occasional notes and reviews to the *Pall Mall Gazette*, and, inevitably, became a reviewer for *The Times* as well. In her memoirs she recalled that 'for the *Times* I wrote a good many long, separate articles before 1884, on "Spanish Novels," "American Novels," and so forth; the "leader" on the death of Anthony Trollope; and various elaborate reviews of books on Christian origins' (p. 192).

These were years of extensive reading for her. 'I wish I could get through books quicker', she complained to her husband on 14 October 1882. 'Three or four volumes of these novels a week is about all that I can do & that seems to go no way.' Yet even the reviews for *The Times*, massive by our standards today, did not absorb all of her astonishing energies. In the autumn of 1881 she proposed to the *Guardian*, the High Church newspaper, a monthly column to be entitled 'Foreign Table-Talk' for a salary of £10 per column.[9] In the first instalment, 1 March 1882, she wrote:

The mass of foreign periodicals grows more and more overwhelming year by year. The range and variety of this current literature, and the amount of intellectual energy spent upon its maintenance, is very little realised in England, except by professed students. . . . Out of all this variety of writing we propose to notice, from time to time, in the first place, such articles as are of general literary interest, and in the next such special work as seems likely to attract English readers (p. 323)

In this particular column she summarized and analyzed the contents of six French journals and three German ones; later she was to turn her attention also to Spanish and Italian periodicals. Between March and September 1882 she wrote eight such 'Foreign Table-Talk' columns, most of them occupying the better part of a newspaper-size page in small type.

At about this time Mrs Ward also began to think again about her old dream of writing a book, preferably on Spain. During the Oxford years she had begun a primer of English literature but abandoned it when, as Stopford Brooke laconically remarked, she 'took a fancy to *Beowulf*, and wrote twenty pages on it! At this rate the book would have run to more than a thousand pages.'[10] And she of course contributed to *The English Poets* volumes which Humphry edited in 1880. But by 1880 Mrs Ward was convinced that she wanted to synthesize her published work of recent years by writing a book-length treatment of Spanish literature. Humphry explained to the Macmillans that his wife had decided to put aside a history of France she once had thought of writing:

What she really desires to do is a book of papers, something after the model of her Uncle M. Arnold's Essays, which shall really tell the student of early Spanish Literature something about the subject, & which though made as light & attractive in style as possible—& especially light because the subject is remote—shall really contain research. Such a book, containing perhaps eight essays, some of them . . . republished, she thinks she could prepare in a year and a half or so—or even in less time, perhaps.[11]

As a first step towards producing the book, she offered in 1882 to write one or two articles on modern Spanish poets for *Macmillan's Magazine*.[12]

The response to this proposal was so favourable that on 29 November 1882 she wrote her father:

Quite between ourselves, I have got what I think I may call a promise of the editorship of *Macmillan* whenever it next falls vacant. Both Mr. [George] Craik and Mr. Macmillan have written about it in such a way that I don't know what else they can mean if not that. And Mr. [George] Grove may retire at any time as whenever the Royal College of Music is started he will have to devote himself to it. . . . I should like it, for it would give me I suppose about £400 a year, & with the help of a girl-secretary for two or three hours in the day, I should have much more time to write a serious book than I ever shall have if I go on journalising.

The first in her new series of Spanish articles appeared in the February 1883 number of *Macmillan's*, and Grove retired, as predicted, in April. The editorship, however, went to John Morley, who, during his previous editorships of the *Fortnightly Review* and the *Pall Mall Gazette*, had accepted contributions by Mrs Ward; therefore he now turned to her for 'a literary article once a month—in the shape of a *comte rendu* of some new books, English or French. It is highly desirable', he added, 'that the treatment should be as lively and readable as possible—not erudite and academic, but literary, or socio-literary, as Ste Beuve was.'[13]

It was a happy assignment for Mrs Ward. The 17 articles which she wrote for *Macmillan's* between 1883 and 1885 constitute, with the possible exception of her later Brontë introductions, her most polished critical studies. Moreover, the range of topics covered in these articles reflects the gradual popularization of her style (which had hitherto been rather heavily academic) and the shifting of her literary interests, under the tutelage of Morley, to the contemporary English scene. The *Macmillan's* series began with Gustavo Becquer and Francis Garnier; it ended by treating writers such as Tennyson and Pater. Morley, in his efforts to bring her into the modern world, sometimes declined articles on more remote subjects:

"Popularise foreign thought" with all my heart [he wrote to her on one occasion], but at intervals, with breathing space. . . . Can you not—casting your keen eye over the field of contemporary English literature . . . —find something to say about it all. I want to tempt you out of mere writing about books into judgements of your own upon something or anything that is actually passing in this world.[14]

In her plans for a book, Mrs Ward also decided to abandon the antiquarianism of her Spanish studies in favour of a treatment of modern French literature. Writing to Alexander Macmillan on 19 July 1883, she reminded him of his earlier offer of £250 for a book on Spain. 'Well, since we have come to London, I have come to feel that if one wants to interest the wider world of readers, one must write of something more

near to them than early Spain.' Though she planned an appendix for the benefit of scholars, the French book 'should
be *literary* before everything, and as readable as possible'. Mrs
Ward requested a £250 advance, which Macmillan sent her at
once, but the book was never written, doubtless because she
had so many other literary projects underway; she eventually
repaid the advance in 1888 by forgoing some of her royalties
from the Colonial Edition of *Robert Elsmere* published by
Macmillan.

One of these other undertakings was a translation of the
journal of Amiel, which she read while on a holiday in Switz-
erland in 1883 because Pattison had told her that 'in *importance* it seemed to him that nothing of its kind had equalled
it since Rousseau's *Confessions*'.[15] Her translation, published
by Macmillan in 1885 with an introduction and extensive
notes, was a decided success. Gladstone admired it, Browning
urged her to make an enlarged second edition,[16] and Matthew
Arnold praised it in one of his essays. By 26 February 1887
Mrs Ward was able to tell her mother that there were 'only
350 [copies] left out of 1250, besides a cheap one vol. edition published in America' and that the assistant editor of the
Century Magazine had reported 'the book was making a great
mark in America'.

Mrs Ward stopped writing for *Macmillan's* in the spring of
1885, because she was beginning to plan a successor to *Miss
Bretherton*. At this point Mrs Ward had no idea that the writing of *Robert Elsmere* would take all of her time for nearly
three years, since she actually intended to return to her *Macmillan's Magazine* work in November or December 1885.
However, in September Morley resigned as editor, to be replaced by Mowbray Morris, whom she disliked. She did not
write again for the magazine thereafter. She also considered
producing a monthly column for the new *Murray's Magazine*,[17] but the writing and revising of *Robert Elsmere* ruled
out that possibility as well.

Once *Robert Elsmere* was published in 1888, of course,
Mrs Ward was theoretically free to return to criticism, but in

fact the overwhelming popular success of her novel now made impossible a continued career as a critic. For a while in 1888 she actually planned to do a book-length study based on Theodor Keim's *Die Geschichte Jesu von Nazara* (1867-72), but by October she put it aside. 'The impulse to write another story is very strong in me', she told George Smith on 12 October 1888, '& perhaps later on if I live there will be time for critical work.'

In 1894 she outlined to George Smith a proposal for a collection of her old *Macmillan's* articles, to be supplemented by new essays on Stevenson, Tolstoy, and Pater, but the book was never done, for by now she had become dependent upon the royalties of another novel every year. Her correspondence with Smith shows that she continually longed to return to criticism; her literary conscience seems to have been troubled (though of course she did not say this directly) by the need to produce novels in quick succession. However, what little literary and religious criticism she wrote after 1888 had to be squeezed in between the more lucrative fiction. 'My health is not strong, and I begin to feel the burden of it more than I once did', she wrote to Edmund Gosse in 1899. 'When the income earning work of the year is done, I must take the time which intervenes between the completion of one task [i.e., novel] & the beginning of another, either for holiday or else for those things which greatly & specially attract me.' Her current work on hand, she added, was 'three or four papers on New Testament Interpretation, which I think will be new to the English public & which seem to me a carrying further of my uncle's work in *Literature and Dogma*'.[18] But except for her Brontë introductions and the introductions to her own collected works, Mrs Ward did not complete any major critical undertaking during the rest of her life. Her non-fictional writings of these years were limited chiefly to polemics on theology and women's suffrage, a few reviews of books by friends, letters to *The Times* appealing for funds for her various humanitarian activities, three wartime propaganda books, and her memoirs.

II

When Gladstone published his celebrated critique of *Robert Elsmere* in the May 1888 number of the *Nineteenth Century*, Mrs Ward was almost persuaded by the editor, James Knowles, to write an immediate reply. However, she carefully pondered the theological questions raised by Gladstone for many months, and not until March 1889 did her response, entitled 'The New Reformation', appear in the *Nineteenth Century*. The article, a careful, detailed analysis of the significance of recent German Biblical criticism for English Christians, revealed Mrs Ward's professional grasp of theological scholarship. She said later of it that

it gave me a certain admitted right to speak, in the years that followed, not on behalf of scholarship or criticism, in themselves, for that I never dreamed of claiming, but as an interpreter and reporter to the wide lay public of a certain kind of scholarly and historical work, profoundly affecting the thought and action of daily life, and too little known or realised in England.[19]

Though an able popularization, 'The New Reformation' was a specialized and technical study, and therefore if we wish to understand the larger implications of Mrs Ward's religious writings, we must also rescue from obscurity some of her other articles and speeches.

Her first serious introduction to the historical origins of Christianity came in 1879, when Henry Wace, afterwards Dean of Canterbury, invited her to write the lives of the early Spanish saints and ecclesiastics for his *Dictionary of Christian Biography* (1877-87). During the two following years Mrs Ward contributed 209 articles to volumes ii (1880) and iii (1882) of the *Dictionary*, ranging in length from one sentence to several pages of small type. What this experience taught her was that 'to adopt the witness of those centuries to matters of fact, without translating it at every step, into the historical language of our own day, a language which the long education of time has brought closer to the realities of things—would be to end by knowing nothing, actually and truly, about their life'.[20] In the articles Mrs Ward was to complain repeatedly of the 'curious upgrowth of legend, or miraculous appearances, forged privileges, and so forth' (ii, 110) and the 'chaos [of Spanish ecclesiastical history], through which, in the present state of information, it is almost impossible to see one's way' (ii, 562). Fighting her way through this tangle of legend and myth, Mrs Ward reached the conclusion that the historical basis of Christianity was very shaky indeed. And if the Fathers and even the Apostles were unreliable as witnesses because of their bias towards miraculous explanations of events, then what was one to make of the doctrine of the bodily resurrection of Jesus?

It was precisely this question which was to shake Robert Elsmere's faith. As Langham points out to him,

History depends on *testimony*. What is the nature and the value of testimony at given times? In other words, did the man of the third century understand, or report, or interpret facts in the same way as the man of the sixteenth or the nineteenth? And if not, what are the differences, and what are the deductions to be made from them, if any? (i, 358)

Robert acknowledges that this is 'enormously important', but Langham adds ominously, 'I should think it is; the whole of orthodox Christianity is in it, for instance!' In an anonymous review of the *Dictionary* published in *The Times* on 12 December 1883, Mrs Ward explored at some length this very historical problem which was to be at the centre of her novel. It was in fact a familiar dilemma for Anglican and Protestant apologists: if Scriptural miracles are to be accepted as historically true, why not later ecclesiastical miracles as well? Roman Catholics and rationalists could at least claim greater consistency in their approach to the problem, since the former accepted the historicity of both categories of miracles, while the latter rejected both.

Though Mrs Ward found herself in the company of the rationalists in her scepticism of all miracles, she was a rationalist with a difference. In her opening address at University Hall, published as a pamphlet in 1891, she asserted that the crude, *a priori* denial of miracles by the thinkers of the Enlightenment failed to take into account either historical considerations or the legitimate religious impulses of human beings. 'The theological and the historical generalisations of the Aufklärung', she declared, 'were alike imperfect and premature' (p. 11). By contrast, the German critics of the nineteenth century had broadened and deepened the denial of Christianity's miraculous element through historical inquiry, while at the same time German philosophy (i.e., Professor Green's Hegelianism) was offering a basis for a 'reconstructed Christianity'.

There were, then, two Liberalisms. That of the eighteenth century was purely negative, characterized by 'the mocking destruction wrought by Voltairian thought' (p. 19); the new Liberalism had grown out of a patient study of Christian history, fortified by the conviction that a demythologized Christianity, stripped of its legendary accretions, would still speak to the spiritual needs of mankind. According to Mrs Ward, the fundamental questions suggested by modern Biblical scholarship were these:

Leaving miracle and dogma aside, are we essentially nearer than the eighteenth century to a true picture of Jesus of Nazareth and the first Christian communities; can we penetrate closer to the eternal need and passion at the heart of Christianity than the philosophers, and, finding it to be our own need and passion, in spite of all disguises, can we take up the Christian work afresh, under the altered conditions of thought, and carry it forward with a new enthusiasm of faith? (p. 30)

Mrs Ward gave a good deal of attention to two problems associated with this reconstructed Christianity which she envisioned. First, she pondered how it could be taught to children and the poor, who might have difficulty in grasping the subtle distinction between spiritual truth and the inaccurate history within which it was embedded. A speech which she delivered in 1892, *New Forms of Christian Education*, and the third volume of *Robert Elsmere* reveal the broad outlines of her solution. What was specially needed, she believed, was an English life of Christ which would portray simply and

accurately the universal spiritual appeal of his character yet
would make no untenable dogmatic claims. (In 1906 she
nearly persuaded herself to write such a life and abandoned
the scheme only with great reluctance.[21]) Second, Mrs Ward
recognized that this New Reformation would have to fill the
imaginative and artistic void left by the disintegration of
orthodoxy. In another speech, published under the title *Unitarians and the Future* (1894), she painted a compelling picture of the cathedral of the new faith:

I remember, some years ago, dreaming in the Cathedral of Pisa of
what the younger faith might in time produce of 'fair seeming show,' to
hold the same working place within it as these marvellous churches of
the past have done within Catholicism. The Church of Pisa has always
been to me one of the most eloquent of all because of the great figure
of the Messianic Christ, the Christ in judgement which, from its high
seat in the golden apse, looks down with extraordinary majesty upon
the church beneath, giving meaning and voice to the whole. . . . Catholicism at its greatest and best, and Catholicism only, speaks from the
awful figure holding the orb, and from the church sculptured or painted
with the miracle and legend which have sprung from that original Messianic conception, as flower from the seed. But let the new Christianity
now stealing into men's hearts but rise to the height of its own mission,
and it too will find its art. It will replace that frowning figure in the
apse by the form of the Teacher whose works and death are wrought
into the life of Europe; it will surround him by the Apostles of his word
—not necessarily the Twelve!—it will cover the walls of the church with
the parables and sayings about which Catholicism in art cares so little,
while in the side-chapels it will still paint with love and tenderness the
apologues and fairy-tales of the primitive faith, its miraculous births,
healings and resurrections. And when it has done this, or something like
it, in the midst of our English life, the new faith will have taken the
next great step in its pilgrimage. (pp. 55-7)

Robert Elsmere was intended to be such a cathedral of the
new faith, in literary form, erected by Mrs Ward herself.

III

Though Mrs Ward treated an astonishing variety of subjects
in her criticism, the one kind of book in which she was specially interested was the spiritual autobiography. The English,

as she remarked, were not as accomplished as the French in
the art of self-revelation, and consequently the greatest Victorian autobiographies, such as Mill's, tended to be dry and
reserved. Mrs Ward contended that the true inner spiritual
struggles of the age were recorded more faithfully, on the
whole, in confessions that purported to be novels but were
actually concealed autobiographies—in books, that is to say,
like Carlyle's *Sartor Resartus*, Froude's *Nemesis of Faith*,
Shorthouse's *John Inglesant*, and Pater's *Marius the Epicurean*. (And of course *Robert Elsmere* belongs to this same
category of confessional fiction, though Mrs Ward obscured
that fact somewhat by afterwards insisting that her novel expressed the religious aspirations of an entire generation.)

'The literature of introspection' was the phrase that she
coined to describe this type of literary work, which cut
across the usual generic boundaries of fiction, non-fictional
prose, and poetry. In an article by that title, published in the
Macmillan's Magazine of January 1884, she argued that such
literary acts of self-revelation were a direct result of the
decline of Christian orthodoxy:

> Modern times have witnessed an enormous development of the liter-
> ature of feeling. With us in Europe the facts of spiritual experience had
> for many centuries but one language, the language of the great religion
> which had absorbed into itself all the older philosophical and spiritual
> enthusiasms of the world. But in the multiplication of sensations and
> experiences which the West has seen since the Renaissance, the language
> of religion has not expanded fast enough to meet the new needs of the
> soul. They have to find for themselves a fresh and supplementary lan-
> guage, expressing shades and subtleties of relation between man and the
> great spectacle of the universe, unknown to older generations (p. 192)

Rousseau, with his sensitivity to both landscapes and
human feelings, was the great prototype, but, according to
Mrs Ward, 'a much higher degree of inwardness has been
reached in the modern world than was possible to Rousseau'
(p. 192). The literature of introspection assumes a variety of
forms in the nineteenth century: it may be nature poetry
(Wordsworth), fictionalized autobiography (Carlyle), or the

'literature of despair' (Senancour and Amiel). What these seemingly diverse forms share is a common 'voice of reverie, the note of delicate and sincere introspection' (p. 197).

The one spiritual autobiography which affected Mrs Ward most profoundly—and about which she said little in her published writings—was *Sartor Resartus*. We have seen in an earlier chapter how infatuated she was with it during late adolescence, and indeed it would be entirely possible to analyze *Robert Elsmere* in Carlylean terms—to see his struggle towards the light as a repetition of the experience of Carlyle's Diogenes Teufelsdröckh, who taught so many Victorian intellectuals how to move from the 'Everlasting No' of modern unbelief through the 'Centre of Indifference' to the 'Everlasting Yea' of nonsectarian religious affirmation. Moreover, the central clothes-metaphor of *Sartor* is pervasively present in Mrs Ward's works. To cite only one conspicuous example: in her Introduction to *Robert Elsmere* she writes of the 'empty churches and ever diminishing hold of the Christian tradition in its older forms' but adds that 'Christianity, as a spirit and a life, is imperishable; the loom of Time has woven steadily in these twenty years; and there will be a new birth for the Church of England' (I, xxvi-xxvii). Teufelsdröckh, in almost identical language, had spoken of 'religion, in unnoticed nooks, weaving for herself new Vestures'.[22]

It is tempting to regard Newman's *Apologia Pro Vita Sua* as another unacknowledged influence upon Mrs Ward's fiction, since she rarely mentions it either, while there do seem to be significant parallels between Newman's career and Robert Elsmere's. Both men have their Anglican faith shaken by a study of early ecclesiastical history; both abandon the priesthood of the Church of England as a matter of conscience; and both devote the remainder of their lives to ministering to the needs of the urban poor. (The title of Book Seven of *Robert Elsmere*, 'Gain and Loss', is an inversion of the title of Newman's autobiographical novel.) Obviously Mrs Ward knew the main incidents of Newman's life, and may in fact have had it in mind when writing *Robert Elsmere*. But we

know from a letter she wrote to her father on 10 August
1890 that she was not familiar with the *Apologia* before that
date:

I am working through [T. H.] Green's *Prolegomena to Ethics*,—and at
the same time I have been reading the *Apologia*. Will you quarrel with
me if I say that the *ethical* tone of Green is to me far more inspiring
than that of Newman! There is an egotism & an irritability about the
Apologia which is surprising and painful to me. I had never read more
than pieces from it before.

That Mrs Ward should have responded so coldly to the greatest of all Victorian spiritual autobiographies tells a good deal
about the scars left by her childhood.

Two examples of the literature of introspection upon
which she did write at some length are *John Inglesant* (1881)
by Joseph Henry Shorthouse and *Marius the Epicurean*
(1885). In fact, Mrs Ward played a vital role in finding a publisher for *Inglesant*, and in an anonymous review (which
Shorthouse called 'very flattering and beautifully written'[23])
of it in the *Saturday Review* she praised the author's spiritual
sensitivity even while she took him to task for his 'academic
High Churchism'.[24] Writing later in *Macmillan's* on 'The Literature of Introspection' (January 1884), she made even
greater claims for Shorthouse's book: 'In that remarkable
novel of two seasons ago, *John Inglesant*, there was more of
the true power of reverie than has yet appeared among our
prose-writers; and its success seems to show that there is after
all some future for the literature of reverie in England' (p.
197).

Marius, on the other hand, received more extensive treatment by Mrs Ward in one of her *Macmillan's* articles (June
1885), for not only was she intimate with the author but the
novel also dealt explicitly with many of the themes which she
was to explore in *Robert Elsmere*. Mrs Ward's review has
recently been described by the editor of Pater's letters as 'the
most discerning contemporary notice of the book', and Pater
himself told Mrs Ward that he thought it 'graceful and pains-
taking'.[25] Yet despite her adroitness in explaining the literary

and religious significance of Pater's novel to the readers of *Macmillan's*, Mrs Ward had little sympathy for an epicurean philosophy which had its basis in 'exquisite moments' rather than a solid ethical system. Mankind, she wrote,

has tried to fix and distil the essence of innumerable impressions in one great tradition—the ethical tradition—which is at once the product and the condition of human life. To live in the mere pursuit of sensations, however refined, is to live outside this tradition, so far as is possible, and therefore outside the broad main stream of human history. (p. 136)

In *Eleanor* (1900) Mrs Ward was to create in the figure of Edward Manisty one who, like Pater, is captivated by the romance of Catholicism but stands comfortably outside it. 'How great is the gulf between a literary and a practical Christianity', she remarked caustically of Manisty's stance (p. 141).

Paradoxically, Pater's total scepticism permitted him to feel more at ease with existing religious institutions than did Mrs Ward. From her point of view, Marius had no more right than Robert Elsmere to toy with Christianity, to pay lip service to a creed which he rejected intellectually. Pater's reply to this objection—one might almost say, his answer to her review of *Marius*—is to be found in his review of *Robert Elsmere* which appeared in the *Guardian* in 1888.[26] Though Pater admired her novel, he complained of Elsmere's rash decision to leave the Church; Elsmere, said Pater, was too 'sudden and trenchant in dealing with so great and complex a question'. But Marius, as Mrs Ward saw it, was guilty of intellectual dishonesty by not breaking with the Church. This pair of reviews constitutes what is, in effect, a curious dialogue between the authors of the two most famous religious novels of the Victorian period.

But the book which evoked from Mrs Ward her most careful reflections upon the literature of introspection was not an English autobiography or novel but the *Journal Intime* of Henri-Frédéric Amiel, the Swiss philosopher and poet, which was published in French in 1882-3. Mrs Ward, attracted by Amiel's distinctive fusion of mysticism and rationalism, wrote an article on the *Journal* for *Macmillan's* (February 1884) and completed her English translation of it the following year.

What was the source of Amiel's appeal to her? 'Amiel is not simply a Protestant, he is an orthodox Protestant, very much opposed to liberal Protestantism', wrote Ernest Renan. 'He speaks of sin, salvation, redemption, conversion, as though they were realities.' Renan said that the difference between a lapsed Catholic like himself and an 'emancipated Protestant' like Amiel was that Amiel retained 'some touch of melancholy, a depth of intellectual austerity'. Though the old dogmas had dissolved, the Protestant sense of sin remained solidly implanted in the soul.[27] As Amiel himself complained in his *Journal*, he had 'a Christian heart and a pagan head' (p. 246).

In her *Macmillan's* article Mrs Ward especially emphasized this tension within the personality of Amiel, because she undoubtedly recognized its correspondence to the Arnoldian ethic and to her own experience:

In a day of confusion and transition, is not the world more in need than ever of such inspirers and pioneers of thought, so free intellectually, so stable and satisfying morally? They stand, as it were, between the two certitudes, the metaphysical or the theological, with which they have practically nothing in common, and the scientific with which they have a great deal, but which yet is never able to obtain complete possession of them. For the scientific certitude proclaims that there is nothing knowable beyond phenomena. Whereas a mind like Amiel's, while intellectually it feels all the force of the arguments urged by science, is yet practically persuaded that beyond and below phenomena there is 'a deepest depth' in which love and duty have their source, a Divine consciousness which is the root of ours. It is to these composite natures, one may prophesy, that the shaping of the future belongs. (p. 278)

Because of this double commitment to reason and intuition, Amiel was, in Mrs Ward's eyes, a member of that 'small transfigured band' which included Jowett, Green, and Matthew Arnold. 'To me', she told her father, 'Amiel is the reasonable & Saint Theresa the unreasonable mystic.'[28]

Yet there was a darker side to Amiel's character which

caused Arnold to describe the *Journal* as a study in pathological behaviour, and which enabled Mark Pattison to see in it
a mirror of his own despair and enervation.[29] Mrs Ward herself recognized that Amiel's endless, brooding self-analysis
symbolized the distintegration of the modern personality.
Amiel was Renan's 'emancipated Protestant', alienated from
the religious institutions of the past, yet always painfully conscious of the burden of self, of the futility of action in a
world emptied of spiritual meaning. Ultimately a victim of
moral paralysis, Amiel represented the transformation, in the
nineteenth century, of the old Protestant tradition of spiritual introspection into an unstrung will, an ennui that was a
sympton of deep spiritual sickness.

In other words, Mrs Ward's attempt to portray Amiel as a
liberal hero, a synthesizer of the best insights of religion and
science, was doomed to failure, for he was in reality an embodiment of the *mal du siècle* or of what Thomas Hardy was
later to call the modern disease of thought. Just as Matthew
Arnold found it necessary at last to leave behind Obermann,
Amiel's fictional counterpart, Mrs Ward, by the time she
wrote *Robert Elsmere*, saw the danger of introspection not
balanced by action in the world of men. In Elsmere's Oxford
tutor she created, by her own admission, an English Amiel—
a man whose paralysis of will contrasts sharply and unfa-
vourably with the vigorous optimism of Elsmere. Deeply as
her Protestant instincts responded to the lonely, austere note
of 'the literature of introspection', Mrs Ward eventually concluded that the truly reasonable mystic was not Amiel but
Robert Elsmere.

IV

Mrs Ward's literary articles in *Macmillan's Magazine* and
elsewhere naturally were not confined to actual and disguised
spiritual autobiographies, much as she might be drawn to that
topic; she also wrote a good deal on English and French novelists of the nineteenth century, and these essays, as might be
expected, tell us much about her literary values and aims.

When *Robert Elsmere* was published, it was generally said by reviewers that Mrs Ward was 'George Eliot's successor', with frequent references to their similar religious views, but Eliot is conspicuously absent from the list of novelists she treated in her criticism. The omission was not accidental. The occasional passing references to Eliot in her published writings (aside from an account of meeting her at Oxford in *A Writer's Recollections*) are uniformly unflattering. In the Introduction to *Amiel's Journal*, for example, Mrs Ward declared that Amiel's verse had 'no plastic power, none of the incommunicable magic which a George Eliot seeks in vain, while it comes unasked, to deck with imperishable charm the commonplace metaphysic and the simpler emotions of a Tennyson or a Burns' (pp. xlvii-xlviii). And in an essay on Elizabeth Barrett Browning published in an obscure magazine, she wrote that George Eliot possessed 'far greater general power and competence than either [Jane Austen or Charlotte Brontë], but [was] subject in compensation to more aggressive faults'.[30]

Mrs Ward's unpublished letters reveal even more clearly her distaste for Eliot's novels. Writing to George Smith on 22 October 1896, she confessed that she always enjoyed any book by or about Charlotte Brontë,

while here I am bored—tell it not!—by *Adam Bede* and obliged to give up an article I had half promised Mr. Dudley Warner on George Eliot, because I cannot be wholly or even mostly on my knees, and it is not seemly for me to be anything else. What a prig is Adam, & what a Sunday school tone much of it has. The Hale farm, Mrs. Poyser, Hetty, Dinah—these remain; but the whole handling of the seduction, compared to what Turgieneff or Tolstoy would have made of it, seems to me superficial & conventional. There!—to no one else would I have written these sentiments—please put them in the waste paper basket!

When Blackwood suggested in 1898 that Mrs Ward write a monograph on Eliot, she declined by explaining that 'the book . . . would give me great trouble, and I do not feel naturally drawn to it, great as my admiration for her is'.[31]

And yet her letters to Smith during the writing of *Robert*

Elsmere show that George Eliot was never entirely absent from Mrs Ward's consciousness. On 3 October 1887 she requested that the chapters be numbered consecutively throughout the four books of the novel 'as in *Middlemarch*', and she probably also was thinking of *Middlemarch* as a model when she asked Smith to issue *Elsmere* in green covers. After her novel was published, Mrs Ward suggested to Smith that he reprint *Elsmere* in a two-volume edition as had been done with *Adam Bede*. 'I don't mean to compare myself to G.E', she added with evident embarrassment (2 May 1888), 'whatever foolish & "irresponsible reviewers" may do!' But the comparison was inescapable, even if Mrs Ward recognized that it was a false one. James Knowles reported to Gladstone in 1888 that she 'reminds me more or less of George Eliot: I cannot say why—but she gives me the impression of wishing to be Elisha to Geo. Eliot's Elijah—& I cannot see why she may not become so'.[32]

Mrs Ward, however, rejected the analogy, because she knew that whatever the superficial similarities between her personality and novels and those of Eliot, it was really the Brontë sisters, particularly Charlotte, who had left their mark upon her fiction. At the age of 17 she had been given a copy of Mrs Gaskell's *Life* of Charlotte Brontë by Aunt Fan, and the book made a striking impression upon her, as she recalled in old age:

The story of the gifted children in the small grim Yorkshire parsonage, with its graveyard in front and its moors behind; their books, their plays, their life in dream worlds of their own, more real to them than the village world outside:—I knew it once by heart. I could see the parlour in the firelight, with the three whispering to each other; I could hear Martha and Tabby, their two maids, in the kitchen. The long village street, the high moors behind the parsonage, the night winds blowing over them, the glory of the heather in the summer, and the snow that covered them in winter; they were all familiar to me through Mrs. Gaskell's art—as to many others—before ever I set eyes on the real Haworth.

But to young Mary Arnold, 'who had been from her childhood scribbling on her own account', the most exciting part of the Brontë story was the anonymous publication of *Jane Eyre* and *Wuthering Heights* and Charlotte's sudden, dramatic appearance in George Smith's office in order to prove her identity. When Mary, a year after reading the *Life*, visited London, she at once insisted upon finding the site of the Chapter Coffee House where Charlotte and Ann had stayed.[33]

The Brontë influence can be seen in nearly all of her novels. At least three of her male protagonists—Helbeck, Edward Manisty (in *Eleanor*), and Squire Wendover—are partially derived from the figure of Mr Rochester in *Jane Eyre*. There is also in *Eleanor* an entire scene—the nocturnal visit of Manisty's demented sister to Lucy's bedroom—taken virtually intact from *Jane Eyre*. In *David Grieve* Mrs Ward temporarily puts aside her story and devotes a chapter to a tour of Haworth, accompanied by a lecture on the Brontës, that has absolutely nothing to do with her hero's fortunes. The episode is patently extraneous, and she makes no effort to justify or explain it. Mrs Ward had such a passionate love for the Brontës that she would drag them into her novels quite unashamedly with no pretext at all.

The most ambitious—and successful—critical effort of Mrs Ward's career was a series of introductions which she wrote at the request of George Smith for the seven-volume Haworth Edition of the Brontë sisters' novels (1899-1900). Drawing upon her wide knowledge of Continental romanticism, she was able to see the unique achievement of *Wuthering Heights* and was nearly the first critic of her century to proclaim its superiority to *Jane Eyre*. But it was *Jane Eyre*, whose surface realism conceals a fairy-tale substratum, that remained Mrs Ward's personal favourite, because it expressed many of the hidden anxieties and fantasies of her own childhood. In the lonely, orphaned, strong-willed Jane who is sent off to a grim boarding-school, Mrs Ward must have found a terrifying echo of her youthful memories, and in Jane's ultimate triumph over adversity she found a model to emulate.

Nevertheless, Mrs Ward's Introduction to *Jane Eyre* is a

balanced piece of criticism in which she boldly outlines the case that can be made against the novel. The arguments of the devil's advocate—whom she describes as 'a reader of more subtlety and range than his fellows' (p. xi)—were in fact supplied by Henry James, who had privately debated with her two years before that the 'Brontë legend', an extraliterary factor, was the real source of Charlotte's fame. The Introduction is largely a record of this fascinating conversation between Mrs Ward and James on the nature of the novel.[34] James, characteristically, claimed that *Jane Eyre* and the other Brontë novels must be judged by their artistry rather than by the pathos of their authors' lives; Mrs Ward, on the other hand, insisted that Charlotte's personality, far from being an extraliterary consideration, actually constituted the major attraction of her novels. Mrs Ward rejected the theory of the autonomy of art just as firmly as she had, in her youthful fiction, denied the autonomy of the intellect, for it seemed to her that James' position represented a retreat to the selfish isolation of Tennyson's Palace of Art, whereas she clung fiercely to the Victorian ideal of an indissoluble marriage between art and 'life' (by which she generally meant morality).

She (or rather James) says that *Jane Eyre* is 'one of the signs, no doubt, that mark the transition from the old novel to the new, from the old novel of plot and coincidence to the new novel of psychology and character' (pp. xviii-xix), and the description might well be applied to Mrs Ward's own novels. Though she was fascinated by the psychological subtlety of James and certain French novelists, she was alarmed by their neglect of the traditional elements of story-telling. In an article on 'Recent Fiction in England and France' published in *Macmillan's* (August 1884), she wrote: '*What, after all, does the plot matter? In these few words we have the secret of the whole decay and deterioration which seems to be overtaking one French novelist after another' (p. 256). Mrs Ward, as usual, tried to reconcile the best of both worlds: she wanted the technical sophistication of the French novel mingled with the 'simplicity' and conservative morality of the English novel. As her artist-hero in *Fenwick's Career* (1906) expresses it: 'English poetic feeling, combined with as much of French technique as it could assimilate—there was the line of progress' (p. 176).

Mrs Ward's feelings about French novelists, and French culture in general, were characterized by an ambivalence sharper even than that of most Victorians. 'Long as I have admired and loved the French', she wrote in *Towards the Goal* (1917), 'I have often . . . felt and fretted against the kind of barrier that seemed to exist between their life and ours' (p. 184). Like most of her contemporaries, she was genuinely horrified by French morality even though she envied other aspects of French culture. While writing *Sir George Tressady* (1896) she lamented to Louise Creighton that 'if I could treat the subject with French or Tolstoi-ish frankness I fancy one could make something very fine out of it, but the limitations imposed partly by my own idiosyncrasy[,] partly by English custom seem to stand in the way'.[35]

This problem was even more acute in *The History of David Grieve*, in which her hero has a prolonged affair in France with a beautiful young artist. (It may be useful to observe that many of the seductions or attempted seductions in her novels take place in France.) To her brother William, Mrs Ward confided:

This French part is frightfully difficult. Without overstepping the bounds prescribed to an English writer, & strongly upheld by my own feeling, how is one to render the effect produced upon a pure-minded but romantic & excitable English lad by the life & talk of the Paris rapin? Zola's *L'oeuvre* is disgusting beyond words, even when one has learnt the art of skipping as I have, & the whole life seems to me so *stupid* & brutal, with its single pinchbeck ideal of *la gloire*. Much good it would do them if they got it![36]

Of *David Grieve* Mrs Ward said that only in *Helbeck of Bannisdale* 'did I ever draw so deep again on the source of personal feeling'.[37] Yet there is almost no literally autobiographical material in *Grieve*. For Mrs Ward, its personal significance lay partially in David's vacillations between England and France—or, to translate these obviously symbolic terms, between industriousness, sobriety, and moral restraint on the one hand, and cultural sophistication, sexual passion, and freedom from ethical inhibitions on the other hand. David has his fling in France, but in the end he returns to Manchester, marries an English girl, and settles down to a virtuous life as a bookseller. Mrs Ward, like her hero, though she knew the charms of Hellenism, ultimately chose Hebraism.

But in 1884, when she was offering her survey of 'Recent Fiction in England and France' in *Macmillan's*, Mrs Ward was still searching for a critical view of the novel that would embrace the finest spiritual and artistic qualities of both nations. The article concluded with this peroration:

The influence of the French novel at the present moment is a proof of what the novel can do when it has a sufficient force of intellectual energy behind it, and when it throws itself frankly and fearlessly upon life. To many of us this influence, in the shape which it has taken of late years, is a cause for alarm; we see in it a menace to the sense of beauty, to the power of conscience, and to all the sweeter and finer elements of imagination. The English race, with its story-telling gifts, its rich romantic tradition, its strong exuberant temperament, ought to be able to produce an art of fiction equal in diffusiveness and tenacity of life to that of the French. We have done such great things in the past that it is hard indeed to believe our day is over. It is pleasanter to press along the barren road which is just now our portion, in the belief and hope that before long some turn, as yet unforeseen, may bring into view figures as impressive, as life-like, and as rich in promise of immortality as those we parted with when George Eliot and Thackeray and Mrs. Gaskell and Charlotte Brontë died. (p. 260)

Was it merely coincidental that three of the four novelists mentioned in the final sentence were women? Perhaps not, for Mrs Ward was completing her first novel when the article appeared, and within a year she was to begin *Robert Elsmere*. In the inner recesses of her heart she was undoubtedly hoping that the mantle of the great mid-Victorian women novelists would after all descend upon her.

Chapter 6
THE WRITING OF *ROBERT ELSMERE*

I think this book *must* interest a certain number of people. I certainly feel as if I were writing parts of it with my heart's blood!
—Mrs Ward (1886)[1]

I

Milly and Olly, a children's story by Mrs Ward published in 1881, was not a specially successful venture: of the 3,000 copies printed by Macmillan, nearly 900 were still unsold in 1888.[2] Nevertheless, her old dream of writing fiction lingered, and in 1884 she proposed to John Morley that she write a short story for *Macmillan's Magazine* in lieu of one of her usual articles. When Morley read the manuscript of *Miss Bretherton* in October, however, he told Mrs Ward that it would not be suitable for serial publication, because 'there is not story enough—not enough of well-marked action—not a sufficient succession of definite actions'. The story, he said, despite 'all the excellences of criticism and vivid literary intelligence', lacked the 'glimpse of *passion*' and '*glow*' of a true romance.[3]

When, at Morley's suggestion, Macmillan published *Miss Bretherton* as a book later that year, the reviewers generally agreed with his analysis. *Miss Bretherton*, though an exceptionally good first effort, seemed to them not a real novel but merely a critical essay masquerading as fiction. Whatever small fame the book achieved for Mrs Ward grew out of the evident similarities between Miss Bretherton and Mary Anderson, the popular American actress then performing in London. 'A friend of mine tells me in one or two instances your heroine resembles me somewhat', Miss Anderson wrote Mrs Ward. 'You may be sure that I felt highly flattered at hearing this.'[4] Mrs Ward sent an indignant letter to the *Athenaeum* denying that her heroine was a literal portrait of any public figure[5]—a position she was also to maintain later in connexion with some of the characters in *Robert Elsmere*—but she did not always maintain this pretence. While attending a Private View at the Grosvenor on New Year's Day, 1887, Mrs Ward unexpectedly encountered Mary Anderson, and, as she wrote to her mother the following day, 'We shook hands & she said to me "I am in Paris studying—music, and resting"— the first half sounded to me so like a fulfillment of Miss B that I had a start.'

Mrs Ward savoured the minor literary achievement of *Miss Bretherton*, sending a packet of the congratulatory letters she had received to her mother at Oxford. Creighton, her father, her brother Willie, Henry James, Pater, and Edmond Scherer all wrote enthusiastically about the book, and Julia read and shrewdly appraised each. 'Your father's letter is odd, but then he is odd—& gets odder', she observed. 'Miss [Rhoda] Broughton [the novelist] is enchanted with the book but she says as Mr. Creighton does that it is not a novel.'[6]

Miss Bretherton, which described the artistic growth of an actress when her natural gifts are supplemented by an intellectual understanding of drama, may seem at first glance to be far removed from the morally strenuous world of *Robert Elsmere*. Whereas Miss Bretherton's distrust of French actresses, particularly a Madame Desforêts, is regarded as evidence of her cultural narrowness, in *Elsmere* Mrs Ward argues with great vehemence that Desforêts (who is again much discussed) is indeed immoral and disreputable. *Miss Bretherton*, with its stress upon the claims of art rather than morality, represents Mrs Ward's thinking at the moment in her life when she was least Arnoldian, least 'earnest', least Hebraic. By the time of *Robert Elsmere* she was already retreating from this brief excursion into Hellenism.

But some of the themes and ideas of *Miss Bretherton* do foreshadow those of her later fiction. The education of a naive provincial character is explored again and again in Mrs Ward's novels, doubtless because she was trying to express what her own intellectual development at Oxford had meant. The relationship between Miss Bretherton and her mentor Kendal is very much like that between Rose and Langham in *Robert Elsmere*. The Oxford, Surrey, and Italian settings of the book were to be used again on other occasions. And, though it is only a passing reference, there is in *Miss Bretherton* a Magdelen tutor who has been turned out for an 'atheistical' book (pp. 313-4).

As soon as *Miss Bretherton* was off the press, Mrs Ward began to talk of another novel. 'I am so glad to hear about "the next" which is in your head and only hope that it may not tax you too much and that you may find ample opportunity & strength to work out your thought', wrote C. P. Scott of the *Manchester Guardian* on the first day of 1885. 'It seems almost an impertinence to say so but I have no doubt of your success.'[7] On 24 January, Morley congratulated her on the favourable reception of *Miss Bretherton*, assuring her that he would be willing to consider the new story for publication in *Macmillan's Magazine*.[8] A month later (26 February) Mrs Ward sent to the Macmillan Company a definite overture: 'The story will be in two volumes altogether a longer and more substantial piece than "Miss B." & its subject will be one of more general interest.' She asked for a flat payment of £250, 'subject to the resumption of my right in it after 2000 copies had been sold'.

But George Craik of Macmillan pointed out to her that *Miss Bretherton*, despite some critical acclaim, had made no profits for the firm and had actually produced a deficit of £22.[9] She therefore made the same proposal to George Smith, head of Smith, Elder and Company:

When, in 1885, I drew a bow at a venture, and in a hurried note to Mr. Smith, whom I knew only as my uncle's publisher, asked him to saddle himself with the publication of 'Robert Elsmere'—of which not a word was then written [this, incidentally, refutes the popular legend, fostered by Mrs Ward's daughter, that Macmillan had foolishly declined the actual manuscript of *Robert Elsmere*]—and to promise, me, moreover, certain sums on publication [£250], I had no standing or repute as a writer of fiction. . . . Mr. Smith, however, took the leap. I can see myself now in the old hall of our Russell Square house, taking his letter from the letter-box, and reading with a throb of delight the few courteous words in which he accepted my rather audacious proposals.[10]

Smith's words (on 2 March 1885) were these: 'I hasten to say that having read "Miss Bretherton" I have no hesitation in accepting your novel on the terms mentioned in your letter.' George Craik wrote Mrs Ward that though he was disappointed she had 'left us', 'I am glad you have been able to get better terms than we could give. . . . That we are not to be the pilots does not in the least take away my interest in the book and my sincere wish that it may be a success.'[11]

The choice of Smith was a fortunate one, and his firm remained the English publisher of nearly all her books until 1916. Though ugly rumours were spread in newspapers about Mrs Ward's greed in extracting favourable terms from her publishers, in fact she was so generous to Smith that she occasionally chose to forgo some of her royalties so that he might make a greater profit. It is of course true that Mrs Ward was excessively preoccupied with earning large sums of money from her writings, especially in her dealings with American publishers—and often the literary level of the novels suffered in consequence—but she never tried to increase her income at the expense of her faithful English publisher. Smith, who had enjoyed a similarly warm relationship with Ruskin, Charlotte Brontë, Thackeray, and Mrs Gaskell, served as Mrs Ward's confidant, financial and literary adviser, and (as he sometimes complained) her banker. When in 1890 he was helping her find a suitable property for the University Hall settlement, Mrs Ward told him that if he succeeded in this attempt, 'you will seem to me more than ever like the mother in Swiss Family Robinson who always had the exact article that anybody on a desert island could possibly require!'[12]

To her annoyance, the *Athenaeum* announced on 28 Feb-

ruary 1885 that 'Mrs. Humphry Ward is writing another novel', but she did not actually put any words on paper until the
following autumn. What was passing through her mind during
this long period of gestation?

We have Mrs Ward's own testimony that the germ of her
novel is to be found in a pamphlet entitled *Unbelief and Sin*[13]
which she had written in March 1881 at Oxford after hearing
the first of the year's Bampton Lectures by the Revd John
Wordsworth, then a fellow and tutor of Brasenose. Sitting in
the darkness under the gallery of St Mary's, Mrs Ward heard
the poet's great-nephew declare that unbelief was fostered
chiefly by 'a secret inclination to sin' on the part of the
doubter. The 'morbid conscience', he said, wishes above all to
slumber, and it can do so only by denying the reality of the
light of God's revelation to man.[14] Mrs Ward was infuriated
by what she interpreted as a frontal attack upon her liberal
heroes—Stanley, Jowett, T. H. Green, Matthew Arnold—and
she couched her pamphlet in much stronger language than
she was ever to use again in assaulting the orthodox position.

The pamphlet contrasted the careers of two young men at
Oxford, A and C, the former of whom is a shadowy prototype of Robert Elsmere in his quest for a system of religious
truth that is tenable in the nineteenth century. A (like Mrs
Ward), by wide reading in the Bodleian, comes to recognize
at last 'that the whole vast system of dogmatic Christianity,
with all its lovely and imposing associations, is but one of
many systems that human nature has in turn framed for its
shelter and support, that like all other theologies the world
has seen, it is the product of human needs and human skill'
(p. 15). C, though he shares the same intellectual opportunities at Oxford, drifts timidly into Holy Orders, 'no longer
able to read a critical book with fairness and intelligence, or
to understand any but the coarsest aspects of the liberal and
scientific school of thought' (p. 21). The inference, for Mrs
Ward, was obvious: that 'unbelief' was a result not of 'sin'
but of A's greater responsiveness to the important intellectual
currents of his age.

Despite the fact that the latter half of *Unbelief and Sin* outlines the main features of a reverent Theism, or a 'reconstructed' Christianity, the pamphlet as whole reflects the radicalism of Pattison rather than the moderation of Jowett and the Arnolds. John Morley was another influence who pushed Mrs Ward in the direction of a fiercer onslaught against Christian orthodoxy. 'I shall never', she wrote, 'lose the impression that "Compromise," with its almost savage appeal for sincerity in word and deed, made upon me—an impression which had its share in "Robert Elsmere".'[15] The thesis of Morley's book *On Compromise* (1874) was that truth ought not to be suppressed merely because it will disturb some people. In particular, he rejected the view that one should outwardly conform to the Church for the sake of its ceremony and ritual or its supposed benefits to society while at the same time repudiating its doctrines. Dogma and liturgy, he said, were inseparable. Naturally Morley had no liking for the liberal clergyman who nurses his doubts in private, nor for the husband who conceals his religious opinions from an orthodox wife. Frequently, according to Morley, a marriage is threatened by a man's discovery *after* the wedding that he can no longer conscientiously profess Christianity, for he has readier access than his wife to 'the best kinds of literary and scientific training' (p. 137). In such a divided home, the husband must not argue incessantly with his wife about religion, but neither should he fear to speak his convictions plainly when the occasion demands. The husband must recognize the value of his wife's 'superstitions' if her religious spirit 'shows itself in cheerfulness, in pity, in charity and tolerance, in forgiveness, in a sense of the largeness and the mystery of things' (p. 138). If such a spirit of generosity is maintained on both sides, then a doubting husband and a believing wife may live together in harmony.

It is impossible not to conclude that in *On Compromise* Mrs Ward found a compelling description of the tense domestic situation (reinforced of course by memories of her own father and mother) that was to be at the centre of *Robert*

Elsmere. The embryonic Elsmere, the Mr A of *Unbelief and Sin*, would be contrasted not with another Oxonian but with a sweetly devout wife who, by reason of her sex, had been deprived of a proper literary and scientific education. Thus the theological debate of *Unbelief and Sin* could be transformed into a narrative of human love frustrated by theological obstacles. As Mrs Ward was to write in a cancelled passage of *Elsmere*: 'This is not a religious pamphlet, but the history of a human relationship.'[16]

The story of Elsmere himself, in other words, was quite fully developed in Mrs Ward's mind by the spring of 1885. Her sister-in-law, Gertrude Ward (to whom much of *Miss Bretherton* had been dictated), left this record in a diary entry written in May of that year:

> The new story is to be written this summer. The first time she told me the scheme of it was one evening last November: she was sitting by the drawing room fire & sketched to me the career of the hero & the development of his opinions. I remember saying I hoped I should not have to write [i.e., transcribe] it as it was so serious & so sad. She has been working it out in her mind ever since, & many a time has been burning to write the first chapter, but she determined to finish up other things first, especially Amiel. Not a line of the new story is written yet. Next week we are going to the Lakes where the opening scene is to be laid.

Visiting the Cropper family (to whom she was distantly related) in Burneside, Mrs Ward went one day to Longsleddale, a beautiful valley which, though only a few miles north-west of Kendal, retains even in the twentieth century a remarkable air of serenity and remoteness. In 1836 Joseph Locke had considered laying the Grand Junction line between Preston and Glasgow through Longsleddale,[17] and again in 1965 there was talk of an underground pipeline for the Manchester Corporation being run through the valley; but in both instances the plans were frustrated, and Longsleddale, somewhat removed from the usual tourist routes, still looks very much as Mrs Ward described it in the first chapter of *Robert Elsmere*. As she travelled up to the head of the valley that June day, she picked out the vicarage and the two farmhouses that would figure in the story, and, more importantly (as she afterwards said), 'the figure of Catherine grew plain to me'.[18]

The little dark blue notebook in which Mrs Ward jotted down the first sketch of *Robert Elsmere* (reproduced below in Appendix A) supplies important evidence about how she envisioned her novel at this stage of its development. The document is perhaps most notable for its omissions: there is no mention of Elsmere himself (though we can assume that this was because his character was already clear to the author), Squire Wendover, Langham, Mr Grey, or any of the other major' characters—except in some notes added several months later. Instead Mrs Ward limited herself to lists of Westmorland dialect words, a full description of Longsleddale, and delineations of Catherine and her family.

Catherine conforms precisely to the feminine pattern described by Morley. Though she has 'intellectual limitations', 'prejudice [is] made beautiful in her'. In *A Writer's Recollections* Mrs Ward said that 'Catherine had been suggested to me by an old friend of my youth' (p. 196)—presumably Mrs Cunliffe, the vicar's wife at Shifnal—but the type of narrow, earnest Evangelical woman represented by Robert's wife had been familiar to Mrs Ward since early childhood. Moreover, Catherine also had literary antecedents in the writings of George Eliot and Wordsworth, as we shall see.

Catherine's sister Agnes is, according to the notebook, 'like Nelly'—i.e., Matthew Arnold's second daughter, Eleanor. Agnes' importance in the first book of *Robert Elsmere*, followed by her almost total disappearance from the scene during the remainder of the novel, has led some of Mrs Ward's readers, including Taine, to speculate that she was originally intended to play a large role throughout.[19] However, the novel's manuscript lends little support to this view, though in it Agnes is allowed to display her astringent wit, reminiscent of Jane Austen's heroines, somewhat more frequently than in the published version.

Of Catherine's other sister, Rose, the notebook says little, and there is no hint at all of her very important relationship with Robert's tutor. We do learn, however, that Catherine's father was modelled in part upon Dr John Percival, President of Trinity College, Oxford, and that Lady Charlotte Wynnstay and her social circle were inspired by Mrs Ward's reading of Macaulay's letters from Holland House.

The most useful type of evidence supplied by the notebook is the occasional clues as to the form of the earliest version of Book One, which was later drastically rewritten and about which practically no other information has survived. In the notebook Mrs Ward records that some 30 years before in Longsleddale a horse was killed and its rider mortally injured when they fell from a bridge. A few paragraphs later she adds: 'The accident on the bridge / Catherine's share in it. (Reminiscent of the death of Winwood Reade).' Reade, a well-known Secularist, had while on his deathbed suffered the indignity of an unauthorized invasion of his bedroom by a fanatical Christian woman who prayed wildly over his prostrate form until she was forcibly removed.[20] That Mrs Ward, in the initial draft of her novel, could have associated Catherine with such a notorious episode suggests that Catherine, as first conceived, was characterized by a more ugly bigotry than in later drafts. (Another early sketch of the opening chapters alludes to 'the free thinking neighbour', presumably the man who died following 'the accident on the bridge' described in the notebook.)

In the last chapter of *Robert Elsmere*, in its published form, we see a much softened and subdued version of the Winwood Reade story, when Catherine creeps into the bedroom of her sick husband and prays fervently (but silently) that he may experience the classic deathbed conversion. Mrs Ward suggests that the traditional Christian preoccupation with a man's final words is misguided, but in fact she exploits the emotional potential of the scene just as thoroughly in her own way as does Catherine. Catherine wants to save her husband's soul before he passes into the afterlife, and she uses every weapon at her command, including his physical weakness. But Mrs Ward also lingers over the episode, because she in turn wants to show us the death of a martyr of the new faith. Hence what was originally no doubt a crude incident in the novel, calculated only to expose the fanatical cruelty of the orthodox believer, was transformed into a good Victorian death scene (albeit with an inversion of the customary theological 'message') in which the husband's refusal to recant fails to break the bond of human love between himself and his Christian wife. John Morley had argued that such a couple could overleap the barriers of religious opinions, and Mrs Ward attempted to show how it could be done, even at the moment of death.

II

Through much of the autumn of 1885 Mrs Ward was kept busy seeing *Amiel's Journal* through the press, but by 18 November she was able to tell her mother that 'the novel gets on, but rather slowly. It is very difficult to write & the farther I get the harder it is.' On 16 December she reported to her brother Willie that the first section—which she described as 'very tame & domestic' with a 'parochial air'—was now nearly completed and that she would send him a typewritten draft for criticism as soon as possible. 'The first part seems to me at present too long & to want condensing', she said. 'The least encouragement would make me do it, but I should be glad to have the view of one who would come to it fresh & see it as a whole. Both Humphry and I have seen it too much in fragments and detail.'

On 8 March she wrote to her father that 'the novel is getting on. I have now about half done it', she added, 'but all the most difficult and strenuous part of the story is to come.' Yet the social distractions of London nearly brought her writing to a standstill, and during April, in a desperate effort to find a more quiet environment, Mrs Ward moved to Borough Farm, the house near Godalming where the Wards usually spent their summers; there she wrote 16, 18, and even 20 pages of manuscript a day. On 23 May 1886 Gertrude Ward, whose orthodox sensibilities were much disturbed by the

book, summarized in her diary *Robert Elsmere*'s progress to
date:

"Robert Elsmere" was begun before Christmas '85—not until Amiel
was quite done with. Amiel was published in October '85, and then the
novel began to grow. Mary works a great deal at it; much has been entirely re-written, some parts I think have been corrected & written two
or three times over. The greater part of the second volume was written
at Borough in April; I think I never was so moved by any book as by
her reading aloud of the chapter where Robert becomes aware that his
faith is gone. I used to dream of him as a real person, and could think
of nothing else but his difficulties. I think Mary was rather pleased at
the impression it made. Here in London it is impossible to get much
done: scarcely anything but corrections has been done since the end of
April.

During July and August, Mrs Ward predicted to her mother
on 11 June, she would have to 'stick to my book like grim
death, if I am to keep my promise to George Smith', yet even
at Borough Farm, as she steeped herself in Biblical criticism
and wrote constantly, the novel went more slowly than she
had expected. 'Alas! alas! I shan't have got the 2nd vol. done
in spite of all my labours', she wrote her mother on 4 August.
'I have practically re-written the whole of it, & it won't be
done for another fortnight.'

During this spring and summer of 1886 Mrs Ward began to
suffer the pyschological and physical symptoms which were
always to accompany the act of composition for the rest of
her life. Her right arm would become so numb and painful
that she was occasionally reduced to dictating to Gertrude;
she would plunge ever more energetically into her writing
until at last she collapsed from nervous exhaustion; then
there would be prolonged holidays on the Continent or at
Fox How while she convalesced. Afterwards, as soon as she
recovered her strength, the cycle would begin all over again.
Without indulging irresponsibly in medical theories, one is
surely justified in seeing in this pattern some obvious indications of compulsive, neurotic behaviour. However, the fre-
netic pace of Mrs Ward's literary career, punctuated so frequently by serious illnesses of a psychosomatic nature, can

perhaps best be interpreted from a Carlylean rather than a Freudian perspective. Carlyle's advice to Victorian doubters, reiterated in *Sartor Resartus* and elsewhere, was 'Produce! Produce!': do not allow yourself to be paralyzed by mere negations and scepticisms; banish your spiritual anxieties not by rational argument but by leaping headlong into the world of action. Robert Elsmere, having lost his Chrstian faith, finds solace in his heroic endeavours on behalf of the New Brotherhood of Christ. Indeed, he seems almost to court martyrdom by working himself to death. Mrs Ward followed his example by always engaging in a frenzy of political, charitable, and literary activities. If thinking became too painful, there was always blessed peace in sheer hard work. As Carlyle's favourite Biblical text admonished, 'Whatsoever thy hand findeth to do, do it with thy whole might.' The Carlylean Gospel of Labour should not be sneered at, for it lay behind the gigantic accomplishments of many of the great Victorians; but in some cases (certainly in Clough's case and perhaps in Mrs Ward's) this attempt to silence the rational intellect by a feverish round of activity strikes us as unwholesome and even self-destructive. Mrs Ward's alternating bursts of creative energy and periods of illness and depression are probably the symptoms of a mind more spiritually troubled than she was ever willing to acknowledge.

Plagued increasingly by nervousness and low spirits, Mrs Ward fled during August 1886 to the Isle of Wight. 'I am better but not well', she wrote her husband from there on 12 August. 'I am afraid I must have been overworking this tiresome head, and I am trying to manage myself as cleverly as possible so as [to] get free as soon as I can of this sense of oppression.' Though she was writing very little, 'my book seems to get on my nerves'. In October, aware by now that the early chapters would have to be rewritten again, she spent several weeks at Fox Ghyll, the Forsters' summer home just down the road from Fox How, where she read aloud 'the chapter describing Murewell and the Squire's library' (Chapter 14) and 'a scene between Robert and Mr. Grey at Oxford'

(Chapter 37) to a gathering of friends. Describing the occasion to her mother on 17 October, she wrote:

If the effect of those chapters on the public judgement is anything like what it was yesterday I shall be happy indeed. Sometimes I can hardly bear to think of the book's appearance. I shall certainly hardly read any reviews of it. I will not let it go till I am satisfied with it,—and alas! it takes a long time to get oneself satisfied with it.

Volume ii was completed at Fox Ghyll, but Mrs Ward was horrified to discover that, through an error, Smith, Elder were already advertising *Robert Elsmere* as 'in the Press'. On 20 October she therefore offered to George Smith this report of her progress:

The fact is when I got down to the country with it in July, I soon convinced myself that the second volume as it then stood was quite unsatisfactory and that I could do it better. I accordingly threw it into the waste-paper basket & began again. Since July 1 I have written practically a volume and a third, for what was the first volume has now been shortened to a preliminary *Book* ['Westmoreland'], I am now working at the rate of about 50 pages of print a week, and I hope at least to let you have the whole book by the end of December for publication say in February.

Her revisions in volumes i and ii had been so extensive, she said, that the novel was now 'a different thing altogether'.

In December she and Gertrude retreated again to the solitude of Borough Farm, where, as she wrote her mother (16 December), 'with the exception of meals exercise & reading I work all day and am getting on famously'. Her goal now was to complete all but the final six chapters by Christmas and to be done with those by 10 January. 'Then a fortnight or three weeks for what revision still remains & I shall have finished the longest &—I hope—the best piece of work I have ever done. But the end is still so far off that I don't dare to let myself think about it much.'

However, the end was farther off than either Mrs Ward or her publisher realized. 'There are still three chapters to do', she declared in a letter to her mother on 1 February 1887. 'The book is certainly working up towards the end. The scene between Madame de Netteville & Robert tell Ethel [Mrs Ward's sister] is most French novelish! I think many of my relations will be shocked!' Again, on 16 February, she admitted that 'these last chapters are worrying me tremendously'. Later in the month, to her brother, she wrote: 'Still two chapters of *Robert Elsmere*. It seems interminable. But it cannot take more than three weeks now. It is not a *novel* at all.' On 9 March 1887 she finished the last words of the final chapter in her London house, and, as she described the moment in *A Writer's Recollections*, she 'came out afterwards, from my tiny writing-room at the end of the drawing-room, shaken with tears, and wondering as I sat alone on the floor, by the fire, in the front room, what life would be like now that the book was done!' (p. 288).

In 1890 Mrs Ward confessed to Frances Power Cobbe that 'I have never quite recovered from the strain of *Robert Elsmere*'.[21] The writing of the novel had specially taxed Mrs Ward's resources because in describing the religious dilemma of Robert she was recording the inner struggle of her own conflicting tendencies towards rationalism and mysticism. But *Elsmere* also presented serious technical difficulties, for Mrs Ward had set herself the task of creating a story that would simultaneously possess intrinsic literary merit and serve as a vehicle for certain ideas. In her memoirs she analyzed the perplexities produced by such a double aim in novel-writing:

> The problem, then, in intellectual poetry or fiction, is so to suggest the argument, that both the expert and the popular consciousness may feel its force. And to do this without overstepping the bounds of poetry or fiction; without turning either into mere ratiocination, and so losing the 'simple, sensuous, passionate' element which is their true life.
>
> It was this problem which made 'Robert Elsmere' take three years to write instead of one. (p. 232)

Mrs Ward's late novels reveal, in fact, an alarming dichotomy between plot and intellectual content; both uneasily co-exist, with only the slightest coherence, between the covers of each book. In *Robert Elsmere*, however, story and idea are admirably fused, and only in the third volume does Mrs Ward's notorious didacticism become really objectionable.

But this unity was achieved in the rewritten version rather than the early drafts of the book. Fortunately, there are two extant groups of manuscripts and proofs of *Robert Elsmere*— one in the Honnold Library of Claremont University, the other in the Berg Collection of the New York Public Library —and by comparing these with the 1885 notebook and Mrs Ward's correspondence with George Smith during 1887, it is possible to determine fairly accurately the changes which were introduced during the process of rewriting. The Honnold materials consist chiefly of fair copies of certain chapters which are very similar to the published text, though there are a few significant variants. The Berg materials, on the other hand, represent a more miscellaneous collection of preliminary notes, early drafts, revised proofs, and fragments. (To simplify references, citations from the Berg Collection documents will be identified as 'Berg', whereas citations from the Honnold manuscripts will not carry any identification.) One astonishing fact which emerges from the Berg materials is how extensively Mrs Ward rewrote the novel after it was in proofs: sometimes only an occasional paragraph from the proofs was retained in the final version. This was a bad habit (bad, at least, from a publisher's point of view) which Mrs Ward never fully overcame and which diminished Smith's profits from all her later books.

Mrs Ward once confessed to a 'tendency to interminableness',[22] a trait which is much in evidence in the *Elsmere* manuscripts and proofs. The *objets d'art* of Wendover Hall and the titles in the Squire's library are catalogued exhaustively; Oxford is described with affectionate thoroughness; Robert's sermons are reported at wearisome length. Indeed, some of the chapters are twice their published length in these early drafts: Chapter 31 (Berg), for example, originally contained a full account of Rose's unhappy experiences in Long Whindale after her visit to Berlin, including an unsuccessful proposal of marriage from Mr Mayhew. Excisions of such details were of course readily made by Mrs Ward, even before Smith began to complain of her book's excessive length; but there were other changes, some not introduced merely in the interest of conciseness, which fundamentally altered the structure and tone of the novel.

We have already seen that Book One was, in its original form, much longer, describing (according to some Berg notes) a series of episodes intended to reveal the spiritual differences between Robert and Catherine. This was greatly condensed, and the consequent omission of the 'Winwood Reade' episode had the effect of offering a less harsh estimate of Catherine's Puritan character. The early version also followed a more strictly chronological order. What other revisions were made in Book One is difficult to ascertain, because only a few pages of the first draft of this section are available today, and the other surviving manuscript portions of Book One are almost identical to the published text, as they represent a later draft.

The one important category of revisions which Mrs Ward afterwards publicly discussed was the condensation of Robert's theological and historical discussions with Squire Wendover. 'As the human interest of the story gained upon me I began to shorten these sections of the story, until in the third year, immediately before publication, I desperately reduced them', she wrote in her later Introduction to *Robert Elsmere* (I, xxix). This statement by Mrs Ward is misleading in two respects. First, the cuts were made not with disinterested literary motives but because George Smith was vigorously demanding a shorter book. Second, most of the Squire's speeches were retained; it was Robert's responses which were trimmed and altered. In the manuscript Robert offers frequent and cogent objections to Wendover's 'science of testimony', making the obvious point that a disbelief in miracles rests upon a set of assumptions about the nature of the universe no more absolutely demonstrable than the assumptions underlying Christian supernaturalism. But in the published text Robert is so crushed by Wendover's arguments that he offers only the most pitiful sort of resistance. These revisions resulted in not only a deliberate weakening of the case for Christianity, as Gladstone and other reviewers complained, but also a weakening of Elsmere's character. Mrs Ward insisted to Meredith Townsend that Robert 'was not really weak but only exceptionally sensitive & responsive',[23] yet even readers sympathetic to Elsmere's religious point of view have often found him excessively passive and too easily swayed by the influence of stronger personalities—first Grey, then Catherine, and finally Wendover.

Likewise, the contrasting theological viewpoints of Elsmere and Armistead, his clerical successor at Murewell, are developed (in an early Berg draft) in a manner reminiscent of the diverging careers of Mr A and Mr C in *Unbelief and Sin*. Most of this schematic parallelism has disappeared in the published text.

Another section of the novel heavily rewritten by Mrs Ward was Chapter 43, which describes Madame de Netteville's attempted seduction of Robert. The author may have professed to relish the 'French novelish' tone of this chapter, but her Victorian sense of morality was also disturbed, with the result that this portion of the manuscript is filled with numerous false starts, deleted sentences and paragraphs, and interlinear additions. Similarly, Mrs Ward groped around a good deal in trying the define the precise relationship between Rose and Edward Langham. In the manuscript their encounters are generally seen through the eyes of Rose, who is willing to shoulder the blame for the failure of Langham's courtship, whereas in the final text Mrs Ward shifts our attention almost entirely to his spiritual and emotional impotence. The figure of Langham, who represents a great achievement of psychological insight in the novel, was much less impressive as originally conceived. (Incidentally, it is Robert, not Catherine, who first senses in the manuscript that Rose and Langham may be romantically attracted to each other.)

Unquestionably this alteration in perspective produced a considerable improvement in the novel, but the revising of the Rose-Langham subplot also resulted in the excision of several exceptionally fine passages. For example, in Chapter 15 of the manuscript, as Catherine and Langham are strolling about the Murewell rectory garden, Rose stands by an open window in the drawing room and begins to play her violin:

Langham stood beside her [Catherine], his back to the sun which was just struggling through the clouds beyond the corn field, & promising a finer afternoon. Rose finished the Allegro & began the Andante. She was playing in a tumult of feeling, playing she knew not why. She took no heed of her fingers; her music remained unturned; she went on playing by heart the delicate majestic melody rising & falling in response to the variations of an inward debate which swept on side by side with the music. Suddenly she moved a little nearer without knowing it to the window which was open to the ground & beyond it, only five or six yards from her her eyes caught the figure of Langham, dark, erect & motionless against the light-filled sky. He on his side started as he saw the little swaying form, the raised arm & wrist, which had till now been hidden from him by the curtains, and she noticed with a thrill his quick change of attitude.

   I will draw him in—he *shall* come!—she thought, her breath coming faster, as her bow lingered over the last chords of the Andante.

But Langham, oppressed by his customary dark vision of human destiny, resists the seductive notes. Rose's attempt to allure him through her music is explicitly sexual; the scene is a brilliant one, and by comparison, Madame de Netteville's later rendezvous with Robert seems the stuff of crude melodrama.

   It is clear from some of Mrs Ward's preliminary notes (Berg) that the final chapters of *Robert Elsmere* were once very different, but it is only with much difficulty that the original plot can be reconstructed. The evidence—unfortunately fragmentary—indicates that Robert, speaking at a Sunday lecture about the Resurrection, was to have collapsed before Catherine's eyes; Robert then goes off to the Alps to die, Rose and Flaxman become engaged while with him there, and as a final gesture Robert sends for Langham. Another set of Mrs Ward's notes (Berg), obviously belonging to a later stage of composition, lists a nearly identical series of events, except that by then she had shifted the locale to Algiers. In short, Flaxman's proposal in Long Whindale and Langham's absence from Robert's deathbed do not represent Mrs Ward's earliest intentions.

The miscellaneous small revisions in the novel may be listed more briefly. Robert's mother remains alive to the end of the manuscript, whereas in the published version she dies in Chapter 11. The manuscript occasionally gives more detailed information about Robert's life as a vicar: we are told, for instance, that he has offended the neighbouring Tory farmers by favouring the county franchise bill. Robert's climactic encounter with Henslow, the Squire's agent, is moved to a different chapter and made less physically violent. The symbolism of the Medusa sculpture and the Greuze portrait (associated with the Squire and Rose, respectively) at Wendover Hall is underscored more obviously in the manuscript. The spelling of the name of Robert's wife was changed from 'Catharine' to 'Catherine'. Lengthy descriptions of landscapes and characters were ruthlessly pruned. A few of the chapters were rearranged, divided, and combined, and all of the chapters were renumbered. Finally, it should be recorded that in a few of the Berg drafts, Elsmere's name appears as 'Ellesmere'.

III

These were some of the modifications to *Robert Elsmere* which Mrs Ward was to make in 1887. In the first flush of excitement after completing the manuscript draft on 9 March, she naively wrote her father that 'there is still about a fortnight's hard work before me in revision and correction, but still I feel as if the worst were over'. And in a letter to her mother on 17 March she also expressed confidence that the process of revising would take only a few weeks:

I am now revising and rewriting hard. It is very difficult work & will take to the beginning of April & more. But there is a sort of satisfaction in it. It is like rubbing up a picture or polishing a piece of plate. The book will certainly be greatly improved by it.

The reason for these unrealistic prophecies is that the reworking of the first volume went very swiftly, as it had already been revised earlier. 'I have all but re-written 3 chapters of the 1st Vol', she told Julia on 26 March. 'I have only one more to re-write—the rest only want correcting & retrenching.' Four days later she promised that 'the book must be out sometime in May'.

Early in April she took the manuscript with her to Borough Farm, reflecting as she did so on 'how lost I shall feel when it has all gone to press',[24] but distractions began to increase. Julia's illness required a visit to Oxford, and Mrs Ward herself once again displayed the usual symptoms of nervous exhaustion. On 29 April she promised Smith that the following day she would give him a typescript of a large portion of the book, urging him to set it up in type as she gradually furnished the final draft. 'It will be a very long book', she admitted in an understatement that Smith must have afterwards regarded with amusement. 'I reckon that the first two vols will contain about 280 pages each. . . . The third volume will contain about 50 pages more.'

The first proofs, which arrived on 7 May, showed an alarming amplitude, persuading Mrs Ward that there would have to be more lines per page and thinner paper. 'It is certainly a long novel, though not I think, when all is considered, too long', she wrote Smith the next day. By the middle of May she was under a doctor's care and able to do little correcting of proofs. Worse yet, Smith was beginning to argue that the proportions of *Robert Elsmere* were too spacious even for a three-decker novel. On the thirteenth he sent Mrs Ward this analysis:

We find that the length of the 1st volume of your novel exceeds very considerably the estimate of 280 pages you gave us. We estimate that, if chapter 14 of volume 1 is of the same length as the other chapters, the volume, if set up after the manner of the proofs, will contain 412 pages. This will make the novel a much longer one than the ordinary three volume novel. Our experience is that great length in a novel militates against its chances of success with the novel reading public. The only two alternatives which suggest themselves are that you should either reduce the length of the book, if such is possible, or that we should use a solid page (like the enclosed), though such a page is seldom used for novels. . . . Before setting up any more manuscript it will be wiser, I think you will agree with me, that we should have the whole of the manuscript in our hands.

The letter sent Mrs Ward into a state of despair, though she grimly set about slashing large chunks out of the manuscript and proofs, a process which was to continue for more than six months.

However, there was encouraging news from Willie Arnold, who was on the staff of the *Manchester Guardian*. Having read the proofs of the first volume, he wrote his sister on 15 May that 'it is the biggest thing that has been done for years', and to Julia Arnold he reported on the same day that

I was deeply touched and interested by it. It promises to be a really considerable book and I look forward to its making a great mark. It has a much firmer grip of character, more humour, and more flexibility than I confess I had expected. The landscape is admirable—Westmorland has never been better done—and there is plenty of the milk of human kindness. You may look forward to finding yourself the mother of a celebrated woman![25]

But in the meantime Smith continued to send dismal reports from the printer. His revised estimate, on 17 May, was that the book would run to an unprecedented 1358 pages. 'We are really quite at a loss to know what to do with a novel which so much exceeds the length of an ordinary three volume novel', his letter concluded. Mrs Ward, in a reply written the same day, agreed to proceed with excisions, though she hesitated to touch the third volume, which 'contains the best work I have ever done or could do'. She also quoted her brother's praise of the book (identifying him as 'a literary man' rather than a relation) and told Smith that 'M. Edmond Scherer the "French critic on Goethe" in whom Uncle Matt believes, was so much struck by the Oxford chapters that he is to review it in the *Temps* directly it appears, & Mr. Walter Pater has already arranged to write about it'. Writing also to her mother on the 17th, she conceded that she was now so ill that the second volume could not be revised in time for the current publishing season. 'I have over-thought & over-felt, and I believe I should spoil the book if I were to rush through it now.' Nevertheless, she intended 'to stick out for printing the 3rd vol almost exactly as it is. I am convinced it will be much the most interesting to the general public.'

Progress during the summer was slow. The Long Vacation was spent at Lady Margaret Hall so that she could be near her mother, whose health was rapidly failing, and in September the Wards enjoyed a brief holiday in Eastbourne. Even there Mrs Ward continued to trim and revise the manuscript, which she now hoped could be published in November. She and Smith agreed that the increased printing expenses resulting from the extensive alterations in proof would be borne by the author. She returned to London 'in a state of utter fatigue & . . . under the doctor's hands . . . doing as little as possible'.[26]

Throughout October she devoted all of her dwindling physical resources to the novel but continued to suffer from a paralyzed right arm, headaches, and insomnia. On 25 October she completed the revision of page proofs of the first two volumes, though, as she wrote her mother, 'the third vol. is still to be pushed through'. The final volume required more rewriting than she had supposed it would, and by 5 November she confessed to Smith, 'I am afraid it is no use—I cannot get this book ready for a November publication. I cannot sleep, & therefore I cannot work at high-pressure. The doctors say go to the Riviera, & I am afraid I must.' She relinquished all claim to further advances or royalties 'till the sale of the book reaches—if ever—1000 copies'. Yet at the same time Mrs Ward was capable of expressing optimism about her novel. She told her publisher that Lord Arthur Russell had said 'that it can hardly fail to make a profound impression', and Bernard Bosanquet, who had also seen the proofs, called it 'splendid'.

The journey to Italy was only partially successful in restoring Mrs Ward to good health. Packets of proofs and manuscript followed her everywhere by post, Humphry was ill for a week at San Remo, the weather was poor, and at Florence 'we got bad news of my mother which brought us suddenly home'.[27] She completed the final revisions in London during late December. Responding to the printer's unhappy report that the third volume had reached 440 pages, Mrs Ward promised (on 10 January 1888) to remove even more material from the proofs and to assume responsibility for the additional expenses.

The book was to be dedicated to T. H. Green and Laura Lyttelton, both dead, and so a proof of the dedication was submitted to Laura's husband, Alfred Lyttelton, who tactfully suggested that it should 'convey that sympathy of mind and character rather than identity of opinion was the basis of your love for Laura and of hers for you'. The revised dedication, however, so pleased him that he read it 'with blinding tears'.[28]

Mrs Ward's long struggle, the product of which was to alter the direction of her life and literary career, was finally over. On 27 January she returned the last proof to the printer. She hoped Smith would make arrangements for publication in America, as *Amiel's Journal* had sold well there, and she told him that she feared the public's absorption in the Irish question might distract attention from her novel. *Robert Elsmere* was published on 24 February. Meanwhile, Julia Arnold lay dying at Oxford. For Mrs Ward, the juxtaposition of these two events, followed by the death of Matthew Arnold in April, produced a mood which alternated between exultation and despair throughout that remarkable spring of 1888. It was, as T. S. Eliot says in 'Journey of the Magi', a Birth that was 'hard and bitter agony . . . , like Death'.

Chapter 7
ROBERT ELSMERE: AN ANALYSIS

[Scepticism] is a crisis in the history of the mind which must occur, but cannot be fabricated. When this condition does seize a great and developed intellect, it is the most deeply interesting phenomenon that the human mind offers for our study. . . . [It] is a disease that can only take hold of a sincere mind; for it is caused by the endeavour to reach a foundation for opinion, and the struggle is desperate because it is felt to be one for life or death.

—Mark Pattison[1]

I

Robert Elsmere was published at exactly the right moment to capture the popular imagination. Had it appeared a decade earlier, its exposition of the principles of higher criticism would hardly have found an audience outside Oxford and Cambridge, for Victorian readers had been remarkably successful in insulating themselves from Continental Biblical scholarship. Had the novel been issued during the 1890s, it would have seemed *déjà vu* to a generation no longer capable of becoming alarmed over the apparent crumbling of Christian orthodoxy. But in 1888 a story about a doubting clergyman possessed interest for a large number of readers, partly because Charles Bradlaugh's repeated efforts to take his seat in Parliament had made atheism a popular topic of discussion during the decade, and partly because higher criticism was suddenly becoming disturbingly visible to ordinary Englishmen. At the Church Congress in Manchester that year there was a lengthy debate on higher criticism and the Old Testament, and the consensus among Anglican clergy and bishops seemed to be that the main conclusions of the critics regarding the Old Testament could no longer be resisted—though there was still no comparable acceptance of advanced critical views upon the New Testament. Matthew Arnold, in the preface to the Popular Edition (1887) of *St Paul and Protestantism*, marvelled at the transformation of English Protestant theology in the 16 years since his book was written: 'Where are now those great and grave doctrines which so possessed the thoughts of religious England formerly?'[2]

Mrs Ward sensed the timeliness of her novel and emphasized it by giving the story a contemporary setting, modelling her characters upon real persons, and offering vivid, realistic descriptions of English spiritual and intellectual life in various quarters. Robert Elsmere himself bears the heavy symbolic burden of being the representative modern doubter; not content with barren scepticism, he is the founder of a new faith, a revitalized Christianity, thus pointing the way—as Mrs Ward fervently hoped—to the next phase in Europe's religious development.

The internal chronology of *Robert Elsmere* is quite precise: the story takes place over a four-year period between May 1882, when Robert visits Long Whindale, and March 1886, when he dies in Algiers.[3] Nevertheless, the claim to contemporaneity is belied by the fact that the plot, as Mrs Ward herself privately confessed, reflects the spiritual struggles of an earlier period. To Mandell Creighton she wrote:

I entirely agree that Elsmere's change, though I think the nature & elements of it are typical, is not as a story typical of the present day. The pressure now is distributed from so many sides, & the alternatives offered are on the whole so much more attractive & inspiring than they were, that a man may often pass through the whole process without much sense of painful giving up. . . . Certainly Elsmere's story is true to the experience of a past generation, the generation of John Stirling [*sic*], of the *Nemesis of Faith*, of Blanco White.[4]

Since Joseph Blanco White became a Unitarian in 1835, John Sterling died in 1844, and Froude's *Nemesis of Faith* was published in 1849, this statement pushes the 'true' chronology of *Robert Elsmere* very far back indeed. Despite its topical nature, then, Mrs Ward's novel is mainly about the past rather than the present, not only because any work of popularization must necessarily treat ideas already familiar to specialists, but also because the author's emotional and imaginative life had not kept pace with her intellectual development. Mrs Ward described *Robert Elsmere* as 'the work of one who, in spite of—or perhaps because of—her long immersion in a learned and literary society was in many respects younger than her years'.[5] Mrs Ward's mind was filled with the latest critical theories from Germany, but her heart, as every page of *Robert Elsmere* reveals, still belonged to the mid-Victorian world of Charlotte Mary Yonge. Elsmere's naïveté, his single-minded absorption in theological problems, and his moral zeal perhaps tell us less than is usually supposed about late nineteenth-century English life, but they do disclose much about the personality of the author.

The illusion of topicality, however, was fostered by the *roman à clef* form which Mrs Ward adopted in nearly all of her novels. To those who knew Victorian Oxford, *Robert Elsmere* was filled with characters recognizably drawn from life: Mr Grey was T. H. Green (Mrs Ward never attempted to deny this identification); the Provost of St Anselm's was obviously Jowett; it was whispered that Langham was Pater; Squire Wendover bore a close resemblance to Mark Pattison; and there were even rumours afloat about the identity of Elsmere. Lady Helen Varley seems to have been a fictionalized picture of Laura Tennant, afterwards Mrs Lyttelton. Jowett offered to Margot Tennant this sarcastic summary of the conjectures he had heard: 'People say that in *Robert Elsmere* Rose is intended for you, Catherine for your sister Laura, the Squire for Mark Pattison, the Provost for me, etc., and Mr. Grey for Professor Green. All the portraits are about equally unlike the originals.'[6] Henry Sidgwick was surprised to discover in May 1888 that 'there is a widespread feeling in Oxford that the portrait of Green is something that ought not to have been done'. After all, Sidgwick argued, 'it is at once faithful and friendly', and he himself would be grateful for this particular kind of posthumous fame.[7] (It is a fact, incidentally, that Green's ideas reached a larger audience through *Robert Elsmere* than through his own books and lectures. Generally after 1888, particularly in America, he was identified as 'the Mr Grey of *Robert Elsmere*' whenever his name was mentioned in print.)

But Mrs Ward was made understandably nervous by all such talk, even though her novel actually seemed to encourage loose speculations. In her Introduction to *Marcella*, she declared, 'Until the stuff of what we call real life has been re-created and transformed by the independent, possessive, impetuous forces of imagination, it has no value for the artist, and in so far as it remains "real," i.e., a mere literal copy of something seen or heard, it represents a dead and lifeless element in an artist's work' (I, xii). Yet *Robert Elsmere* is weighted down by precisely such inert, untransformed matter, and Mrs Ward's energetic denials that her characters were modelled upon 'real' people merely confirm her uneasiness about her own practice. 'There is not a single character drawn from the life in *Robert Elsmere* except Mr. Grey, & a sketch among the minor characters', she told C. K. Shorter,[8] but her assertion will not hold up under close examination.

Elsmere himself is a composite figure, with bits and pieces taken from a number of clergymen whom Mrs Ward knew or about whom she had read—or, as she phrased it, 'inspired and coloured, as all such figures are, by the actual human experience amid which he was conceived'.[9] As early as 1881, in *Unbelief and Sin*, she had described his religious views in great detail, and his spiritual crisis was patterned after Mrs Ward's own experience while writing articles for the *Dictionary of Christian Biography*; but his behaviour and physical appearance were drawn from observation and reading. Mrs Ward acknowledged, for instance, that 'some of the *colouring* of the country parish part' was suggested by the *Life* of Charles Kingsley, 'a very favourite book of mine'.[10] Elsmere emulates Kingsley in both his clerical activities—industriously organizing clubs in the parish and caring for the needs of the poor—and his penchant for fishing, about which he talked 'as Kingsley might have talked of it, and, indeed, with constant quotations from Kingsley' (i, 320). Unfortunately this adoption of Kingsley's habits produces some artistic fissures in Elsmere's personality, for we are asked to believe that he is simultaneously a robust Muscular Christian and a sick, nervous, sensitive seeker after truth.

Elsmere's mornings of strenuous study recall the regimen of Mandell Creighton in his Northumberland parish, and his physiognomy and temperament are close to those of John Sterling, whose biography by Carlyle Mrs Ward had undoubtedly read. Carlyle describes Sterling as impetuous, unhesitating in word and act, possessing a bodily frame that was 'thin, excitable' and displaying 'animation rather than strength'.[11] Another similar somatic type whom Mrs Ward may have had in mind was her friend J. R. Green, whose brilliant career as a historian was cut short in 1883 by tuberculosis, though she explicitly denied that Green was in any sense a model for her hero. Green, like Elsmere, had abandoned the Anglican priesthood because of religious doubts (as well as ill health) and had looked forward with anticipation to a faith of the future that would absorb both mysticism and freedom of thought and inquiry. Elsmere's remarkable capacity for moving socially back and forth between the slums of London and the West End, his gift for brilliant conversation, and the manner of his death are all directly reminiscent of Green, despite Mrs Ward's protestations to the contrary.

There were of course numerous precedents for Elsmere's decision to renounce holy orders. In Robert Elsmere itself Mrs Ward cites the case of Ernest Renan, whose faith had been completely shaken by the discovery that the book of Daniel was a 'strange product of Jewish patriotism in the second century before Christ' (ii, 46-7). Leslie Stephen, whom Mrs Ward knew well, had left the priesthood of the Church of England when he became convinced that Noah's flood was a

fiction.[12] After the novel was published, one contributor to
the *National Review* claimed that the 'real' Robert Elsmere
was the Revd James Cranbrook, a Presbyterian minister who,
having offended orthodox sensibilities in his congregation,
resigned his pastorate and attempted to found a new and
more tolerant religious body.[13] The example most likely to
have influenced Mrs Ward's treatment of her hero, however,
was set by Stopford Brooke, whose wife stayed with the
Wards at Oxford on the occasion when Brooke delivered his
last sermon as an Anglican from the university pulpit. Mrs
Ward heard the sermon, and in later years when he became a
Unitarian she regularly attended his services at Bedford
Chapel in London.[14]

Finally, one cannot ignore the parallels between Elsmere's
career and Tom Arnold's. Though Arnold was never ordained
as either a Roman Catholic or an Anglican, he risked financial
ruin and endured domestic unhappiness in his quixotic search
for truth. In making Robert Elsmere leave the Church just as
he was on the verge of great success as a clergyman, Mrs Ward
must have been recalling that day in Oxford when she burst
into the home of the T. H. Greens and announced with tears
that papa had once again become a Catholic—this time on the
eve of his election to a university professorship.

II

Archibald Tait once observed, 'The great evil is—that the
liberals are deficient in religion and the religious are deficient
in liberality.'[15] This was the profound religious dilemma of
the Victorian age to which Mrs Ward addressed herself in
Robert Elsmere. How could a young man like Elsmere be
both religious and liberal (i.e., intellectually enlightened)?
The solution which she offered to her contemporaries was
based upon the familiar Arnoldian dialectic: the destruction
of orthodoxy by modern rationalism must be followed by a
new synthesis which would offer a reasonable religion for
nineteenth-century men and women. The three stages of the
dialectic are suggested in several ways. First, Robert himself

undergoes a change as the story progresses. He begins as a conventional Christian, falls unsuspectingly into a morass of unbelief, and at last regains his footing by discovering what Matthew Arnold called the 'joy whose grounds are true'.[16] Second, the Arnoldian dialectic is reflected in the characters who dominate each of the three volumes of the novel. The first volume belongs to Catherine, the representative of orthodoxy; the second belongs to Wendover, an embittered sceptic; and the third to Robert, the founder of the purified new faith.

Even the settings of *Robert Elsmere* evoke a similar dialectical pattern. The moral centre of volume i is Long Whindale (i.e., Longsleddale), a Westmorland valley of Wordsworthian beauty and freshness which symbolizes the simplicity of the earlier faith. In volume ii the really decisive actions take place in Squire Wendover's library, which is filled with poisonous books that nearly ensnare Robert's soul. They do in fact capture his mind, but his deepest spiritual life is untouched, so that in the third volume he is able to create in the East End of London (outwardly the City of Destruction) a City of God —though in an Arnoldian rather than an Augustinian sense. Like Dr Arnold in the closing lines of 'Rugby Chapel', Elsmere becomes an inspiring Carlylean hero, a modern Moses, leading the confused ranks of humanity through the wilderness of this world 'On, to the bound of the waste, / On, to the City of God'.

Yet such a schematic view of the novel overlooks the hints of change that are evident in Long Whindale, in Catherine, and in the old faith. The opening chapter of *Robert Elsmere*, which has often been admired for its beautiful portrayal of the arrival of spring in a Westmorland valley, is more than a clever exercise in Ruskinian landscape description. From the first paragraph onward, we learn that the impression of changelessness in Long Whindale is an illusion. It is not only the season which is robbing the valley of its natural austerity; there are signs everywhere of a more advanced civilization encroaching upon the ancient fells. Burwood Farm, Catherine

Leyburn's home, has a bow window, neat flower-beds, and close-shaven lawn, all of which were unknown in Long Whindale a generation or two before:

The windows in [the sheds] were new, the doors fresh-painted and closely shut; curtains of some soft outlandish make showed themselves in what had once been a stable, and the turf stretched smoothly up to a narrow gravelled path in front of them, unbroken by a single footmark. No, evidently the old farm, for such it undoubtedly was, had been but lately, or comparatively lately, transformed to new and softer uses; that rough patriarchal life of which it had once been a symbol and centre no longer bustled and clattered through it. It had become the shelter of new ideals, the home of another and a milder race than had once possessed it. (i, 6)

There is a new church in the valley, and the vicar is a typically middle-class Victorian clergyman incapable of achieving the intimate relationships with the peasants that his predecessors had enjoyed. Even the description in Chapter 1 of Rose playing her violin at Burwood, with the music floating and eddying about the valley, which may appear to be an echo of Wordsworth's 'The Solitary Reaper', is in fact something quite different: the song is not of 'old, unhappy, far-off things' but a modern Andante by Spohr.

All of this is important because it points forward to the later, almost imperceptible changes in Catherine and her religious faith. After Robert has abandoned Christianity, Mrs Ward supplies this analysis of the corresponding but more subtle transformation of his wife:

She would live and die steadfast to the old faiths. But her present mind and its outlook was no more the mind of her early married life than the Christian philosophy of to-day is the Christian philosophy of the Middle Ages. She was not conscious of change, but change there was. She had, in fact, undergone that dissociation of the moral judgement from a special series of religious formulae which is the crucial, the epoch-making fact of our time. (ii, 471-2)

Many reviewers, including Gladstone, were bewildered by Mrs Ward's assertion in the penultimate paragraph of the novel that Catherine quietly attended the services of the New

Brotherhood of Christ after the death of Robert, because they felt it was out of character for her. Yet from the very beginning of *Robert Elsmere* Mrs Ward had been warning her readers that Catherine and her faith were no more exempt from the universal law of ceaseless, inexorable change than was Long Whindale.

Given this close symbolic relationship between the heroine and landscape of Book One, it is not surprising that Mrs Ward was able to create Catherine only after her visit in 1885 to Longsleddale. (Mrs Ward nearly always had to find settings for her novels before she could people them with characters.) Catherine towers over the other characters in Book One, because she is in her natural element, while her sisters and Robert have deeper affinities to the modern world outside the valley:

[Her] complexion had caught the freshness and purity of Westmore-land air and Westmoreland streams. About face and figure there was a delicate austere charm, something which harmonised with the bare stretches and lonely crags of the fells, something which seemed to make her a true daughter of the mountains, partaker at once of their gentle-ness and their severity. *She* was in her place here, beside the homely Westmoreland house and under the shelter of the fells. (i, 13)

Catherine moves with 'a beautiful dignity and freedom, as of mountain winds and mountain streams' (i, 136); in her more tender moments she reminds Robert of March flowers break-ing through the Westmorland soil (i, 132); and when Robert compares her to the 'mountains, to the exquisite river, to that great purple peak', even the unsentimental Rose acknowl-edges the justice of the analogy with her cynical response that 'she is not unlike that high cold peak!' (i, 168-9).

If Mrs Gaskell had not already appropriated the title, Mrs Ward might well have called her novel *North and South*, for the important conflicts of the story all hinge—as they often do also in Scott's fiction that she read so assiduously in child-hood—upon psychological and social contrasts resulting from geography. The North is the past, a pre-industrial world char-acterized by unspoilt natural beauty and simple faith. The

South is the present, the familiar Victorian world of modern knowledge and doubt. When Robert finds himself a guest at the vicarage of Long Whindale, he realizes with delight that he has moved backward in time to a less complicated era. Though his decision to marry Catherine, whom he meets in this tranquil valley, suggests Robert's desire to wed himself to the moral simplicities of her world, ultimately he is an intruder in Long Whindale, a citizen of the intellectually sophisticated South, who cannot live comfortably with Catherine's naive religion. He belongs to the present, and she belongs to the past. This, rather than any specific theological differences that develop between them, is the source of trouble in their marriage.

The movement of the characters about the valley and its environs is keyed to the same geographical symbolism. Significantly, Long Whindale, which lies on a north-west–south-east axis, is tame and featureless throughout its lower half but is bordered by steep, rugged crags at the northern head of the valley. Shanmoor (the real name of which is Kentmere), the neighbouring valley to the south-west, is more heavily populated and 'civilized'; it is while on a picnic there that Catherine's resistance to Robert's charms begins to weaken. But Marrisdale (i.e., Bannisdale), the valley to the north-east, is completely uninhabited; and it is there that Catherine goes alone to wrestle with her desires and temporarily persuade herself that she cannot marry Robert. In order to stiffen her will, she instinctively turns to the north.

Long Whindale itself is a series of time-layers, as if it were an archaeologist's *tell* in which the deepest strata are uncovered as one moves north. The earliest form of human civilization is represented at the craggy northern end by High Ghyll (which recalls Wuthering Heights), the farmhouse of the Backhouses, with its atmosphere of superstition, brutality, and ignorance. At approximately the centre of the valley are the church, the vicarage, and Burwood Farm. At the southern tip of Long Whindale is the road that leads to the nearest city, Whinborough (Kendal). The church, in other words, occupies an intermediate position between primitive superstition and modern civilization. 'There are no fairies and no ghosts . . . any more', wrote Froude in *The Nemesis of Faith*; 'only the church bells and the church music have anything of the old tones, and they are silent, too, except at rare, mournful, gusty intervals' (p. 28). Robert, in his pursuit of Catherine, penetrates ever deeper into this mysterious past, even beyond the Long Whindale church, until he proposes to her at last on a ghostly path above High Ghyll at midnight on Midsummer's Eve.

The frequent allusions to Wordsworth in Book One (Catherine, for example, is compared with his 'Louisa' [i, 174], and Richard Leyburn's portrait resembles that of the poet [i, 16]) function in the same way as do the Wordsworthian references in Matthew Arnold's poetry—that is to say, they evoke memories of an earlier age of innocence and simple religious trust. The Wordsworthian 'forest-glade'[17] and Christianity alike belong to the uncomplicated past, which can be viewed only from a distance with longing and nostalgia by modern personalities like Elsmere.

Mrs Ward's Westmorland valley, like Hardy's Wessex or Emily Brontë's Yorkshire moors, is a powerful spiritual force which shapes the lives of its inhabitants. In an unpublished lecture (1909) on Hardy,[18] Mrs Ward argued that the greatest literary figures, such as Shakespeare and Goethe, transcend any tie with a local scene; but she admired and emulated nevertheless 'that Antaean band of writers'—most notably Hardy and Emily Brontë—'which draws its life from a particular soil, and must constantly renew it there'. Mrs Ward's roots were in Westmorland, and she was always at her best when writing about it. For her the Cumbrian fells were richly alive, speaking to harried nineteenth-century men and women of the serene (but, alas, discredited) faith of their ancestors.

Catherine, far from being a 'repellent, evangelical monster' (as one critic has described her),[19] is the *genius loci* of this pastoral setting, a beautiful spirit who hovers over the valley's poor peasants like 'Sister Dora', Mark Pattison's sister, among the miners of Walsall (i, 63), and who, like George Eliot's Dorothea Brooke (in *Middlemarch*), is a saint that has had the misfortune of being born in the wrong century. Of course Catherine's religious ardour has its less attractive side, which is amply documented in the novel. Langham calls her 'the Thirty-nine Articles in the flesh' (i, 293), and Rose, when Agnes suggests that Catherine may marry, exclaims: 'Marry! ... You might as well talk of marrying Westminster Abbey' (i, 130). Mrs Ward makes no attempt to conceal the substratum of fanaticism in her heroine. In the *Elsmere* notebook and twice in the novel itself (ii, 137, 142) she is identified with Madame Guyon, the ascetic, self-tormenting mystic of the Quietist school. Mrs Ward also notes the resemblance between Catherine and her bigoted Methodist aunt (i, 155, 198) and sees her as secretly sympathizing with Newcome, another religious fanatic (i, 297). Mrs Ward obviously regards Catherine with strongly ambivalent feelings: she responds to her heroine's intense spiritual fervour yet insists that such a childish faith in the modern age is, intellectually speaking, an anachronism. When Catherine is swept unwillingly into the nineteenth century by her marriage to Robert, some kind of catastrophe is inevitable. 'Half the tragedy of our time', writes Mrs Ward, 'lies in this perpetual clashing of two estimates of life—the estimate which is the offspring of the scientific spirit, and which is for ever making the visible world fairer and more desirable in mortal eyes; and the estimate of Saint Augustine' (i, 235).

But in the Westmorland section of *Robert Elsmere* such portents are merely hinted at in muted tones. Book One is, as Mrs Ward said, 'very tame & domestic', possessing the flavour of a provincial comedy of manners done by Jane Austen. Mrs Thornburgh, bustling self-importantly about in her matchmaking efforts, is Mrs Bennett of *Pride and Prejudice* transplanted in Westmorland; Mr Thornburgh, the vicar of Long Whindale, who emerges from his study occasionally to offer ironic comments on his wife's activities, plays the part of Mr Bennett. 'One does not see these types, [Robert] said to himself, in the cultivated monotony of Oxford or London. [Mrs Thornburgh] was like a bit of a bygone world—Miss Austen's or Miss Ferrier's—unearthed for his amusement' (i, 41). 'How Miss Austenish it sounded' to Robert at Mrs Thornburgh's party: 'the managing rector's wife, her still more managing old maid of a sister, the neighbouring clergyman who played the flute, the local doctor, and a pretty daughter just out' (i, 42).

The 'Miss Austenish' tone is executed surprisingly well by Mrs Ward, particularly in a marvellously comic scene describing a musical duet by the vicar of Shanmoor and the inimitable Miss Barks (i, 69-71), but for Mrs Ward such drawing-room satire is not the essence of her novel, as it was for Jane Austen, but only a light-spirited prelude to the ensuing crisis in the history of Robert's mind.

III

Though much of the second volume of *Robert Elsmere* is ostensibly devoted to a description of the hero as a happily married and energetic young country parson in Surrey, fishing and preaching with equal enthusiasm, Mrs Ward had little first-hand knowledge of rural life. She was, as she said, 'a townswoman, living in Oxford or London',[20] and the photographic realism of the passages about Murewell Rectory (which was in reality Peperharrow Vicarage, where the Wards had lived in the summer of 1882) cannot conceal her apparent ignorance of the lives led by Robert's parishioners. Robert, we are told, had known the people of Murewell since early childhood, yet despite this assertion, none of them really emerges as a distinct individual in these chapters. What really matters in the Surrey section of the novel is the clash of ideas that takes place within Robert's mind. If Catherine, the spokesman of orthodoxy (as Mrs Ward understands orthodoxy), is the dominant figure of the first volume, then here the strongest personality is the local squire, an embodiment of atheistic rationalism; and, caught between these two powerful forces, Robert is nearly crushed.

Roger Wendover (whose name, ironically, is that of a medieval chronicler of ecclesiastical miracles) is in both physical appearance and cast of mind, though not in the external circumstances of his life, a fictionalized version of Mark Pattison.[21] Pattison and Wendover both devote their lives to a literary *magnum opus* which is never completed; each has an insane father; each has associated with Newman but later turns to scepticism; each exalts the life of the mind above a life of action; each dies a bitter, frustrated, painful death. In the manuscript drafts of the novel the resemblance between the two men is even more pronounced. A cancelled passage in Chapter 18 portrays a long-standing quarrel between Wendover and the Provost of St Anselm's (i.e., Jowett) over the true nature of a university. Pattison, as Rector of Lincoln, attempted to foster research and scholarship in the German fashion, whereas Jowett, as Master of Balliol, subscribed to the rival theory that his college should offer a liberal education to prepare young men for public service. Wendover—in almost the exact language which Pattison had used in *Suggestions on Academical Organisation* (1868) to denounce Jowett's ideals—complains that the Provost has 'ruined a University' by turning it into a 'boarding-house university'.

In the *Robert Elsmere* manuscripts there are several cancelled references to an unhappy love-affair of Wendover's which immediately calls to mind Pattison's marital difficulties. Wendover proposes clumsily to the beautiful young daughter of Lord Windermere, who accepts him but then throws him over at the last moment for a cousin her own age. This episode (as in Pattison's case) deepens the Squire's melancholia and compels him to find solace in study and travel.

Why, then, did Mrs Ward claim (in 1888) that 'the Squire is in no sense a portrait of Pattison', and (in 1909) that ' "the Rector" suggested the Squire only so far as outward aspect, a few personal traits, and the two main facts of great learning and a general impatience of fools are concerned'?[22] The answer, of course, is that the picture of Wendover, a spiritually sick man, is hardly flattering, and there can be no doubt that

Mrs Ward genuinely loved Pattison. Yet, as she wrote in *A Writer's Recollections*, 'When his "Memoirs" appeared [in February 1885, just as she was proposing *Robert Elsmere* to Macmillan], after his death, a book of which Mr. Gladstone once said to me that he reckoned it as among the most tragic and the most memorable books of the nineteenth century, I understood him more clearly, and more tenderly, than I could have done as a girl' (p. 106). Squire Wendover was Mrs Ward's affectionate tribute to Pattison's role in shaping her own mind, tempered by an awareness that his complete rationalism had led in the end to a cul-de-sac of despair.

Mrs Ward did not accept the view that 'unbelief' was an expression of secret 'sin' (at one point in the novel [ii, 472] she directly quotes John Wordsworth's lecture in order to refute it), but she was convinced that an exclusively intellectual life could damage a man's moral instincts. To dwell continually in the realm of thought was to behold Medusa directly and thus take the chance of being turned into stone. On the mantelpiece of the Squire's library Robert observes

a head of Medusa, and the frightful stony calm of it struck on Elsmere's ruffled nerves with extraordinary force. It flashed across him that here was an apt symbol of that absorbing and overgrown life of the intellect which blights the heart and chills the senses. And to that spiritual Medusa, the man before him was not the first victim he had known. (i, 465)

Wendover—like Pattison and those furtive inhabitants of the Bodleian that Mrs Ward had watched years before, and like Edith Lansdale of 'Lansdale Manor'—has incurred a 'fearful risk' by his pathological craving for knowledge. In his 'Godlike isolation' from the poor at his gates, he plays out the part of the soul in 'The Palace of Art' and Wendover Hall, 'as beautiful as a dream' (i, 289), becomes inevitably a nightmare filled with Tennysonian 'white-eyed phantasms' which haunt him as death nears.

In depicting the moral catastrophe which overtakes the Squire, Mrs Ward may also have had in mind Matthew Arnold's Empedocles, who tells himself, as he toils up the 'charred, blacked, melancholy waste' of Etna, that 'some-thing has impaired thy spirit's strength, / And dried its self-sufficing fount of joy'. Now a slave to thought and 'dead to every natural joy', Empedocles looks back upon the serene spiritual harmony of the past (both his own past and that of the human race) as an illusion whose unreality must be af-firmed by every enlightened thinker. Wendover is attracted to Robert for the same reason that Empedocles listens with gratitude (but also sorrow) to the simple nature-myths sung by his companion, Callicles: the youth poignantly reminds the older man of what he himself once was. However, Wen-dover's attempt to make a disciple and surrogate son of Rob-ert has sinister implications, for he is feeding parasitically upon the emotional vitality of another to compensate for his own state of dessication. 'Nothing but a devouring flame of thought— / But a naked, eternally restless mind!' (as Empe-docles says of himself), Squire Wendover is for Mrs Ward an object lesson in the terrors of modern rational thought divorced from ethical considerations.

Mrs Ward offers us a lengthy analysis of the contents of the Squire's library not only because she is fond of describing books (similar passages appear in several of her novels) but also because she is providing what amounts to an annotated bibliography of nineteenth-century intellectual history. As Langham detects the gradual shifts in the Squire's interests as reflected in his library—'from the Fathers to the Philoso-phers, from Hooker to Hume'—he comments, 'How history repeats itself in the individual!' (i, 352). In the manuscript of *Robert Elsmere* (Chapter 20) Mrs Ward emphasizes that Rob-ert's intellectual transformation is also a paradigm of 'that tumult and agony of the modern mind, which spreads itself year by year in ever wider circles of disturbance, troubling profundities of feeling & breaking up calm surfaces of life':

What was taking place in Robert during this period of his young intel-lectual development was the reproduction in miniature of what takes place on a large scale in any of the critical moments of human history. *It was the slow & gradual substitution of one set of preconceptions for*

another; the steady imperceptible advance from the presuppositions of
English orthodoxy, involving a double order of things, spiritual & material, continually interrupting & intersecting each other, to the presuppositions of science, in which the mind assumes the "rationality of the
world" & the unity of all experience. Just as the world moves from the
generalisation of St. Thomas Aquinas to that of Bacon & Locke, from
the generalisation of Hegel to that of Comte, or from that of Rousseau
to that of the modern student of anthropology and primitive culture,
and for the common understanding of man the great kaleidescope of
experience changes, & passes into ever fresh combinations & leading
patterns, with every alteration of the point of view; so, in the history of
the individual the same moments of crisis occur, preceded by the same
periods of half-conscious preparation. All that vast confusion of circumstance which had been to a greater or less degree enslaved and brought
to order by one master set of conceptions resumes as it were its inher-
ent right of sway, and dictates another system of the mind, as a nation
changes the form of its government. . . .
    And with this fundamental change everything changes. Opinion in all
directions throws itself into fresh lines; and action seeks for itself new
outlets.

Mrs Ward saw the nineteenth century as one of these epochs
of far-reaching intellectual change, and she regarded her own
hours of quiet struggle in the Bodleian (which she attributed
to Robert in the Squire's library) as a symbol of the contemporary upheaval in systems of ideas.
    Though the Squire and his library operate as a catalyst,
they are not the underlying cause of Robert's loss of faith. 'I
recognise that his influence immensely accelerated a process
already begun', explains Elsmere (ii, 105). Mrs Ward also
remarks that 'now at every step the ideas, impressions, arguments bred in him by his months of historical work and ordinary converse with the squire rushed in . . . to cripple resistance, to check an emerging answer, to justify Mr. Wendover'
(ii, 40). In a letter to Meredith Townsend written in 1888,
Mrs Ward argued this thesis even more vigorously: 'The
Squire's influence is described as only the match which ultimately lights the mine. I have tried to show that everything
really depended not on the Squire but on the nature of the
historical training which had gone before.'[23]

The *Elsmere* notebook indicates that Mrs Ward at first intended to describe the 'converging pressure of science & history', and Darwin's name is listed under 'Books wanted' in the notebook (a character in *The Testing of Diana Mallory* [1908] declares that 'Darwin has transformed the main conceptions of the human mind' [p. 366]); but, as Mrs Ward wrote in the subsequent Introduction to *Robert Elsmere*:

As far as my personal recollection goes, the men of science entered but little into the struggle of ideas that was going on [in the 1870s]. The main Darwinian battle had been won long before 1870; science was quietly verifying and exploring along the new lines; it was in literature, history, and theology that evolutionary conceptions were most visibly and dramatically at work. (I, xxii)

What shakes Robert's belief in Christianity is neither the Squire nor Darwinism but his own patient study of the documents and records of the late Roman Empire. In a half-hearted effort to conceal the confessional element in the novel, Mrs Ward has her hero absorbed in French rather than Spanish history, but nevertheless his conclusion is identical to the position she had adopted after preparing the Spanish articles for the *Dictionary of Christian Biography*: that the 'kings, bishops, judges, poets, priests, men of letters' (i, 495) of the early Christian era lived in such an atmosphere of credulity and superstition that the entire historical basis of Christianity must be called into question.

The climactic moment arrives when Robert realizes (in the words of Matthew Arnold) that 'miracles do not happen' (ii, 84)—meaning particularly the miraculous resurrection of Jesus. Mrs Ward repeatedly asserted that this crucial statement was a result of inductive historical reasoning, yet she failed to acknowledge the obvious fact that a disbelief in miracles rests upon certain *a priori* assumptions about the operation of 'natural' laws. By embracing a dogmatic monism that was completely uncritical in its acceptance of 'reason', Elsmere, it might be argued, merely leaped from one system of authority to another. Instinctively a true believer, Mrs Ward was evidently incapable of genuine agnosticism; orthodox Christianity had to be discarded, but she (and Robert Elsmere) turned at once to constructing a new faith from the wreckage of the old. As Dr Arnold remarked in one of his sermons, 'For indeed to be for ever wavering in doubt is an extreme misery.'[24]

What is disappointing about the culmination of Robert's mental struggles is that his cry of agony, though intense and heart-felt, seems to be expressed in the most banal terms: 'O God! My wife—my work!' (ii, 86). To modern readers accustomed to acknowledging the redemptive value of total despair, this response may sound very tame, and we are not surprised to learn that 'at his worst there was never a moment when Elsmere felt himself *utterly* forsaken' (ii, 94). Yet if Elsmere's *angst* strikes us as almost cosily domestic, it should be said, in fairness to Mrs Ward, that she was not unaware of the potential depths of spiritual anguish. Robert weathers the storm with relative ease because he (like Mrs Ward) discovers almost instantly a middle ground between unreasonable orthodoxy and destructive rationalism. Laura Fountain in *Helbeck of Bannisdale*, who is unable to find such a convenient synthesis, commits suicide; Robert, however, is never really forced to peer into the abyss (though he is conscious at times that it is there beneath his feet), since Mrs Ward has already prepared an escape route for him.

Robert accordingly turns to a celebration of the human Christ and to a Theism which cannot be discredited by historical research. Mr Grey says to him:

Spiritually you have gone through the last wrench, I promise it you! You being what you are, nothing can cut this ground from under your feet. Whatever may have been the forms of belief, *faith*, the faith which saves, has always been rooted here! All things change,—creeds and philosophies and outward systems,—but God remains! (ii, 110)

But it is a faith based on intuition rather than historical evidence or revealed Scriptures. Robert argues that the chief distinction between Christianity and Theism is that the latter '*can never be disproved*', for 'at the worst it must always remain in the position of an alternative hypothesis' (ii, 203).

The dramatic interest of the novel turns primarily upon the struggle of will between Robert and Catherine after he has made his decision to leave the Church and his clerical vocation. The preservation of Catherine's love is supremely important to Robert, because it is for him the primary evidence of divine love and a reassuring link with the old faith. Robert, in fact, regards his wife as a symbol of the deep spirituality of Christianity: she has a 'Madonna-like face' (i, 22), and Robert addresses her as 'Madonna mine' (ii, 28). A cancelled passage in the *Elsmere* manuscript (Chapter 25) reveals even more explicitly the significance of Catherine in Robert's religious life:

A sort of allegory of himself ran vaguely through his mind. He felt as though he had been forcing his way for weeks through some dense & baffling forest, tangled by the creeper[s], bewildered by the closeness of the trees, stifled for lack of air, crushed by the sense of the impenetratable [*sic*] distance & discoverable issues. And suddenly the trees thin around him, the air grows lighter, the wood falls back, and under the blessed sky & wind of an uncovered heaven, there rises in a clearing made by pious hands a white & tender image,—a vision of the Mother & Child. And forgetting all the passion & the desperation of that long struggle through the blinding hindering branches, he falls on his knees, the heart crying out with joy, the black oppression lifted.

This dream-fantasy, filled with phrases from the opening canto of the *Divine Comedy*, discloses the symbolic weight of the recurrent scenes in which Robert stumbles through the dark Surrey woods. On the very night that he renounces Christianity, he moves mechanically along a darkened lane until 'the trees before him thinned' and he hears the voice of Catherine calling for him (ii, 85-6). After returning from Oxford, he must pass through a 'frowning mass of wood' before he can dimly see Catherine's figure behind the muslin curtains of the rectory window (ii, 113-6). When his wife temporarily flees the rectory, he searches for her among 'a thick interwoven mass of young trees' until he at last finds her in a clearing (ii, 138). Much later, in a delirium produced by fatigue and illness, Robert again catches a glimpse of his Madonna, whose faith he has formally rejected but whose

spiritual beauty is nevertheless a solace to his troubled soul:
'The strangest whirlwind of thoughts fled through him in the
darkness, suggested very often by the figures on the seven-
teenth-century tapestry which lined the walls. Were those the
trees in the wood-path? Surely that was Catherine's figure
... ?' (ii, 534-5).

The Surrey portion of *Robert Elsmere* is also richer in colourful incident and characterization than the foregoing analysis might suggest. The brooding figure of the Squire casts an
appalling shadow over the pastoral landscape. His sister, Mrs
Darcy (who, incidentally, is a portrait of the wife of E. H.
Craddock, Principal of Brasenose),[25] lends an appropriately
demented quality to the atmosphere of Wendover Hall. Newcome (whose name and mannerisms may have been suggested
by Newman), the High Church clergyman, is a grotesque figure out of a child's nightmare. Above all, there is the strange,
remote personality of Edward Langham, spiritual kin to the
Squire, in whom unbelief has produced the moral paralysis of
an Obermann or an Amiel. Mrs Ward claimed, in fact, that
Langham was modelled exclusively upon these two introspec-
tive personalities, but he is also reminiscent of both Pater and
Clough, particularly in his unsuccessful resolve to leave Oxford. His courtship of Rose—which is one the most fascinating episodes of the novel though admittedly too long for a
mere subplot—owes much to Clough's 'Amours de Voyage'
and Matthew Arnold's 'Marguerite' poems. Thematically the
courtship is related to the main story, for we are meant to see
that Langham's passivity, even when in love, contrasts unfa-
vourably with Robert's earlier vigour as a suitor.

Rose herself is a refreshing character in a novel peopled so
largely with intensely religious personalities. She is beautiful,
vivacious, 'aesthetic' (indeed, in many respects very much
like Emilia Pattison),[26] yet Mrs Ward must punish her at least
lightly because she is too self-assertive. As her juvenile tales
demonstrate, Mrs Ward was preoccupied with the idea that a
frivolous girl is morally strengthened only through an unhappy love affair. Hence we are informed that after Langham

breaks off their engagement, 'deep undeveloped forces of character [begin to] stir within her' (ii, 284). Henry James, however, recognized the real implications of Rose's eventual 'third volume-y' marriage to Flaxman, the wealthy, handsome, but very colourless aristocrat. James sensed that Mrs Ward had provided such a conventional husband for Rose precisely because (perhaps at a subconscious level) the author's Puritan instincts disapproved of Rose's artistic ambitions. 'I can't help wishing that you had made her serious, deeply so, in her own line, as Catherine, for instance, is serious in hers', James wrote.[27] But Mrs Ward, like Robert Elsmere, still worshipped the traditional religious and cultural values represented by the shrine in the forest clearing, and art and scholarship, though valuable in themselves, were lower in her scale of values than a strict standard of morality.

IV

Mrs Ward believed that the final third of *Robert Elsmere*, which is set largely in the East End of London, was the finest part of her novel, but most readers would probably be inclined to apply to it T. S. Eliot's famous observation on Tennyson's *In Memoriam* that the author's doubt is a more intense and vivid reality than his faith. Elsmere, never a strong personality, is flattened into an instrument of propaganda once he is no longer afflicted by scepticism. 'One fears a little sometimes', James remarked wryly to Mrs Ward, 'that he may suffer a sunstroke, damaging if not fatal, from the high, oblique light of your admiration for him.'[28] Elsmere's sufferings in Surrey compel our sympathy; his apotheosis in London as the saint of a new cult becomes a dull spectacle.

Mrs Ward also again laboured under the handicap of placing her hero in a milieu about which she knew little. When Robert is writing articles in his house in Bedford Square (which corresponds to descriptions of the Wards' house in Russell Square) or moves in the glittering social world of Madame de Netteville, Mrs Ward is obviously on familiar ground, but her descriptions of slum life are based on only a few visits to the East End in the company of her sister-in-law, who was a nurse, and conscientious research in printed sources. Though Mrs Ward was of course a perceptive observer, such a superficial acquaintance with working-class existence was hardly sufficient for one who professed to offer a new religion to the poor. When she made similar brief ventures into the world of the lower classes while writing *David Grieve*, Alice Green (the widow of J. R. Green) remarked sarcastically that Mrs Ward was going to Manchester 'for a three day study of the working class'.[29]

From the *Elsmere* notebook and her letters written between 1885 and 1887, we know some of the books which Mrs Ward read to inform herself about the alien world of the East End. In the notebook one of the titles listed is Gissing's *Demos: A Story of English Socialism* (1886). She also studied the published letters of Edward Denison (1872), who spent much time among the London poor trying to teach them the elements of Christianity.[30] James Knowles thought that Walter Besant's novel *All Sorts and Conditions of Men* (1884) had influenced Mrs Ward's treatment of 'Elgood Street', but there is no solid evidence to support this view.[31] She was, however, intrigued by the problems of instructing the poor, and she turned to the lectures of Joseph Payne and Huxley's *Lay Sermons* (1870) for suggestions as to how scientific concepts could be communicated in simple fashion. She read widely in the autobiographies and memoirs of working men such as William Lovett and Thomas Cooper.

Having abandoned the Church and living now in the shadow of the British Museum, Elsmere would seem to be destined for a scholarly career, but his eyes turn quickly to the brutalized masses, devoid of any religious sentiments, that crowd the eastern and southern edges of London. Though he briefly engages in charitable work under the direction of a Broad Church vicar, Robert concludes that the Revd Mr Vernon is involved 'in endless contradictions and practical falsities of speech and action' because the essence of the Broad Church strategy is the concealment of one's opinions (ii,

213-4). The vein of Pattisonian radicalism in Mrs Ward's thinking made her impatient with such apparent duplicity, just as she had strongly disapproved of Jowett's willingness to subscribe to the Thirty-nine Articles. In a letter written in 1895, Mrs Ward remarked, 'I deeply regret—& wrote *Robert Elsmere* to shew it—the whole action and attitude of the Broad churchmen of those days.'[32] Elsmere declares (in language reminiscent of John Morley's) that there is no room for compromise:

Miracle is to our time what the law was to the early Christians. We *must* make up our minds about it one way or the other. And if we decide to throw it over as Paul threw over the law, then we must *fight* as he did. There is no help in subterfuge, no help in anything but a perfect sincerity. . . . The ground must be cleared; then may come the rebuilding. (ii, 555)

Robert also has encounters with High Churchmen, Comtists (whose 'potent spirit of social help' he admires [ii, 311]), Unitarians (with whom he identifies intellectually but not emotionally), and every variety of Secularist and Socialist, all of them moving helplessly about under the cloud of spiritual darkness that covers the East End. Eventually he decides that he must establish his own centre of activities, free of all sectarian ties, in an empty warehouse on Elgood Street. Undoubtedly with the example of Toynbee Hall in mind, Robert creates the New Brotherhood of Christ, described by one sceptical witness as 'a new church' (ii, 463), which offers a multitude of social, educational, and religious activities for the working people of the neighbourhood.

Superficially, the New Brotherhood appears to be a 'purified' or attenuated version of Christianity. The faith has only two articles ('In Thee, O Eternal, have I put my trust' and 'This do in remembrance of me' [ii, 509]), and its simple liturgy recalls that of James Martineau's Unitarian prayer book, which first appeared in 1862. The walls of the Elgood Street hall are lined with recesses which will hold the names of present and deceased members of the New Brotherhood, reminding us that Mrs Ward had once thus envisioned the cathedral of the new faith. In short, the New Brotherhood gives the impression of offering a modest, unpolemical alternative to orthodox Christianity that is nonetheless deeply Christian in spirit and ethics. That is evidently how Mrs Ward wished the third volume of her novel to be read. However, the Arnoldian theme of reconciliation and the Pattisonian theme of intransigence are always straining against each other in Mrs Ward's religious fiction, and there are frequent indications that the ultimate goal of the New Brotherhood is not to modify but to supplant traditional Christianity. The one sermon we hear Robert preach at Murewell is on the Messianic text 'This day is the scripture fulfilled in your ears!', for he is destined to become the Christ of Mrs Ward's neo-Christianity. As he declares in a lecture to a crowd of working men on Easter Eve:

No—an idea cannot be killed from without—it can only be supplanted, transformed, by another idea, and that one of equal virtue and magic. Strange paradox! In the moral world you cannot pull down except by gentleness—you cannot revolutionise except by sympathy. Jesus only superseded Judaism by absorbing and recreating all that was best in it. (ii, 357)

Clearly the implication is that the New Brotherhood today stands in the same relationship to Christianity as Christianity did in the first century to Judaism. Like Jesus, Robert gathers round himself a small circle of disciples who will carry on the work of Elgood Street after his martyrdom; but even before his death, pious legends and myths are beginning to be associated with Robert's name, thus suggesting how the earliest oral accounts of Jesus' ministry eventually developed into the versions found in the Synoptic Gospels.

Some readers and reviewers of *Robert Elsmere*, recognizing its revolutionary implications, have wondered why Mrs Ward chose to disguise this fundamentally new religion as a reformed Christianity. Was it merely timidity on her part? In *The Future of University Hall*, a lecture delivered and published in 1892, she explained that Christianity had so interwoven itself with European history and culture that the modern Englishman cannot escape it 'without wasteful and paralysing revolt' (p. 24). Theoretically Buddhist mysticism might be of equal spiritual value to Christian mysticism, but in fact —as she told Felicia Skene in 1889—Christianity was superior to other religions because it had been associated with the greatest of all human cultures.[33] The Christian colouration of the New Brotherhood, then, is a result of convenience and historical accident rather than of any intrinsic merit which the faith of Jesus might possess that would distinguish it from other religions.

One of the temptations in the urban wilderness which Robert as the new Christ must face and overcome is the siren call of an alluring Frenchwoman, Madame de Netteville. In several of her novels Mrs Ward created a similar feminine type, intellectually gifted but morally depraved (and nearly always of French birth or descent), who presides over a brilliant salon. Madame de Netteville's attempted seduction of Robert has class as well as sexual overtones. Her drawing room represents the most beautifully decorated room in the Palace of Art, and she wishes to lure Robert into it so that he will stop his ears to the cries of the poor without. But Robert, his mind filled with painful images of the suffering he has witnessed in Elgood Street, declines to separate himself from the moral realities of that world beyond the gates of the Palace of Art:

When, every now and then, in the pauses of their own conversation, Elsmere caught something of the chatter going on at the other end of the table, or when the party became fused into one for a while under the genial influence of a good story or the exhilaration of a personal skirmish, the whole scene—the dainty oval room, the lights, the servants, the exquisite fruit and flowers, the gleaming silver, the tapestried walls —would seem to him for an instant like a mirage, a dream, yet with something glittering and arid about it which a dream never has. (ii, 406-7)

The grim paradox—which Mrs Ward was to explore often in her later novels—was that this drawing room, both in its furnishings and guests, symbolized the finest aspects of modern civilization, yet it was threatened with extinction by the moral indifference of those who frequented Madame de Netteville's salon. Like Squire Wendover's library, the fashionable drawing room, admirable in many ways, becomes crowded with daemonic shapes when it attempts to ignore its obligations to the peasants in the valley below.

On the same night that Robert spurns the advances of Madame de Netteville, Catherine for the first time learns from Hugh Flaxman the full story of her husband's self-sacrificial labours among the London poor. Having experienced these simultaneous moral crises, 'Elsmere and his wife', we are told, 'were lovers as of old' (ii, 424). The reconciliation which John Morley had predicted was finally achieved. The last chapter begins: 'There is little more to tell. The man who lived so fast was no long time dying' (ii, 537). Fatally ill with throat cancer in Algiers (where the Wards had visited in 1881), Robert remains faithful to the new creed until the end, never wavering in his trust of God, though he professes ignorance of what form of existence may await him in the afterlife.

The gospel according to Robert Elsmere may seem in some respects a hasty and premature theological synthesis, but it is impossible not to admire the eloquence and fervour with which Mrs Ward proclaimed it both in this novel and throughout the rest of her life. Though her religious ideas were tainted by the facile optimism of her century, she never lost touch— despite, as it were, her official ideology—with the tragic element of life which she had learned from orthodox Christianity. It is not enough to say that Robert Elsmere dies because Mrs Ward has the usual Victorian weakness for sentimental death-bed scenes. He dies because (in words that echo the closing paragraph of *Middlemarch*) 'his effort was but a fraction of the effort of the race' (ii, 599), and only through the martyrdom of humanity's most precious spirits can the rest of us climb upward on the shadowy ladder of faith that leads to God.

On the last page of *Robert Elsmere* Mrs Ward quotes (or rather slightly misquotes) these lines from Clough's 'Come, Poet, Come':

> *Others, I doubt not, if not we,*
> *The issue of our toils shall see;*
> *And (they forgotten and unknown)*
> *Young children gather as their own*
> *The harvest that the dead have sown.*

The lines had earlier appeared as an epigraph at the beginning of *Unbelief and Sin*; in 1920 they were inscribed by Mrs Ward's family on her tombstone in Aldbury churchyard.

Chapter 8

ROBERT ELSMERE AND ITS READERS

No agitation, on the platform or in the newspaper, no demand for a political revolution, ever achieved anything like the publicity or roused anything like the emotion of the earnest attempt of this quiet English lady to tell an interesting story, to present an imaginary case. "Robert Elsmere," in the course of a few weeks, put her name in the mouths of the immeasurable English-reading multitude. The book was not merely an extraordinarily successful novel; it was, as reflected in contemporary conversation, a momentous public event.

—Henry James[1]

I

Like Byron, Mrs Ward in the spring of 1888 awoke to find herself famous. Widely reviewed and the subject of endless literary small-talk, *Robert Elsmere* was already in a fourth edition before Gladstone's article in the May number of the *Nineteenth Century* pushed sales even higher. By March 1889 it was said that between 30,000 and 40,000 copies had been sold in England and 200,000 copies in the United States. In 1909, writing in the Introduction to the Westmoreland Edition of *Robert Elsmere*, Mrs Ward estimated that 'something, probably, not very far short of a million copies of the work have been distributed in the English-speaking countries, and translations of it have appeared in most foreign languages' (I, xiii).[2]

There is no indication that either Mrs Ward or George Smith had anticipated such an unusual reception for the novel. Even in her most optimistic moments, Mrs Ward seems

159

to have envisioned at best a *succès d'estime* that would appeal to a relatively small group of intellectuals who, likế herself, were troubled by the impotence of traditional Christianity in the modern world. Instead she discovered that she had written the best-seller of the decade, a novel that was parodied and imitated on both sides of the Atlantic, abused from countless pulpits, reviewed by a former Prime Minister and a future Archbishop of Canterbury, and dramatized on the New York stage. Clearly *Robert Elsmere* was a 'symptom', as everyone said, but exactly what this remarkable public response signified was less obvious. While High Churchmen and conservative Evangelicals fulminated against Elsmere's heresies, agnostics complained that—as one American wrote—'it will revive interest in theology and retard the progress of rationalism'.[3] But however it was interpreted, *Robert Elsmere* was universally regarded as a Sign of the Times which would supply the careful reader with a clue to the present theological and intellectual state of England.

Some liberals claimed that *Robert Elsmere* merely recited the critical commonplaces of an earlier generation. Moncure Conway, the American Unitarian clergyman, called it 'a cockcrow over yesterday's sunrise'. Jowett observed that 'its success is really due to its saying what everybody is thinking' but added that he was astonished by Mrs Ward's 'knowing so much about German theology'. James Martineau, though he thought her 'a genuine and thorough student of the origins of Christianity', was unimpressed by *Robert Elsmere*. On the other hand, E. S. Talbot, a liberal Anglo-Catholic who later contributed to *Lux Mundi*, found *Robert Elsmere* so unsettling that reading it was 'rather a cloud upon the holiday'. Randall Davidson, then Dean of Windsor, described it as a 'strangely harmful book'. J. H. Shorthouse, the Quaker novelist, declined even to read it, as he had 'no sympathy with what I understand to be its tendency'. The novel made such a deep impression on young Julian Huxley, who was Mrs Ward's nephew, that it helped to convert him to religious humanism 'but without belief in a personal God'.[4]

Amid the theological furore evoked by *Robert Elsmere*, only a few readers paid attention to its literary qualities. Mark Twain said its effect on him

was exactly as though a singer of street ballads were to hear excellent music from a church organ. I didn't stop to ask whether the music was legitimate or necessary. I listened, and I liked what I heard. I am speaking of the grace and beauty of the style.[5]

Pater (in a review in the *Guardian* of 28 March 1888) also praised *Robert Elsmere* as 'a *chef d'oeuvre* of that kind of quiet evolution of character through circumstance, introduced into English literature by Miss Austen, and carried to perfection in France by George Sand'. Mrs Ward, said Pater, 'might well have written a novel which should have been all shrewd impressions of society, or all humourous impressions of country life, or all quiet fun and genial caricature. Actually she has chosen to combine something of each of these with a sincerely felt religious interest.' Unlike other reviewers, Pater denied that religion was an inappropriate subject for the modern novel, and he admired the subtlety and skill with which Mrs Ward had introduced it into the 'many varieties of average mundane life' described in the book.

Not surprisingly, the only other critic to discuss *Robert Elsmere* from a strictly literary point of view was Henry James, who first expressed his opinion of the novel in two letters to Mrs Ward[6] and later in a review published in the *English Illustrated Magazine* (1892). Writing privately to the author, James was of course entirely complimentary (except for his reservations about Rose's fate and the idealization of Robert), but the review, though also apparently enthusiastic about the book's merits, was phrased with studied ambiguity:

The whole complicated picture is of a slow, expansive evocation, bathed in an air of reflection, infinitely thought out and constructed. It suggests the image of a large, slow-moving, slightly oid-fashioned ship, buoyant enough and well out of water, but with a close-packed cargo in every inch of stowage-room. One feels that the author has set afloat in it a complete treasure of intellectual and moral experience, the memory of all her contacts and phases, all her speculations and studies.

The operative word in this passage is probably 'old-fashioned', for James admitted to a friend that he had written 'only a civil perfunctory payé (with words between the lines)',[7] and his later correspondence with Mrs Ward reveals most plainly their fundamental disagreement about the craft of novel-writing.

However, many of Mrs Ward's readers on the Continent reacted favourably to *Robert Elsmere*. Taine, who found in it a 'new vein of psychology' and the best English novel since George Eliot's death, was pleased that Mrs Ward had treated directly 'one of the two pressing problems of the age,—the gradual transformation of Christianity'. Many years later Mrs Ward was told of a letter written by Taine to his daughter in 1888 in which he declared, 'I have been sitting up three nights over *Robert Elsmere*. C'est le plus beau livre du siècle!'[8] Renan believed himself to be 'partly the original of Robert', and Mrs Ward learned that when Mommsen 'thinks of charm he thinks of Rose'.[9] But Edmond Scherer warned her that *Robert Elsmere* was 'foreign to the French public', for French Catholicism was as yet untouched by the ideas of higher criticism; 15 years afterwards, M. Brunetière, the editor of the *Revue des Deux Mondes*, told Mrs Ward that her novel had at last become relevant to the French religious situation, because of the debates occasioned by the growth of Modernism in the Roman Catholic Church.[10]

In England and America also, various eminent figures of the age had their say about *Robert Elsmere*. Andrew Lang whimsically observed that Elsmere 'is not *my* sort (at least unless you have a ghost, a murder, a duel and some savages)'. Edward Burne-Jones confessed, 'I never thought I should devour a book about parsons'. T. H. Huxley admitted to 'a great deal of sympathy' with Squire Wendover and praised Catherine as 'the gem of the book'. Oliver Wendell Holmes wrote to Mrs Ward that *Elsmere*, though 'medicated', was 'the most effective and popular novel we have had since "Uncle Tom's Cabin" '. In an interview printed in an American newspaper, Robert G. Ingersoll lamented that Mrs Ward's

hero was too conservative in his desire to retain all of Christianity except the miraculous. 'It is an effort', he said, 'to save
and repair the dungeons of the Inquisition for the sake of the
beauty of the vines that have overrun them'.[11]

The most celebrated reaction to *Robert Elsmere*, however,
came from an ex-Prime Minister who unexpectedly turned his
great rhetorical guns upon the book.

II

'Mrs. Humphry Ward deserves the hearty congratulations
of the whole Liberal party', began a leader in the *Pall Mall
Gazette* on 7 April 1888. 'For her new novel has done that
which all other books and all other events have failed to
effect. From December, 1885, to March, 1888, Mr. Gladstone has been able to think of nothing but Ireland and
Home Rule. But Mrs. Ward has changed all that.'[12] What
finally distracted Gladstone's attention from the Irish question (which had led to the downfall of his government in
1886) was the publication of *Robert Elsmere*, the heterodox
tendencies of which he viewed with considerable alarm. Gladstone's review in the *Nineteenth Century* caused nearly as
great a sensation as the novel itself, particularly in America
where it was widely reprinted in pamphlet form, and thereafter other reviewers were afforded the unusual pleasure of
treating both Gladstone and Elsmere (or 'Weg on Bobbie', as
one woman said) together.

Mrs Ward and Gladstone had not met before 1888, though
she had caught an occasional distant glimpse of him in London society, and they had both had a share in promoting
Shorthouse's novel *John Inglesant* (1881). When *Amiel's
Journal* was published in 1885, she hoped that it would
appeal to the same audience as Shorthouse's book and that
possibly Gladstone might 'befriend it as he did John Inglesant'.[13] To make that possible, she sent him a copy through
E. S. Talbot, who was married to Gladstone's niece. Lord
Arthur Russell later reported to Mrs Ward that the Prime
Minister 'spoke with great interest of Amiel',[14] but no review

or breakfast invitation was forthcoming as in Shorthouse's case.

'Would you feel inclined to send a copy of *Robert Elsmere* to Mr. [James] Knowles of the *Nineteenth Century?*' Mrs Ward asked George Smith on 6 March 1888. 'He says that he wants very much to see the book, that he admired *Miss Bretherton* &c &c! Perhaps it might be worth our while!' On 14 March she sent Smith this further report: 'Mr. Knowles seems to be enthusiastic, & is handing on his copy to Mr. Gladstone. But I am afraid Robert Elsmere's opinions will be hardly as congenial to the G.O.M. as John Inglesant's were!' Knowles, writing to Gladstone two days later, apologized for the 'exorbitant & egregious length' of *Robert Elsmere* but hoped that 'for the sake of its great subject & the very considerable ability of its appreciation of the currents of our time, . . . you may think it worth a notice in my review— (which would "make" the author)'.[15]

Gladstone did plunge into the book and soon wrote to his daughter that 'Mamma and I are each of us still separately engaged in a death-grapple with *Robert Elsmere*'. It was, he decided, 'wholly out of the common order' and 'a tremendous book', but he regarded 'with doubt and dread the idea of doing anything on it'.[16] Another correspondent to whom Gladstone described the novel was Lord Acton, who was then in Cannes. 'You perhaps have not heard of "Robert Elsmere" ', Gladstone wrote him on 1 April: 'for I find, without surprise that it makes its way slowly into public notice. It is not far from twice the length of an ordinary novel and the labour & effort of reading it all, I should say, six fold while one could no more stop in it than in reading Thucydides.' But the Theism espoused by Mrs Ward was an inadequate substitute for Christianity, and therein lay Gladstone's concern: 'I am tossed about with doubt', he concluded, 'as to writing on it.'[17] Acton, in a reply on 11 April, agreed that Mrs Ward's explanation of the origin of Christian supernaturalism—that it grew up in an age predisposed to believe in miracles—was absurd. 'I wonder', he wrote, 'that her father, an instructed man, if not her husband, whose information is modern and rather Philistine, let her say such a thing.' Nevertheless Acton cautioned Gladstone against a rash defence of Christianity that was not based on historical facts, and a correspondence between the two men ensued on *Robert Elsmere* for several months.[18]

Knowles, in the meantime, told Gladstone on 2 April what little he knew personally about Mrs Ward. 'She strikes me as very *prim* & rather like a married old-maid in some ways', but he also acknowledged her talent. 'As to "her standing"—that I really & honestly think at the present moment largely rests with yourself. If you can & will expand what you sketch in outline about her & the book in your letter—I believe it will confirm her in a position—towards which she is tending—in literature—of considerable eminence—if not something even more than that.'[19]

Rumours of Gladstone's intentions began to reach Mrs Ward's relatives and the press. On 10 April Matthew Arnold wrote to his sister Frances: 'George Russell was here a day or two ago; he was staying at Aston Clinton with Gladstone, and says it is all true about his interest in [*Elsmere*] : he talked of it incessantly and said he thought he should review it for Knowles.'[20] And on 6 April the following note had appeared in the *Pall Mall Gazette*: 'The London correspondent of the *Manchester Guardian* states that Mr. Gladstone has occupied his holiday in reading Mrs. Humphry Ward's new novel "Robert Elsmere". . . . The correspondent hears that Mr. Gladstone is greatly interested in the book, and will probably contribute a review of it to an early number of the *Nineteenth Century*.'[21] Knowles, who claimed to be innocent of this 'leak', complained to Gladstone on 9 April that 'it is a complete mystery to me where & how these wretched gossipmongers pick up their miserable crumbs!'[22]

At about this time Gladstone and Mrs Ward accidentally found themselves together in Oxford, where Julia Arnold was nearing death. On 5 April Mrs Talbot, whom Gladstone was visiting, walked down from Keble College and gave Mrs Ward an amusing and tantalizing account of her uncle's interest in *Robert Elsmere*:

She says Gladstone is reading R.E. with great intentness marking as he goes, & she comes after him in his marked copy. He is now near the end of the 2nd vol. When he doesn't like a sentiment or a statement he marks it with the Italian *ma!* in the margin[;] when he approves he puts arrows of mysterious meaning known only to himself. Mrs. Talbot says there is a general feeling that the book is going to be much read.[23]

The following day Mrs Talbot sent this note to Bradmore Road: 'Mr. Gladstone read your letter, & he says he would like to talk yr. book over with you, if you could some day make an opportunity of seeing him.'[24] Mrs Ward's mother died on 7 April; a day later, suffering from physical and emotional exhaustion, she wrote to her daughter Dorothy: 'It is announced in some of the papers that Mr. Gladstone is to write an article on *Robert Elsmere* for the *Nineteenth Century* but we do not know if it is true, & I feel as if just now I did not care.'

But, her death-watch over, Mrs Ward that very evening had a memorable encounter with Gladstone in the Talbots' drawing room.[25] For nearly an hour they sat alone together, Gladstone fidgeting on a 'small uncomfortable chair', and talked of Oxford, Newman, Pattison, T. H. Green, charity in London, and a host of other topics suggested by the novel. Gladstone protested that 'if you sweep away miracles you sweep away the Resurrection!' and was about to attack the central propositions of *Robert Elsmere*, when 'the supper bell rang & the clock struck eight'. They agreed to meet again the next morning. During the second conversation Gladstone 'got quite white sometimes & tremulous with interest & excitement' as they engaged in 'a battle royal over the book & Xtian evidence'. 'He was *very* charming personally', Mrs Ward told her husband, 'though at times he looked stern & angry & white to a degree, so that I wondered sometimes how I had the courage to go on—the drawn brows were so formidable.' When she suggested that an account of the Resurrection in the *Acts* was not historically reliable, 'he talked of "trumpery objections!" in his most House of Commons manner'.[26]

Following this interview both left Oxford, Gladstone returning to London and Mrs Ward travelling north to Fox How in order to bury her mother in the Ambleside churchyard. By mid-April he had finished and was correcting his review of *Elsmere*, which he found 'rather stiff work'.[27] Throughout the month he and Mrs Ward continued to exchange letters in which they argued at greath length whether Elsmere's religion was a viable alternative to Christianity. 'You have much courage', Gladstone wrote on 16 April; 'but I doubt whether even you are brave enough to think that, fourteen centuries after its foundation, Elgood Street could have written the Imitation of Christ.'[28]

When Gladstone's article (' "Robert Elsmere" and the Battle of Belief') appeared in the *Nineteenth Century* in May, it was scarcely a literary analysis of the novel, though he did discreetly complain that 'the great, nay, paramount function of character-drawing, the projection upon the canvas of human beings endowed with the true forces of nature and vitality, does not appear to be by any means the master-gift of the authoress'; and, anticipating James' metaphor, he described the plot as so overburdened with irrelevant characters and incidents that 'the cargo is too heavy for the vessel'. The real purpose of the article, however, was not an examination of *Robert Elsmere qua* novel. It was rather a vigorous refutation of the validity of Elsmere's (and Mrs Ward's) quasi-Christian Theism. The weakness of the book, asserted Gladstone, is that in it orthodoxy is defended only by emotion, whereas the attack upon traditional Christianity is supported by all the weapons of intellect: 'A great creed, with the testimony of eighteen centuries at its back, cannot find an articulate word to say in its defence.' The obvious inference, according to Gladstone, was that Mrs Ward had failed to acquaint herself with the vast literature of Christian apologetics. After a detailed treatment of the historical points raised by *Robert Elsmere*, he concluded by offering the penetrating observation that 'if the ancient and continuous creed of Christendom has slipped away from its place in Mrs Ward's brilliant and subtle understanding, it has nevertheless by no means lost a true, if unacknowledged, hold upon the inner sanctuary of her heart'.

George Smith had remarked that Gladstone's article would disappoint him very much 'if it does not give a great stimulus to the sales'.[29] It did have exactly that effect, and it also supplied subsequent reviewers with a stock of solid arguments to be used against the novel's thesis. To Mrs Ward, it seemed that such a lengthy and, on the whole, friendly critique demanded some kind of response, and her first impulse was to write an article immediately for the Nineteenth Century. 'If I do reply', she declared to her husband, 'I shall make it as substantive and constructive as possible. All the attacking, destructive part is so distasteful to me.'[30] But friends succeeded in dissuading her. 'It appears that Frederic Harrison advised her not to do it', Gladstone wrote to Acton on 13 May. 'But Knowles told me that he was labouring to bring her up to the scratch again. There, I said, you show the cloven foot: you want to keep the N.[ineteenth] C.[entury] pot boiling.'[31]

'I am glad you have not answered Gladstone', Stopford Brooke told her. 'If you answer him, if you get into analysis, etc., you will take all the beauty out of the continuance of your book.'[32] However, Mrs Ward did intend to write a reply, but she was determined that it would be dramatic rather than argumentative in style and would avoid a direct confrontation with Gladstone. Benjamin Jowett was nonetheless worried and wrote her on 16 November:

I am rather anxious about the step which you propose to take—of defending your cause in the 19th Century. . . .

1 It will be a great strain & excitement. 2 It takes you out of your natural position, that of an imaginative & dramatic writer into a theological & controversial one. 3 It commits you to what you have said in R.E. which may be a very good basis for a novel, but not really tenable or practicable. Altogether you will be in a false position, I think.[33]

Shortly thereafter Jowett made a special trip to London to press this point of view, but when Mrs Ward's article, 'The New Reformation', appeared in the March 1889 issue of the Nineteenth Century, he admitted it had 'done no harm'.[34]

'The New Reformation'[35] was actually a reply to both
Gladstone's article and another attack upon *Elsmere* by Randall Davidson which had been published in the November
Contemporary Review, though neither name was directly
mentioned by Mrs Ward. Davidson, amplifying Gladstone's
accusation of an ignorance of Christian apologetics, asserted
that internal evidence within the novel demonstrated Mrs
Ward's failure 'to acquire any knowledge of the rational, as
apart from the emotional basis on which the Christian fabric
has been reared and stands'. Mrs Ward, in 'The New Reformation', puts the case for enlightened Biblical criticism into the
form of a dialogue between two young men, one theologi-
cally orthodox and the other a liberal, who resemble the A
and C of *Unbelief and Sin*.

Mrs Ward's article, ostensibly a defence of her novel, was
in reality a defence of her credentials as an authority on Biblical scholarship. As Jowett had predicted, by replying to her
critics Mrs Ward stepped out of the role of novelist and became instead a religious controversialist. T. H. Huxley, in an
article published in the *Nineteenth Century* the following
month, offered unstinted praise of her efforts: 'Mrs. Ward
will, I hope, pardon the comparison, if I say that, her effective clearing away of antiquated incumbrances from the lists
of the controversy, reminds me of nothing so much as the
action of some neat-handed, but strong-wristed, Phyllis, who,
gracefully wielding her long-handled "Turk's head," sweeps
away the accumulated results of the toil of generations of
spiders.'[36] The depth of Mrs Ward's scholarship was indeed
impressive, but her pleasant discovery that she could be a
highly effective polemicist was to have an unhappy effect
upon her subsequent novels.

III

Robert Elsmere was reviewed so extensively in Britain,
America, and elsewhere that I can describe only a representative sample of the published criticism in this chapter. (However, a full list of reviews is provided in the Bibliography.)

One of the first two notices of the book appeared in the *Scotsman* (5 March), which called it 'unquestionably one of the most notable works of fiction that has been produced for years'. In comparing *Elsmere* to George Eliot's novels, the *Scotsman* suggested a theme that was to be repeated with endless variations by later reviewers. 'The Scotsman review ought to help the book in the north', Mrs Ward commented to George Smith on 6 March—'I was delighted with it today.' Another notice, slightly less enthusiastic, appeared on 5 March in the London *Morning Post*. The reviewer complained that in the third volume 'dogma unduly encroaches upon fiction' and, despite his commendation of 'the moral atmosphere of the book', took exception 'to most of the ideas of Elsmere and his friends'.

The *British Weekly* (9 March) described *Robert Elsmere* as a 'very able, thoughtful, and high-toned book', reserving special praise for the literary felicity of the Westmorland chapters. Mrs Ward, 'a disciple of Mr. Arnold', had given her readers 'a most instructive and truthful account of the present attitude of a large section of the cultured class to Christianity, or rather, of what will immediately be their attitude'.

Favourable notices like these were naturally welcomed by Mrs Ward and her publisher, but Smith insisted (on 15 March) that 'what I am truly looking for is a really good review in the "Times" or some other influential Journal, which might have the effect of stimulating the Mudies subscribers'. *The Times* did not break its silence until the following month, but the remaining weeks of March did bring important reviews in the *Academy*, the *Manchester Guardian*, the *Saturday Review*, the *Athenaeum*, and the *Guardian* (by Pater).

Of this group, the *Saturday Review* (24 March) struck the only strongly hostile note. Robert Elsmere, it declared, was 'one of the folk who cannot bear to be without a religion, and for whom the religion which was intellectual enough for St. Paul and St. Augustine and St. Anselm and Butler and Berkeley is too unintellectual, the religion which was spiritual enough for St. John and for Thomas à Kempis and for Jeremy

Taylor too unspiritual'. Elsmere's only sensible act, the re-viewer added, was his death. 'The ugliest piece of bigotry, of fanaticism that I remember having read!' Edmond Scherer remarked of it to Mrs Ward.[37] In fact, the high rhetorical pitch to which the public debate over *Robert Elsmere* was rising began to disturb her. 'Every review of this book, be it praise or blame, is more or less painful to me', she wrote to Meredith Townsend on 30 March.[38]

The *Manchester Guardian* (21 March), by contrast, ap-plauded the merits of *Robert Elsmere* in a review that ex-tended to a full column and a half. Every page of the novel, it said, was weighty, 'executed with elaborate care, and full of condensed thought and vivid experience'. William Sharp ('Fiona Macleod'), in the *Academy* (17 March), predicted a 'wide and potent influence' for *Elsmere*, and, though he objected to its diffuseness of style, he found it keenly inter-esting 'merely as a tale of contemporary English life, a ficti-tious record of the joys and sorrows, loves and antagonisms, fortune and misfortune of men and women more or less like individuals whom most of us know'. Squire Wendover he called one of the most impressive characters in contemporary fiction. The reviewer in the *Athenaeum* (31 March) took the position, by now a familiar one, that despite Mrs Ward's 'ful-ness of knowledge, . . . breadth of appreciation, and . . . criti-cal talent', she was a clumsy novelist who had tried to squeeze too much material into one book.

In April the 'influential Journals' began to speak. The *Pall Mall Gazette* (5 April), while it denied Mrs Ward the supreme compliment of literary creativity, lauded the truthfulness and reverence of *Robert Elsmere* and offered this ironic evalu-ation of its reception:

On the one hand it has already had the misfortune to be greeted with a salvo of mechanical appaluse from the log-rolling fraternity, with whom Mrs. Ward is in high favour. "Behold," they cry, "a greater than George Eliot is here," thereby making themselves more than usually ridiculous. On the other hand, the religious world is supposed to have taken alarm, and such alarm is quite stupid enough to be credible. The book, we are told, is regarded as having an unsettling tendency. Its presence will be discouraged at the circulating libraries. In view of the popularity which always attaches to books denounced as having a dangerous tendency by the orthodox, this must be good news for Mrs. Ward and her publishers.

The Times (7 April), labelling it 'a clever attack upon revealed religion', nevertheless devoted three-fourths of a column to its analysis of *Robert Elsmere*. As the *Pall Mall Gazette* had suggested, such negative yet lengthy responses to the book could only result in increasing its circulation. A more balanced and intelligent critique came from R. H. Hutton in the *Spectator* (7 April), who found *Elsmere* 'a very remarkable book, though by no means a very remarkable novel'. After a discerning treatment of the literary aspects of the story, Hutton took issue with Mrs Ward's religion based on a human Christ. 'But profoundly as we differ from Mrs. Humphry Ward's criticism of Christianity', he wrote, 'we recognise in her book one of the most striking pictures of a sincere religious ideal—(a religious ideal peculiar to the present age)—that has ever been presented to our generation under the guise of a modern novel.'

During the summer and autumn of 1888 the major British monthlies and quarterlies at last offered their views (uniformly negative) on *Robert Elsmere*. Herbert Cowell, in *Blackwood's* (July), devoted a full twenty pages to the topic 'Robert Elsmere and Modern Oxford', admitting openly that 'it is not as a work of art that we undertake to criticise it'. 'We certainly are not prepared to believe', announced Cowell, 'that modern Oxford has much to be proud of when she sends forth a distinguished *alumnus* so indifferently equipped that when, as rector, he presents himself in the squire's hall, it resembles nothing so much as a lamb led to the slaughter.' Once he had warmed to his subject, Cowell, like many other reviewers of *Elsmere*, dropped all pretence of discussing the novel and plunged instead into a fervent defence of Christianity against contemporary scepticism.

The *London Quarterly Review* (July) professed great alarm over the harmful effect *Elsmere* would have upon its readers:

There is a latent scepticism in many a young mind which this book will call to the surface and confirm. The seeds of doubt that are lying idle and harmless in many hearts will be quickened into life by the hints and insinuations of these pages, and the glow of feeling which invests its history of the progress of unbelief.

Echoing the objections of Gladstone, the reviewer complained of the unscientific dogmatism of Elsmere's assertion that 'Miracles do not happen' and declared that the faith of the New Brotherhood 'is, in truth, a last relic of Christianity, retained when the main foundations on which it rests have been cut away'.

There is a nice irony in the fact that the markedly unfavourable review in the *Quarterly* (October) was written (though of course not signed) by Henry Wace, who had in 1879 persuaded Mrs Ward to do the historical research that eventually thrust her out of the Church. Wace later admitted in print that he saw at least the possibility of this connexion:

I am under much obligation to Mrs. Ward for the valuable series of articles which she contributed to the *Dictionary of Christian Biography* under my editorship, upon the obscure but interesting history of the Goths in Spain. I trust that, in her account of the effect upon Robert Elsmere . . . of absorption in the barbarian scene, she is not describing her own experience and the source of her own aberrations.[39]

In his review Wace adopted the same approach as other orthodox critics of the novel. Like Gladstone, he affirmed that 'a success of this kind is proof that a book has touched some general and deep source of public feeling, and has given vivid expression to thoughts or interests which are widely spread'. Like Cowell, Wace lamented the spiritual state of Oxford as portrayed by Mrs Ward. The latter half of the review, again following the usual pattern, was a weighty discussion of the historical generalizations in *Robert Elsmere*. Jowett, when he visited Mrs Ward in November, learned that she planned 'doing battle with the Reviewer in the *Quarterly*',[40] and it seems likely that 'The New Reformation' was in fact as much a reply to Wace as to Gladstone and Davidson.

The response of British religious journals was predictable.

Most simply quarrelled at tedious length with Elsmere's theological formulations, though the *Congregational Review*
(June) did commend Mrs Ward's lack of bitterness towards
Christianity. What is perhaps more striking is the manner in
which *Robert Elsmere* was taken up as a sermon topic by
numerous clergymen. In London the Revd Hugh Haweis, a
well-known Broad Churchman, denounced both Elsmere and
Gladstone from his pulpit, declaring that religious progress
lay in the direction of a moderate liberalism within the
Church of England. Mrs Ward was disturbed by Haweis' sermon, but she reacted even more angrily to the declaration
by Hugh Price Hughes, England's leading Nonconformist
preacher, that he knew the 'originals' of nearly all the characters in *Robert Elsmere*. There was 'scarcely a grain of truth'
in Hughes' utterances, she said, 'and a man has no business,
on such a matter, to assert in public what he has no means of
knowing to be accurate'.[41] In September Dr Stanton Coit, an
Ethical Culturist, spoke on *Elsmere* at South Place Chapel,
observing that 'so far from being likely to further the cause
of free thought or to weaken the bulwarks of Orthodoxy, as
some nervous Christians seemed to think, he regarded it as
likely to strengthen the position of Orthodoxy'. As late as
March 1889 the York Clerical Brotherhood heard a paper on
'Robert Elsmere v. Christianity' by the Revd C. R. Gilbert,
and in June 1890 the Archdeacon of Man delivered a lecture
to the Yorkshire Evangelical Union on *Robert Elsmere* and
Lux Mundi.

Surrounded by all this heavy polemical thundering, a few
reviewers were able to regard the *Elsmere* phenomenon with
less than total solemnity. Robert Y. Tyrrell, in the *Fortnightly Review* (May 1889), wittily noted that 'Mr. Gladstone will not read a novel unless it is at least as dull as a
blue-book'; Andrew Lang, writing in the *Contemporary Review* (June 1888), suggested that what Elsmere really needed
was an extended holiday devoted to golf and fishing—without
his wife. But high seriousness was the tone which characterized most of the British reviews, and when in July the post-

man delivered a large parcel of clippings from across the Atlantic and her husband announced, 'There's America beginning!',[42] Mrs Ward realized that her novel, now an international success, was being discussed earnestly in the United States as well.

IV

For the modest sum of £60, Baron Tauchnitz secured the privilege of including *Robert Elsmere* in his English-language 'Continental Series',[43] and there were also translations published in most of the major European languages. Continental reviewers generally treated the novel with sympathy but with greater detachment than their English counterparts, for the powerful religious conflicts described by Mrs Ward often seemed remote to non-English readers. M. Bentzon, a French reviewer, suggested that his countrymen saw the choice as lying between Catholicism and rationalism; Elsmere's 'halfway house' was therefore incomprehensible to the French mind. Professor Beyschlag, a 'mediating' higher critic, professed to be unconvinced of the validity of Mrs Ward's new religion: such an experiment, he said, had been tried 40 years earlier in Germany and had proved a failure. J. Van Loenen Martinet, reviewing a Dutch translation of *Robert Elsmere*, likewise claimed that the book recalled to his mind the religious controversies which had shaken Holland two generations ago.[44]

In America, however, the publication of *Robert Elsmere* evoked no such complaints about a cultural lag. Indeed, the liberalizing changes in American theological seminaries and the accompanying religious ferment were just beginning there at about the time that Mrs Ward's novel appeared on the scene; hence it and the numerous other novels with religious themes that circulated in the U.S.A. during the 1880s—most notably Margaret Deland's *John Ward, Preacher* (1888), with which *Elsmere* was often compared—attracted an abnormal degree of interest because of their timeliness. If *Robert Elsmere* was a solid success in Britain, it was an unparalleled sensation in America. As one New York journalist summed up the situation in December 1888, *Elsmere*

has been, if anything, more widely read and discussed in America than in England; there is hardly a pulpit from Portland, Maine, to Portland, Oregon, that has not fulminated against the radical tendency of the work. It is reported that a religious paper has refused to publish any more sermons on the subject unless they are paid for, the supply so far exceeds the demand. A newsdealer who has a stand at the entrance to one of the North River ferries told me the other day that he had sold 3,000 copies of the work and had ordered 1,000 more from the publishers; and I am informed on good authority that some 150,000 copies of the book have been sold on this side of the water alone.[45]

The largest single group of readers of *Robert Elsmere* and of all Mrs Ward's later novels was to be found in America. She was speaking the simple truth when she wrote to Annie Fields in 1894, 'Your great American public becomes year by year a larger & larger fact in the consciousness of the English author, it seems to me.'[46]

Aside from the lively popular interest in theological questions, another factor in the large American sales of *Robert Elsmere* was that it was shamelessly pirated in the form of extremely cheap reprints. Because the international copyright law was not then observed in the United States, George Smith began to express concern about issuing an authorized American edition as soon as he realized that the novel was selling well in England. Lippincott was unsuccessfully approached, and Harper also declined it because, as Henry Alden said, 'its purpose was antagonistic to the teachings of our Saviour in vital points—especially as to his resurrection'.[47] At length Macmillan, which had earlier purchased the Colonial rights to *Elsmere*, agreed to issue a one-volume American edition, priced at $1.25, but within a few weeks after its publication on 28 July the pirates began to flood the American market with their less expensive versions.[48]

Wolcott Balestier, on the very day of his arrival in London as a representative of the John W. Lovell Company, had obtained a copy of *Robert Elsmere* from Mudie's and posted it

at once to New York. As a result, Lovell was able to issue a
50¢ paperback version in the last week of August, while a
shipping delay caused the authorized Macmillan edition to go
out of print temporarily. The episode earned for Lovell, who
voluntarily sent Mrs Ward a cheque for £100, the title of
'moral pirate'.[49] The other American pirates who reprinted
Robert Elsmere did not make even such a token payment to
the author. Wretchedly printed and bound and filled with
typographical errors (including the misspelling of 'Humphrey' on the title-page), these editions, many of which had
paper covers, were used for various promotional purposes—
as a gift, for example, to every purchaser of a bar of 'Balsam
Fir Soap'! On 3 January 1889, Mrs Ward sent her sister-in-
law, Henrietta Arnold, this report of the literary uproar in
America:

A young American who came here yesterday gave a most extraordinary
account of the publishers' struggle over it. In Boston there was a great
fight between the big shops—the Whitleys of the place—and the retail
book trade. Until at last, Dutch-auction fashion, one big shop came
down to 4 cents! On the morning when the book was to be sold at this,
there was a *queue* waiting for it, stretching far out on the pavement—so
he says: This could only go on two or three days as on every copy these
worthy persons lost 11 cents—but at any rate they beat their rivals!

Despite the proliferation of reprints, *Publishers' Weekly* revealed that there were actually only four sets of plates in circulation, each pirate having produced editions for others as
well as himself.[50]

In December Macmillan issued a more expensive two-
volume edition of *Robert Elsmere*, but the sales of this and
the earlier Macmillan version probably accounted for only a
fourth of the total number of copies sold in America. *Publishers' Weekly*, in fact, repeatedly commented in its edito-
rials during 1888 and 1889 upon the need for an international copyright agreement as demonstrated by the pirated
editions of *Elsmere*. It estimated that if Mrs Ward had received royalties from all of the American versions, she would
have earned at least $5,000,[51] a fact that certainly did not

escape the notice of the author and her English publisher, particularly since there were indications that the United States Congress would approve new copyright legislation before she had completed another novel. 'Does it not seem strange to you', Smith asked her (21 December 1888), 'that the question of whether a lady living in Russell Square should or should not be a millionairess, is depending on "lobbying" at Washington?'

Robert Elsmere's popularity in America was also surprising in its duration. When each of the nation's major libraries was asked in 1893 to submit a list of the 150 novels most frequently borrowed, *Elsmere* appeared on 30 per cent of the lists.[52] But even Mrs Ward, pleased though she was by her book's fame, could express misgivings about its American reception:

> My feelings about America are very mixed. I feel the book has made a *deep* impression there, & I shouldn't be human if I were not thrilled & delighted by its success. But the vulgarity[,] the lack of all sensitiveness & delicacy which enters into their modes of publication, their reviews, & often, their sermons, is a terrible make weight. I feel it grudging & like the "superior person" to say this. A great wave of human sympathy is a wonderful & a humbling thing. Perhaps one's sense of what is touching & beautiful in it makes one all the more alive to the false & ugly elements, & more afraid lest they should feed what is worst in oneself & make one less capable of good work in the future.[53]

Certainly the packet of periodical clippings which an American friend had sent her must have borne out this impression. Uncritically hailed as the greatest novel of the decade—and sometimes as the greatest novel of the century—*Robert Elsmere* evoked from the American press an extraordinary mixture of accolades and misinformation.

The first notices of the book in the United States sometimes misspelt both the the title and the author's name, offered unfounded speculations about Mrs Ward's parentage, and dwelt obsessively upon Gladstone's review. Nevertheless, American reviewers treated *Elsmere* most kindly. The *New York Times* (5 August) praised Mrs Ward's scholarship and compared the New Brotherhood of Christ to New York mission houses; the *Literary World* (18 August) anticipated 'even a warmer reception here than it has had in England, for it is a great novel'; the reviewer in the Chicago *Dial* (November) could not 'recollect anything which is fairly comparable with it for style or creative power'.

Of course there were dissenters from this chorus of praise, especially among religious journals. The *Catholic World* (September) called Elsmere's religion 'altruistic rubbish' and scoffed at the alleged power of Wendover's rationalism. The *Atlantic Monthly* (November) found a remote, bookish quality in the novel which gave the plot an air of unreality: 'It is amusing to see what a part books play in this story. All the main characters either have written, are writing, or are likely to write.' Yet even hostile reviews testified to the strong impression which the book had made in America. The January 1889 number of the *North American Review*, the most prestigious quarterly in the United States, devoted 20 pages to a symposium on 'Robert Elsmere's Mental Struggles', with contributions from Edward Everett Hale, Julia Ward Howe ('I know of no story, since "Uncle Tom's Cabin," whose appearance has excited so much comment, intellectual interest of so high a character'), and others.

Mrs Ward's complaints about American vulgarity notwithstanding, some of the reviews were very perceptive indeed. James T. Bixby, for example, in the *Unitarian Review* of Boston (November), undertook a careful analysis of the book in relation to *Miss Bretherton* and other recent novels that was unquestionably as informed as any review printed in Britain. An even more remarkable article was published in the *Homiletic Review* (February 1889) by the Revd Albert J. Lyman, of Brooklyn, New York, who had read Matthew Arnold well and recognized Mrs Ward's extensive intellectual indebtedness to her uncle. Like nearly every other American reviewer, Lyman took note of *Robert Elsmere*'s great vogue:

People all admire the style, the art, the dramatic power, the moral dignity of the story. Everybody is a little scared about its theology and is fumbling around for an orthodox club. Everybody secretly blames Catherine, thinks Wendover horribly well done, has a quiet, hidden fondness for the wayward Rose, stands mourner at poor Elsmere's reasonless fate, and is on the whole convinced that here is no milk for theological babes, but a dangerous *tour-de-force*, which depicts in altogether too fascinating outlines the skeptical struggle of the age. In a word, the book is supposed to be *realism*, and statesmen and clergymen rush to the rescue.

Magnificent fiction it might be, but *Robert Elsmere*, according to Lyman, was not realism, for Mrs Ward's hero moved in the theological and intellectual world of the previous generation—a charge made by other reviewers, but documented nowhere else so impressively as in this article.

'Clergymen unlimber the rhetorical cannon, thump the pulpit cushions, and raise the astonished dust', reported Lyman, and certainly *Robert Elsmere* did produce some lively clerical responses in America. At Plymouth church in Chicago an enormous audience, overflowing into the aisles and altar steps, gathered on the night of 21 October to hear the Revd Frank Gunsaulus declare:

'Robert Elsmere' takes hold of men with an almost fatal grasp. Its success lies half in the fact that in so many localities the armor of orthodoxy has become rusty with disuse. But there are fatal defects to be seen in the argument when it is divested of the glamor of the art surrounding it.

Naturally he then proceeded to enumerate those fatal defects, and the Chicago *Tribune* reported his speech on its front page the next morning with breathless enthusiasm. Charles W. Wendte, minister of the First Unitarian Church in Oakland, California, announced to his congregation that he was uniquely qualified to discuss the novel because he had once met Matthew Arnold, whom he took to be the original of Robert Elsmere. Mrs Ward, he said, had not introduced any new arguments against orthodoxy, but she had popularized the old arguments and put them into the hands of the people. 'Where one person reads Hume, Renan, Strauss, Theodore Parker, Spencer, or even Robert Ingersoll, a hundred read "Robert Elsmere".'

As more than one critic complained, *Robert Elsmere* was received by many Americans less as a popular novel than an oracular pronouncement on God and human destiny. 'Do you agree with Robert Elsmere?' became for a year or more in the United States a shibboleth designed to expose every shade of orthodoxy or heterodoxy. 'I think some of my American letters would amuse you!' Mrs Ward confided to George Smith (12 October 1888).

V

The public response to *Robert Elsmere* cannot be measured solely by examining reviews, for there were also attempts to refute the book's thesis through the medium of other novels. In America, Mrs Helena Hetherington and H. D. Burton co-authored *Paul Nugent, Materialist* (1890), a reply to *Robert Elsmere*;[54] in England, Marie Corelli, an extremely popular novelist of the day who has since sunk into obscurity, launched an attack in *Ardath* (1889) upon Elsmerism as merely a revival of Voltairean scepticism. Dr Joseph Parker, of the City Temple, London, had written the bulk of *Curfew Jessell* (1889), an amusing fictional account of popular religion in England, before the publication of *Robert Elsmere*, but when his novel was sent to the printer he interpolated a few indignant speeches about Mrs Ward's hero.[55] 'Whitteker Whimsey' (presumably a pseudonym) furnished in an American periodical what he claimed was an authentic 'omitted chapter' of *Elsmere*, in which Robert's faith in the historical method is momentarily shaken by a conversation with Mr Oxenbode, who argues that miracles testify to a God who is free and unconfined by his own laws.[56]

Mrs Ward received reports of at least two novels which unethically exploited the popularity of *Robert Elsmere*. One American publisher issued a purported sequel with this misleading title-page:

Robert Elsmere's Daughter
A Companion Story to *Robert Elsmere*
by Mrs. Humphry Ward[57]

Smith, in a letter of 8 December 1889, counselled Mrs Ward against taking the matter to court:

If we do not succeed we shall have widely advertized a publication, which is now but little known beyond the kitchen maid class. And in any case, I am afraid that you may appear to be too sensitive in taking serious notice of such a catch-penny production. The councel for the defendant—who would probably not be of a high class—would say all the disagreeable things he could, and it is possible that the judge might say something to the effect that it might have been supposed that Mrs. Humphry Ward could have well afforded to treat such a publication with the contempt it merited.

An equally clumsy sequel first published in German, *Catherine Elsmere's Widowhood* (1893) by E. Chabot, provided sensational episodes that enlivened its otherwise dull discussions of the German religious situation: Sir Reginald, Wendover's rakish heir, tries to seduce Catherine, but she resists, and her son (who of course does not exist in Mrs Ward's novel) inherits both a title and 'Elsmere Castle'.

Another bastardized version of the Elsmere story was written for the stage by the American actor William Gillette, who, however, abandoned the undertaking when Mrs Ward cabled her disapproval. But others completed the play, and it was performed in both Boston and New York during the spring of 1889. In this dramatized *Robert Elsmere*, advertised on the billboards as 'a new four-act society drama', Catherine turns to Newcome as her spiritual adviser, the Squire disappears completely, a comic English gentleman named Cecil Wanless is introduced, and the final curtain falls on a happy tableau of Robert restored to health in the arms of his wife. The religious issues in the novel are scarcely touched.[58] To the manager of a New York theatre who intended to produce the play, Mrs Ward wrote:

Robert Elsmere was never written with any view to the stage. It is entirely unsuited to theatrical presentation and I have refused steadily to allow it to be dramatised in this country. It can only be adapted to the stage by destroying the proportions of the story, by emphasizing what is subordinate and leaving out what is essential,—for I cannot believe that the American or any other public would bear to hear the most intimate and sacred of speculative problems discussed behind the footlights.[59]

Most of the American spectators and drama critics who witnessed it agreed that *Elsmere* on the stage was a dismal failure.

Perhaps the most curious imitation of *Robert Elsmere* was not a literary one at all; it was Mrs Ward's own prolonged effort to translate the dreams of Elsmere's New Brotherhood into the bricks and mortar of an actual institution. 'The New Brotherhood still exists, and grows', the last paragraph of *Robert Elsmere* had declared (ii, 558); and unfriendly reviewers had frequently seized upon that sentence and retorted mockingly that the New Brotherhood was only a figment of Mrs Ward's fevered imagination. In 1890, therefore, she founded a settlement house at University Hall, subsequently metamorphosed into the Passmore Edwards Settlement in Bloomsbury, both of which institutions absorbed much of her time and energy in later years.[60] Mrs Ward publicly insisted that the University Hall settlement had no formal connexion with her novel (and reproved George Smith for calling it the New Brotherhood in his letters to her),[61] but in fact the Hall and Passmore Edwards Settlement were rooted in Elsmerian ideals. Life imitated art, with unfortunate results. Though the Settlement (now known as the Mary Ward Centre) still survives in modified form, it soon became a vehicle chiefly for middle-class self-improvement schemes and charitable activities for poor and crippled children. The primary goal of the New Brotherhood—to inspire working men and women with the religious ideals of Elsmere's neo-Christianity—was never realized. In *Richard Meynell* Mrs Ward obliquely acknowledged this failure when she spoke of Hugh Flaxman's 'supreme and tyrannical common sense' which 'had never allowed him any delusions as to the ultimate permanence of heroic ventures like the New Brotherhood' (p. 248).

But though the achievements of the Passmore Edwards Settlement were more limited than Mrs Ward had hoped

they might be, the very creation of the Settlement is sympto-
matic of the way in which *Robert Elsmere* continued to
make its influence felt in her life. The novel simultaneously
liberated her from the drudgery of literary journalism, opened
up illimitable vistas of fame and wealth, and imprisoned her
in the role of respected spokesman for a particular religious
point of view in her later novels. The effect of *Robert Elsmere* upon Mrs Ward's literary career was not altogether
beneficial, but the fact remains that she would not have had a
career as a novelist without it. In offering a skilfully fictionalized account of her spiritual anxieties—and the confident
resolution of those anxieties—to the Victorian reading public,
Mrs Ward, almost by accident, touched an exposed nerve, and
the applause and noisy denunciations which greeted its appearance in print transformed her suddenly into one of the
most widely read novelists of the century. Nevertheless, surrounded by the evidences of her new prosperity, Mrs Ward
could not forget the deprivations, both financial and emotional, of the past. 'If it had only happened 10 years ago', she
wrote to her father (10 February 1889), '& Mamma could
have shared it!'

Chapter 9
ELSMERE'S HEIRS

But the interesting and touching thing to watch was the gentle and almost imperceptible flowing back of the tide over the sands it had left bare. It may be said, I think, that he [Pater] never returned to Christianity in the orthodox, or intellectual sense. But his heart returned to it. He became once more endlessly interested in it, and haunted by the 'something' in it, which he thought inexplicable.

—A Writer's Recollections (p. 121)

I

Mrs Ward's greatest literary problem after 1888 was to write another novel which was not merely a sequel to, or imitation of, *Robert Elsmere*. In her next story, *The History of David Grieve*, she therefore turned to a different social class (the *petite bourgeoisie*), a different locale (Manchester and, secondarily, Paris), and a different period (the 1870s); yet in the end Grieve arrives at a religious position indistinguishable from Elsmere's. As several reviewers observed, David Grieve would have felt quite comfortable as a member of the New Brotherhood of Christ. A minor figure in the novel—Mr Ancrum, a minister of a small dissenting sect—likewise reveals Mrs Ward's continuing preoccupation with the themes of *Robert Elsmere*, particularly the dilemma of the clergyman who has succumbed to doubt. Though the Giant Despair presumably lay in wait for every faltering Christian of the nineteenth century, Mrs Ward regarded the anguish of the ordained man of God beset by scepticism as a specially touching paradigm of all modern unbelief. Mr Ancrum, whose restless intellect contends with his religious instincts as he suffers silently in his drab little flat in Manchester, is a lineal descendant of Robert Elsmere, but he also anticipates other notable doubting clerics in Mrs Ward's later novels.

In *Helbeck of Bannisdale* (1898), Mrs Ward returned again to the themes of *Robert Elsmere*, but this time there was a curious role reversal, for the heroine, Laura Fountain, is made the sceptic and Helbeck the devout Catholic believer. As with *Elsmere*, the story sprang full blown from her mind as soon as Mrs Ward had discovered an appropriate Westmorland setting (Levens Hall, near Kendal) and a plot that would enable her to translate a theological conflict into a tale of frustrated love. Because it is shorter than *Robert Elsmere* and less diffuse, *Helbeck* achieves a Brontë-like intensity that is violated only in the first chapter of Book Five, when Mrs Ward introduces Dr Friedland, a Cambridge scholar, and through him comments on the religious issues involved. But apart from this brief authorial digression, *Helbeck*, as it moves inexorably towards its tragic conclusion, illustrates the darkening of Mrs Ward's imagination. Without a Dr Friedland or a Robert Elsmere to show her that there is a third alternative, Laura—trapped between her own barren scepticism and Helbeck's life-denying asceticism—must commit suicide.

Except for *Helbeck of Bannisdale*, most of Mrs Ward's novels during the 1890s had primarily social and political rather than religious motifs, and when she began *Eleanor* (1900) she evidently intended to eschew theological questions once more. The plot summary[1] which she sent George Smith early in 1899 makes merely a passing reference to the suspended priest who was to figure so largely in the novel, and it emphasizes that *Eleanor* will be a 'pure love-story' with only casual treatment of 'the great ideas that meet in Rome'. However, as she was in the midst of writing *Eleanor*, Mrs Ward became aware of the cases of Isaac Hecker, Hermann Schell, and Franz Reusch, all of whom, for a variety of reasons, had been either defrocked or excommunicated by

Rome.[2] Borrowing details from their experiences, Mrs Ward
created the character of Father Benecke, the heretical scholar
from a South German university, of whom Edward Manisty
says:

Father Benecke is a priest, but also a professor. He published last year a
rather liberal book—very mildly liberal—some evolution—some Biblical
criticism—just a touch! And a good deal of protest against the way in
which the Jesuits are ruining Catholic university education in Germany.
. . . They put his book on the Index within a month; he has had a year's
grace to submit in; and now, if the submission is not made within a
week or so, he will be first suspended, and then—excommunicated.
(p. 157)

Genuinely touched by the pathetic appeals of the Pope,
Benecke sends him a private letter of submission, which, to
the priest's horror, is treacherously published the next day in
the *Osservatore Romano*. Father Benecke withdraws his
recantation and is excommunicated.

The belated enlargement of Father Benecke's role in *Eleanor* was a direct result of Mrs Ward's growing interest in the
Although his story is only tenuously connected with the
main plot of *Eleanor*, Mrs Ward devotes many pages to describing the moving career of this sincere, truth-seeking cleric
who suddenly finds himself bereft of the supporting strength
of traditional religious institutions. He still speaks the language of Christianity—because 'I can speak no other language'
(p. 438)—and his inner spiritual life is 'now his only support
in rebellion, the plank between him and the abyss' (p. 453);
but what Father Benecke mourns above all is the loss of the
joy and fellowship of the Eucharist. He eventually joins the
Old Catholics and thus once more can share in the mystical
experience of the cross, which, says Mrs Ward, is 'the clue to
the world's secret' (p. 441).

The belated enlargement of Father Benecke's role in *Eleanor* was a direct result of Mrs Ward's growing interest in the
Modernist movement in European Catholicism. Unlike Victorian Broad Churchmanship, which feared ritual and used
the sacraments only perfunctorily, Modernism—whether
Roman Catholic or Anglican—placed great emphasis upon the
communal and mystical aspects of worship.[3] It is not difficult

to understand why this new religious development so strongly appealed to Mrs Ward, for in *Robert Elsmere* she had expressed her distaste for the individualistic, negative character of conventional Anglican liberalism and had groped about instinctively in the third volume of the novel for a neo-Christianity with a strongly social basis. Robert Elsmere's period of secret doubt was merely a prelude to his work of reconstruction in the New Brotherhood, which offered to the men and women of East London a sacramental, corporate form of worship that was at once liberal and Catholic (in the broadest sense). In 1907 Mrs Ward wrote to Louise Creighton:

> But what interests & touches me most—in religion—at the present moment is Liberal Catholicism. It has a bolder freedom than anything in the Anglican church, & a more philosophic and poetic outlook. It seems to me at any rate to combine the mystical and scientific powers, in a wonderful degree. If I only could believe that it could last, & had a future![4]

What Mrs Ward wished to discover, as this letter suggests, was a religion which would embody, as much as possible, the liturgies and forms of devotion of the past yet at the same time would not contradict the intellectual tenets of modern worshippers.

In the year that she was writing *Eleanor* Mrs Ward also began to express publicly her conviction that the Church of England must allow its communicants greater latitude of theological opinion. An earlier hint of this view in her fiction appears in *Marcella* (1894), in which Edward Hallin (who was modelled upon Arnold Toynbee) proposes a 'Church that was to be the people—reflecting their life, their differences—governed by them—growing with them' (ii, 333). Mrs Ward in 1899 sent a very long letter to *The Times* which argued that liberals were entitled to the same freedom within the Church as High Churchmen, and that therefore if Ritualists were permitted to ignore some of the rubrics of the Prayer Book, then greater tolerance must also be extended to those who regarded themselves as Anglicans but had reservations about the historicity of the Creeds.[5] Mrs Ward's proposal that, in effect, the Creeds be dropped from the Anglican liturgy (or at least be drastically modified) provoked numerous angry responses in *The Times* and other periodicals, and she used the controversy she had stirred up as the occasion for writing a sequel to 'The New Reformation' in the *Nineteenth Century*, which pleaded at even greater length for a 'conscience clause for the laity'.[6]

Like most of the religious debates in which Mrs Ward engaged, the problem of credal subscription was rooted more profoundly in her own experience than the published documents might suggest. From other sources it is apparent that during the last two or three years of the century Mrs Ward began to feel great distress at her exclusion from Holy Communion because of her inability to recite the Creeds in good conscience. She wrote an impassioned letter in 1898 to her old friend Mandell Creighton, who was at that time Bishop of London, lamenting 'the injustice which excludes those who hold certain historical & critical opinions from full membership in the National Church, above all from participation in the Lord's Supper'. The present theological stirrings in the Church of England were making her conscious, she said, 'of all sorts of claims and cravings that I have often wished to talk over with you—not as Bishop of London!—but as one with whom, in old days at any rate, I used to talk quite freely'. The quandary of the devout liberal was that in England

no one can have his children confirmed who is not prepared to accept or see them accept certain historical statements which he & they may perhaps not believe. And except as a matter of private bargain & sufferance,—always liable to scandal—neither he nor they—unless these tests have been passed—can join in the Commemoration of their Master's death, which should be to them the food & stimulus & life. Nothing honestly remains to them but exclusion and hunger—or the falling back upon a Unitarianism which has too often unlearned Christ, & to which, at its best, they may not actually belong.[7]

The 'hunger' of which Mrs Ward speaks in this letter was of course her own. A Westmorland acquaintance, Miss Mary

Cropper, wrote to her in 1920 recalling an episode of two decades earlier. 'I wonder if any clergyman has refused you the Holy Communion', inquired Miss Cropper. 'I cannot believe it.' She remembered once asking Mrs Ward to come to church with her on Easter, 'and you feared that if the vicar knew about it he wd. not wish you to come. I thought you were mistaken then, and I think so still more since those 22 years have passed.'[8] But Mrs Ward was unwilling to risk such a confrontation. As she said of one of her characters in *Eltham House* (1915), 'Joyce always went to early Communion on Sundays, wherever they were. "And I can never go with her," thought Carrie. "There are many clergymen, of course, who would refuse to give me Communion if I did go" ' (p. 151).

When Mrs Ward published *The Case of Richard Meynell* in 1911, reviewers inevitably discussed the obvious contrasts between it and *Robert Elsmere*. In the earlier novel, the liberal reformer found it necessary to break with the Established Church in order to preserve his intellectual integrity; in *Meynell* the process of theological renewal was envisioned instead as taking place within the Church. Mrs Ward represented this change in perspective as being the result, in part, of her tardy acceptance of the principle of ecclesiastical comprehensiveness that had been advocated by Jowett and Dr Arnold. Some readers of *Meynell* interpreted her apparent return to Christianity as a symptom of the usual conservatism of an aging writer. But, at a deeper level, Mrs Ward's decision to carry the fight for intellectual freedom into the Church itself had grown out of many years of thought on the subject and reflected her own frustrated need to kneel and receive the consecrated elements of the Eucharist.

II

In her correspondence with Reginald Smith, who had directed the affairs of Smith, Elder since the death of his father-in-law in 1901, the earliest reference to a possible sequel to *Robert Elsmere* appears in a letter from Smith to

Mrs Ward, dated 26 November 1904, in which he proposed that the writing of 'the "Since Robert Elsmere" book' (thereafter described in the correspondence as *Robert Elsmere II*) be postponed until after 1905. It is curious that Mrs Ward should have considered such a novel, for her single previous experience in writing a sequel—*Sir George Tressady* (1896), which attempted to capitalize upon the great vogue of *Marcella* (1894) in America—had not been a happy one. *Tressady* was inferior to *Marcella* in both literary achievement and popular success. As Mrs Ward explained in the Introduction to the Westmoreland Edition of *Tressady*, 'The defect of "sequels" is that they do not and cannot spring from the true story-telling impulse in its freshness. . . . The ideas and images to be handled must be in many respects the same as those from which the long labour of the earlier book has already extracted a first and sharpest savour' (I, ix).

But Mrs Ward throughout her career was always casting about for new novelistic formulae that would retain or recapture her vast reading audience, because she had learned to live too sumptuously and donated large sums of money too generously to her own settlement house and other charitable causes. When the early negotiations with publishers about *David Grieve* were being conducted, she reported to her father (15 June 1891) with naive pleasure that the projected royalties from the book would be £13,000. 'Now', she added, 'I must try & forget all these facts & figures, & write for oneself alone & for that little public of "the best" by whose judgement in the long run one must stand or fall.' The letter has a ring of sincerity, and there is no doubt that she really believed in 1891 that her primary goal in writing novels was artistic rather than financial, but, especially as she grew older, money problems always seemed to dominate her thinking whenever she launched a new story. *The Case of Richard Meynell* was begun in such a frame of mind: writing to her son Arnold (whose gambling debts were seriously draining the family resources) on 15 May 1910, she announced that she would 'soon plunge into the new book, which must somehow re-capture the American public, if future prospects are not to be materially changed!' All the while that *Meynell* was in progress, she worried about what she called 'money-affairs' and wondered if the current novel would repair the damage done to her American reputation by *Daphne* (1909), which had angered some readers because of its unflattering portrayal of permissive divorce laws in the United States.

Richard Meynell was written, therefore, under the shadow of financial stress and at a time in life when her creative powers were ebbing. Yet *Meynell*, despite all its evident shortcomings, displays a certain vitality—the vitality of a good pamphlet if not that of a good novel—because in it Mrs Ward was able to return with obvious pleasure to the old question of how the 'after-shine' of Christianity (Carlyle's phrase) could once again become a spiritual light in the contemporary world. In the latter half of 1909, in a memorandum labelled 'strictly private & confidential', she sent to Reginald Smith the following sketch of the novel:

AN ENGLISH MODERNIST

Stephen Pole, a hard-working English clergyman in suburban parish of superior artisans—as it might be Woolwich—strong Ritualist—affects the population through ritual and symbolism. Becomes affected by criticism—cannot any longer make the historical statements required—but mystical Christianity remains.

Had been in his first youth a hearer of Elsmere and deeply affected by his apparent failure. Yet he finds many in whom the Elsmere impulse persists—within the Church.

In the first chapter Catherine Elsmere introduced. His perception of her saintliness—and her complete aloofness from modern knowledge—entire absence in her of the symbolic poetic imagination. Things have progressed since Elsmere's day. The rise of the Modernist movement. How it is to affect the Church of England.

He finds it gradually impossible to preach as before, and the service, in certain aspects, becomes intolerable. His people insensibly follow him. Intellectual breach with Christian theology. But the Church—the Sacrament—mysticism all important.

He is in love with the daughter of his Bishop—who is enthusiastically with him. He throws down the gauntlet, refuses to read certain portions of the service—preaches advanced criticism on the Virgin Birth and the Resurrection—but will *not* resign his living.

The Bishop and his daughter. The Bishop—clear-headed—subtle—well-trained. Conflict between him and his daughter. He must prosecute. It is his duty.

A heresy trial with fierce excitement. In the middle of it the prosecuting Bishop gradually affected, like Paul, by the view he is attacking—goes over to the enemy. The greater part of his diocese go with him. The book breaks off on the eve of an Anglican Council in which the rights of citizenship within the English Church will be secured to both traditionalists and modernists—depending on the choice of congregations.

The love story between the modernist—Stephen Pole—and the Bishop's daughter Elsie Murray will have to be developed through various vicissitudes not at present clear. There will be a large background of characters belonging to different classes, and to various schools of thought.

Elsie Murray dies at the moment of Stephen Pole's triumph—and he is left to the mission of his life.[9]

Richard Meynell, as it gradually evolved, is very different from this early version. The names of the characters are changed; an elaborate, melodramatic subplot is introduced; the setting is shifted to a colliery district in Staffordshire that Mrs Ward had previously described in *Sir George Tressady*; Meynell is hardly a 'strong Ritualist', though he does display an intelligent interest in liturgical reform; and, most importantly, he falls in love with Mary Elsmere rather than the bishop's daughter (though in both instances Mrs Ward displays her familiar habit of offering a resolution of theological differences by means of a love-affair or marriage).

Stopford Brooke applauded Mrs Ward's plans—which he summarized as 'Robert Elsmere, reborn twenty or thirty years after, and brought up to the twentieth century'—and urged her to proceed with the novel.[10] Reginald Smith also approved, though he insisted that the title would have to be changed, as 'Modernism' probably meant nothing to American readers.[11] *McClure's Magazine*, after inquiring nervously whether the novel dealt with agnosticism, agreed to print it serially in the United States,[12] while in Britain serial rights went to *Cornhill Magazine*, which was published by Smith, Elder. Doubleday and Smith, Elder would then issue a book version in 1911.

By 4 August 1910, Mrs Ward had sent off the first number to the printer, but she admitted to Louise Creighton that 'I am very harassed about the book, which does not lie clear before me by any means'. As usual, she was reading extensively as she wrote: 'William James, and Tyrrell, and Claude Montefiore's book on the Synoptics, and some other theology and history'.[13] To a French correspondent she declared (on 19 August) that 'the book will be very heterodox; it raises all sorts of first principles—so far at any rate as the claims of Christian Dogma are concerned', and she was therefore certain that the editor of the *Revue des Deux Mondes* would not be interested in publishing a translation of it. The title of the novel, she added, would be 'Study of Religious Types', and she hoped to treat orthodoxy fairly; nevertheless, the plot would turn on 'the notion that what the enemies of the English Modernist find it difficult to obtain by law, they make an effort to obtain by slander on personal character'.[14]

The possible reception of her novel in the United States continued to cause anxiety. 'What the public of M'Clure's Magazine will say to it I cannot tell', Mrs Ward confessed to Annie Fields—'for it will be *very* English, *very* theological and America does not yet seem to have forgiven me *Daphne*. But it gives me joy to get back to some of the old lines, with a big canvas, & plenty of space.'[15] She also was feeling the pressure of magazine deadlines. 'It is absurd to have to write such a book hurriedly', she told her son (10 September). But at least she hoped to 'soften its first crudities' before it was published as a book, and by then she was confident that it would not 'excite any *bitterness*, when all is done'.

In September Mrs Ward went for a fortnight to Staffordshire 'to gather some local facts & types for my book',[16] and in March 1911, after speaking to an anti-suffrage rally in Kendal, she and her daughter Dorothy made a brief pilgrimage to Longsleddale, where Mrs Ward spent the afternoon chatting with a farmer's wife and making notes for the final chapters of *Meynell*.[17] The previous October, while visiting the parish church of Alderly, she had also unexpectedly

found herself collecting ideas for the hero of her novel when
the rector, the Revd Hudson Shaw, announced that

he would no longer read the Ten Commandments, the Athanasian
Creed, or the Cursing psalms, or the Preface to the marriage service, &
appealing passionately to the laity—'how can you stand it?—how have
you stood it so long! I have waited for 25 years,—now I take my own
course & stand the consequences!'[18]

Mrs Ward found this a refreshing contrast to the more orthodox services that she often attended at Aldbury, near Stocks.
On 21 August 1910, in one of her *Meynell* notebooks, she
recorded with disgust that even though it was the day after
Florence Nightingale's funeral and the Second Lesson told
the story of the Good Samaritan, the unimaginative cleric at
Aldbury church had offered only 'a feeble discourse on the
love of money'.

As the writing of *Richard Meynell* neared an end, Mrs
Ward's mood became increasingly mellow and relaxed. As she
had remarked earlier to Mrs Creighton, 'It has been delightful
going back to theological & philosophical reading—though I
find that my appetite for Biblical *criticism* is no longer quite
what it was. Perhaps only because one has made up one's
mind, & is more interested in the religious & practical appli-
cation of the new notions.'[19] Mrs Ward never doubted the
need to master the conclusions of higher criticism, but in
Richard Meynell, even more than in *Robert Elsmere*, her outlook was tolerant, constructive, and irenic. The old clothes of
orthodoxy were in tatters; it was now time, she believed, to
weave the new garments of faith. In September 1911, *Meynell* completed, she relaxed on the terrace of Rydal Mount
for several days, reading Wordsworth and reflecting on the
possibility of writing 'a volume of imaginary "sermons &
journals of Richard Meynell" going in detail into many of the
points only touched in the book'.[20] Though *Richard Meynell*
might 'make a good many people angry', she had (as she expressed it in a letter to Henry James) 'been happy in writing
it'.[21]

III

Richard Meynell, the middle-aged rector of Upcote Minor, may be the spiritual heir of Robert Elsmere, but it is obvious at the very beginning of the novel that he faces a different situation from that which confronted Elsmere a generation before. In the first chapter the postman delivers to the rectory a veritable flood of correspondence from liberal theologians all over Europe who share his dreams of reform (p. 6); even Bateson, the dying miner, has volumes by Mill, Huxley, Paine, Renan, Blatchford, Matthew Arnold, Browning, and Ruskin on the bookshelf in his shabby little bedroom (p. 31). At all social levels in the parish there is evidence that the new ideas of science and historical criticism are far more widely diffused than they were in Elsmere's time. The Modernists like Meynell are no longer a lonely, weak force in the Church of England:

> How different from Robert's day! Then the presumption underlying all controversy was of an offended authority ranged against an apologetic rebellion. A tone of moral condemnation on the one side, a touch of casuistry on the other, confused the issues. And now—behind and around the combatants—the clash of equal hosts!—over ground strewn with dead assumptions. The conflict might be no less strenuous; nay! from a series of isolated struggles it had developed into a world-wide battle; but the bitterness between man and man was less. (pp. 275-6)

The two conflicting aspects of Mrs Ward's religious outlook are strikingly evident in this passage: the metaphor of battle (which recurs throughout the novel) suggests that she has declared total war upon Christian orthodoxy, yet simultaneously she can express the belief that the theological and liturgical controversies will be resolved with little bitterness. *The Case of Richard Meynell* is an odd amalgam of these disparate impulses.

Meynell, like *Elsmere*, has an air of topicality about it that is partially illusory. Unquestionably the Christological issues which Mrs Ward had raised in *Elsmere* were now being discussed with great intensity in many quarters of the Church of England. The *Hibbert Journal*, for example, had published an article entitled 'Jesus or Christ? An Appeal for Consistency' in January 1909, and for seven months the journal was inundated with letters, articles, and responses of every variety.[22] A more immediate source of the ideas expressed in *Richard Meynell* was the series of lectures on Catholic Modernism delivered by Paul Sabatier, the French historian and clergyman, at the Passmore Edwards Settlement in February and March 1908 under the auspices of the annual Jowett Lectures organized by Mrs Ward. 'The Church is the traditional home', declared Sabatier. 'Life in it has become very difficult, almost insupportable, and yet the true courage is to remain there; the heroic course is to endure the reign of terror and suspicion which prevails.' Modernism, he argued (in a passage which Mrs Ward was to adopt and amplify in *Richard Meynell*), was a reconciling force: it was Catholic in its emphasis upon the community of believers, yet it was Protestant in its rejection of any mechanical theory of Papal authority.[23]

Meynell's theology also shows signs of his having read the writings of George Tyrrell ('the greatest [religious] figure in the twenty years before the war', according to Mrs Ward[24]), the excommunicated English Catholic priest whose progressive rejection of dogma was accompanied by a growing attraction to mysticism. And as *Richard Meynell* was being written, Mrs Ward followed with interest the case of the Revd James M. Thompson, an Oxford don, whose Modernist book *Miracles in the New Testament* (1911) was censured by the Bishop of Winchester.

Nevertheless, as was true of *Robert Elsmere*, the novel does not belong fully to the contemporary scene which it professes to describe. Both in Mrs Ward's notebooks and in the novel itself there are frequent indications that the heresy trial of Meynell was based upon details drawn from the experiences of R. D. Hampden, Bishop Colenso, Charles Voysey (pp. 48, 75, 508), and the *Essays and Reviews* contributors (p. 486), all of whom, significantly, had captured public attention half a century or more earlier. Cyril Fenton, the dour, ascetic High Churchman in the novel, is an unpleasant caricature of Hurrell Froude, Newman's friend, who died in 1836. There is even a direct reference to John Wordsworth's 1881 Bampton Lecture (p. 138), the premise of which (that theological doubt is a result of hidden sin) forms the basis of the conspiracy against Meynell.

The anachronistic quality of *Richard Meynell* is still more plainly visible in its hackneyed, old-fashioned subplot, described by one of the characters as 'a situation that only occurs in plays to which you don't demean yourself by going!' (p. 266). One of Mrs Ward's most disarming qualities, in fact, is that she knows when she is writing a bad story, and she makes no effort to conceal her own opinion of it. The tangled subplot of intrigue and concealed identities is compared to 'the plot of a novel' (p. 278), presumably not a very good one; a climactic scene reminds one character of 'third-rate drama' (p. 472). In view of Mrs Ward's undeniable literary sensitivity, why did she attach such a stagey, lurid backdrop—involving a completely unbelievable Byronic villain who lives in a ruined abbey and twists his black moustache whenever he is thinking particularly wicked thoughts—to her stirring tale of the triumph of Modernism? Mrs Ward's own subsequent explanation, that she had in mind 'the effect of a popular air amid the clash of a symphony',[25] is unconvincing, for all of her later novels abound in stock situations, flat characters, and sentimentality. Whatever the cause (and surely Mrs Ward's obsession with sales and royalties played some part in it), the deterioration of her fiction in the last decade of her life is both unmistakable and painful to witness.

Meynell himself is not a particularly interesting figure: in contrast with Elsmere, he is afflicted by no doubts or hesitations about ultimate questions. The centre of action has shifted now from the individual conscience to the machinery of the Church, a change in emphasis which inevitably makes *Meynell* a less subtle and compelling book than *Elsmere*. Whereas Robert Elsmere was a fascinating study in the psychology of unbelief, Richard Meynell is merely an efficient propagandist whose confidence in his own cause borders on self-righteousness. On the other hand, Meynell's relationship with Elsmere's legacy is deepened by his courtship of Mary Elsmere, whose religious training has been rigidly administered by Catherine but who is nevertheless 'spiritually . . . her father's child, and not her mother's' (p. 136). Catherine and Rose also reappear in the novel, the former more narrowly orthodox than ever and the latter only slightly less beautiful and witty than when she married Hugh Flaxman some 20 years earlier. Flaxman, who becomes Meynell's chief ally when a campaign of slander is mounted against the rector, is still extremely decent and equally bland.

Among the minor figures in the story, Hester Fox-Wilton is a conspicuous example of that recurring feminine type in Mrs Ward's novels, the restless, flirtatious young woman whose unconventional behaviour ultimately brings destruction upon herself. An entry in one of the *Meynell* notebooks indicates that Mrs Ward's original plan was for Hester to be fatally injured during her elopement with the villainous Philip Meryon, but—no doubt as a result of her visit to Longsleddale in the early spring of 1911—she instead allows Hester to return to England, to repent, and to die peacefully after losing her way in a snowstorm at the head of Long Whindale. Though Mrs Ward's customary insistence upon punishing sinners (particularly rebellious females) is still too apparent in the published version, the decision to move the action of many of the final chapters northward to Long Whindale was a brilliant one, for this was the terrain that she knew best. Catherine's death there in the last paragraph of the book, with only the tranquil country sounds—of the river and birds and a distant sheep dog—floating in through the window of Burwood Farm, is probably the finest passage in the novel, drawing its evocative power from our recollections of *Robert Elsmere* rather than from the story in which it actually appears.

The unhappy fate of Hester Fox-Wilton illustrates once again that Mrs Ward's liberalism in theology was joined to an increasing conservatism in morals. Conduct was for her not simply three-fourths of life, as Matthew Arnold had said, but rather very nearly the whole of it. One of the favourite terms of approbation in Mrs Ward's vocabulary was 'modern', and she regarded intellectual and theological relativism as the hall-mark of the modern mind; yet in the sphere of ethics she remained always an absolutist, insisting upon a total acceptance of traditional Chrstian morality even though she rejected the dogmatic basis of that morality. Biblical criticism did not seem threatening to her, because it undermined only the allegedly historical and scientific statements in the Scriptures and the Creeds. But modern psychology, with its deterministic bias, was another matter, and in her later novels Mrs Ward repeatedly attacked the new scientific fatalism which, in denying human responsibility, weakened the hold of all moral systems upon men and women. Hester's downfall is explicitly connected with her reading 'in the literature—the magazine articles at any rate—of French determinism' (p. 500), for it becomes easier to succumb to sexual temptation when she believes that a 'remorseless fate' is expressing itself through her selfish impulses.

The politician Norham (who, according to a notebook entry, combines the traits of Arthur Lyttelton and Gladstone) states the problem most clearly to Meynell:

'You think you can take what you like of a great historical religion and leave the rest—that you can fall back on its pre-suppositions and build it anew. But the pre-suppositions themselves are all crumbling. "God"—"soul," "free-will," "immortality"—even human identity—is there one of the old fundamental notions that still stands unchallenged? What are we in the eyes of modern psychology—but a world of automata—dancing to stimuli from outside? What has become of conscience—of the moral law—of Kant's imperative—in the minds of writers like these?'

He pointed to two recent novels lying on the table, both of them brilliant glorifications of sordid forms of adultery. (p. 283)

Meynell's reply—'*We* are not anarchists—as those men are'—merely reasserts his own strict code of conduct (which is never called into question except by the plainly malicious characters in the novel), and its implied sweeping rejection of all deterministic theories of human behaviour is perhaps not

far removed from an obscurantism which would have horrified Mrs Ward had the topic of conversation been Biblical
criticism rather than psychology.

Even in his proposed liturgical innovations, which are undeniably radical in nature, Meynell is more tolerant of traditional forms of worship than Elsmere was. A great deal of the
Anglican service is retained; Meynell only wishes to prune out
those passages in the hymnal and the *Book of Common
Prayer*, particularly the Athanasian Creed, which are offen-
sive to the ears of twentieth-century Christians. Despite Mrs
Ward's close ties with Unitarianism, she preferred the liturgi-
cally richer services of the Church of England, and in fact had
distressed many Unitarians in 1893 by complaining (in a letter to the *Manchester Guardian*) that the opening service of
Manchester College was too austerely Protestant in tone.[26]
Mrs Ward's hero was willing to discard the Creeds and some
of the Psalms and to alter the collects, but the final liturgical
form was still recognizably Anglican.

Do these compromises suggest that Mrs Ward was now a
believer in Christianity in some Broad Church sense? Apparently not, for Meynell is just as inflexible as Elsmere in his
denial of a supernatural Christ, a Resurrection, or any distinctive revelation embodied in the Christian religion. Indeed,
Mrs Ward once more invokes the metaphor of the New Reformation by portraying Meynell's appearance before the Com-
mission of Inquiry as a contemporary version of Luther's
public examination at the Diet of Worms. Meynell, like the
Protestant reformer, declines to retract his sermons or his
writings and silences his inquisitors with an eloquent defence
of the new faith.

At the end of the story there is a heresy trial in the Court
of Arches, and beyond this Meynell envisions a direct appeal
to the Privy Council and Parliament in order to secure the
right of Modernists to membership in the Church of England.
Mrs Ward describes entire parishes and at least one diocese
marching under the Modernist banner, a wave of religious enthusiasm sweeping across England, and the Christian Church

everywhere shaken to its foundations as it was in the days of Luther. The underlying assumption of both *Robert Elsmere* and *Richard Meynell* is that men and women by nature desire to worship God and that they are being driven away from the churches only by an outdated theology. Hence Mrs Ward's confident assumption that such extraordinary religious forces would be liberated once the Church of England removed certain legalistic and technical obstacles to membership.

In several important respects Richard Meynell's programme of Church reform is a return to the one suggested by Dr Arnold in 1832. He is directly indebted to Arnold, for example, in his recommendation that more than one type of service be conducted in each parish church on Sunday so as to satisfy the needs of diverse categories of worshippers. Canon Dornal sarcastically identifies Meynell with 'Arnold's game': 'Meynell's dream is not unlike his—to include everybody that would be included' (p. 191). But Meynell frequently also pays tribute to the example and inspiration of Newman, who had rightly perceived the Eucharist to be the centre of the Church's spiritual life. In emulating Arnold's tolerance and Newman's sacramentalism, Meynell represents Mrs Ward's effort to reconcile at last those two opposing forces of English Church life that had pulled her father back and forth and thus had blighted her own childhood. In a passage fraught with personal significance for Mrs Ward, the Bishop of Dunchester declares:

'Herbert, just before I was born there were two great religious leaders in England—Newman and Arnold of Rugby.... To-day we have been listening again, as it were, to the voice of Arnold, the great leader whom the Liberals lost in '42. Arnold was a devoutly orthodox believer, snatched from life in the very birth-hour of that New Learning of which we claim to be the children. But a church of free men, coextensive with the nation, gathering into one fold every English man, woman and child, that was Arnold's dream, just as it is Meynell's.... And yet though the voice, the large heart, the fearless mind, and the broad sympathies were Arnold's, some of the governing ideas were Newman's. As I listened, I seemed'—the old man's look glowed suddenly—'to see the two great leaders, the two foes of a century ago, standing side by side,

twin brethren in a new battle, growing out of the old, with a great mingled host behind them.' (pp. 514-5)

IV

The publication of *The Case of Richard Meynell* brought
Mrs Ward the usual spate of interesting letters. The Revd
Hastings Rashdall, the most eminent Anglican Modernist,
wrote:

I thought you might perhaps like to know the impression which your
creation has made upon one of those milder and more timid Modernists
who are actually to be found in the ranks of the Church of England
clergy. I don't anticipate any such heroic movement as you describe,
though of course one can not say what effect might be produced by a
prophet like your hero if such a prophet did arise: but I think the book
will really help the very Fabian kind of movement that is going on
among us. You will reach thousands whom no volume of sermons or
theological Essays could reach, and the mere suggestion that such a
movement is going on among the clergy will help us, and perhaps do
something to undo the infinite harm which the Bp of Winchester's
action against Thompson has done.[27]

But the Bishop of Winchester (who was in fact E. S. Talbot,
whom Mrs Ward had known well at Oxford) also sent a cor-
dial letter to the author, rejoicing 'that you can draw as much
Gospel as you do from what you accept, for yourself & for
others', though he strongly condemned Meynell's theological
position as untenable.[28]

The widow of T. H. Green found *Richard Meynell* 'extremely interesting' but questioned Meynell's right to stay in
the Church 'till there is a change in the ordination services'.[29]
Frederic Harrison wrote that the novel 'has given me the
most lively interest both as romance—as fine as anything
since *Adam Bede*—and also as controversy—as important as
anything since *Essays and Reviews*'.[30] Perhaps the most curious letter came from Charles Voysey, now 83 years old, who
had read *Meynell* with 'great physical distress': 'But I have
gone through every line of your book with the most *intense*
desire to see where *you* stand after 20 years' experience of
life & religion since you gave us "Robert Elsmere". . . . The

Living Loving God has made Christ, for me, quite super-
fluous, to say the least. But my lack of sympathy with you in
this point shall not diminish my admiration for your grand
effort in the cause of Liberty & Truth.'[31]

On publication day, 26 October 1911, Dorothy Ward recorded the activities at Stocks in her diary:

> The coming out of *Richard Meynell*. I went early to mummy to read
> the reviews with her, & the Times tho' *unseeing* & in fact almost silly
> was on the whole v.[ery] favourable & *Morning Post* excellent & *Man-
> ch[ester] Guardian* for once v.[ery] laudatory, tho' critical too. *D.[aily]
> News* & *D.[aily] Express* nasty rather, nothing in *Standard* & *Tele-
> graph*. After lunch we motored to B[erkham]sted across the park—
> most golden—to fetch ev[e]n[in]g papers, & St. James was rather
> nasty, but Westminster had a long front-page review enthusiastic
> ab[ou]t the theology but severe as to the story—[32]

Such an imposing list of first-day reviews may give the misleading impression that *Richard Meynell* was creating as great
a sensation as *Robert Elsmere* had in 1888, but in reality
nearly all of Mrs Ward's novels—at least until the very last
years of her life—commanded this sort of respectful attention
from newspapers. The irony of Mrs Ward's literary career is
that to the end her books evoked a critical and popular response which would have been envied by any other novelist,
yet her expectations (and financial needs) were so great that
each successive novel brought fresh disappointments. By ordinary standards, *Richard Meynell* was a widely read and reviewed book; by the standards of *Robert Elsmere* or *Marcella*
or *Lady Rose's Daughter*, it was a pitiful failure.

During the period ending 30 January 1912, fewer than
15,000 copies were sold in England. 'In our eyes "Richard
Meynell" is moving steadily, if a little slowly', Reginald Smith
commented on 20 November 1911. But the reports from
Doubleday in America were genuinely alarming. 'I confess to
being somewhat distressed about "Richard Meynell"', the
head of the firm wrote to Smith on 1 December. 'I feel as
strongly as you do the great merit of this book. We have gone
at the job with enthusiasm and spent a lot of money.' At

present, he said, the novel showed an unearned investment of about $15,000, and he expected to have to take a considerable loss on it.[33] In February Humphry Ward had to sell a Rembrandt from his private collection in order to offset the relatively small income from *Meynell*.[34]

Ethel Arnold, then lecturing in America, sent her sister an account of a conversation with Professor Benjamin Bacon, a liberal Congregationalist Biblical scholar at Yale University; when asked whether *Meynell* would be as popular as *Elsmere*, he replied:

> Well, Miss Arnold—to that question I should be inclined to answer 'no'. You see *Robert Elsmere* dealt with fundamentals—i.e. with the eternal and universal conflict between faith and unfaith—the struggle which every human soul that is worth anything experiences sooner or later. 'Richard Meynell' deals on the other hand with religious *politics*, if I may so express it—with questions of expediency and policy raised by the final decision 'I do *not* believe'—rather than the old fundamental primitive problem 'To believe, or not to believe'.[35]

American reviewers, though in general charitably disposed towards *Richard Meynell*, expressed bewilderment at the legal and financial arrangements of the Church of England as described in the novel. The American edition of *Meynell* contained a special preface by Mrs Ward explaining such mattters, in the hope that 'those who twenty years ago welcomed [*Elsmere*]—and how can I ever forget its reception in America!—may perhaps be drawn once again to some of the old themes in their new dress', but there was no concealing the fact that *Meynell* was, as Professor Bacon said, largely concerned with narrowly political questions in the Church of England that held slight interest for American readers.

In Britain reviewers praised Mrs Ward's mastery of novelistic technique, quarrelled (somewhat less shrilly than in 1888) over the book's theology, and agreed that though *Richard Meynell* was a worthy sequel, it could hardly become a cause of scandal as had *Robert Elsmere*. The *Times Literary Supplement* (26 October) thought the novel's obsession with ecclesiastical problems to be out of step with the modern age, and the *Westminster Gazette* (26 October) discerned beneath the 'intellectual boldness' of the book a 'solid and unshaken foundation of conventionality'. Religious periodicals scoffed at Meynell's Modernism, the *Church Times* (17 November) describing it as sophistry and the *Dublin Review* (April 1912) calling it the inevitable consequence of Protestantism. The *Spectator* (11 November) examined Meynell's new liturgy and found it wanting. *T. P.'s Weekly* (3 November) accused Mrs Ward of being 'a special pleader for an impossible position'. But the predominant mood among reviewers was that of polite boredom. 'It is a curious sign of the times, the unconcern with which this book has been received', declared the *Academy* (18 November). 'Twenty years ago, when we approached "Robert Elsmere," it was with a sense of awe and a furtive feeling, as of those who grasp at forbidden fruit. Of Elsmere's rebellion we read with bated breath, vastly moved; of Meynell's antagonism to the Established Church we now read with perfect tranquillity.'

Mrs Ward had studied as thoroughly as anyone of her generation the literature of Modernism (as the thickly strewn allusions and quotations in *Richard Meynell* testify). Where she went astray was not in her scholarship, which was impeccable, but in her reading of the temper of the new century, for Mrs Ward's Victorian sensibility misled her into believing that the majority of men and women were hungering and thirsting for a modernized version of Christianity. She had not taken sufficiently into account the growing secularization of the contemporary world, the decline of all institutional forms of Christianity, whether conservative or liberal, and the widespread indifference to theological questions. The fallacy of *The Case of Richard Meynell* was Mrs Ward's assumption that most of her readers shared her own deep-seated desire to return once again to the Communion rail of the Church in order to recover an elusive peace of mind.

EPILOGUE

There is a natural instinct in us all leading us to arrange, or dramatise, the life we see—according to our moral or aesthetic ideas. But life is rebellious and disappointing. Most of its plots break off or come to no proper end.

Introduction to *The Marriage of William Ashe* (p. xiv)

Mrs Humphry Ward achieved virtually every public recognition of success that late Victorian and Edwardian England could give: she was an internationally recognized literary figure, a spokesman for numerous respected causes, a hardworking organizer of excellent charitable activities, and the intimate friend and adviser of many of the nation's most influential men. At Stocks, her handsome country home, she swept gracefully across the lawn to greet arriving guests, talked happily of her flowers, and surrounded herself with grandchildren, friends, and pets. It was a supremely comfortable existence—it was, in fact, a realization of the visions of aristocratic splendour which recur in Mrs Ward's novels—but behind the serene countenance which she showed to the world lay a disturbing, inexplicable sense of subdued melancholy. Despite the apparent optimism of the third volume of *Robert Elsmere*, the painful renunciation of Christianity continued to trouble her deeply throughout her life, as it had her Uncle Matt. The Neo-Christianity of which she dreamed had not yet found an Elsmere or Meynell to lead the masses. As Arnold had written in 'Stanzas from the Grande Chartreuse', there was no alternative for the reluctant unbeliever but to 'wait forlorn', quietly to shed tears for the beautiful but dead faith of the past, and to look forward with patience to that future which was still powerless to be born.

On a more mundane level, Mrs Ward was troubled during her last two decades by recurrent financial problems. She was not materialistic in any obvious or vulgar fashion, but the enormous royalties from her books were always mysteriously swallowed up by the equally enormous family expenses, with the inevitable result that she found herself thinking more and more about money. In her literary notebooks, plot outlines became interspersed with budgets, lists of tradesmen's bills, and estimates of royalties. During the War her income fell off so badly that she was nearly compelled to sell Stocks. When her will was probated, the net value of her estate was found to be less than £7,000—certainly a small figure when one takes into account the immense sums of money which had passed through her hands since the publication of *Robert Elsmere*. 'I do so dread, as one gets richer losing the capacity for poetry for disinterested enthusiasms for all that really makes life', she had prophetically written in a letter to Humphry many years before (20 April 1899). 'One may easily become blunted & lose capacities that one once had. I constantly fear it for myself.'

The War not only reduced drastically the sales of her novels but also sent Mrs Ward into an uncharacteristic state of depression. The villages near Stocks were filled with soldiers, and the roads crowded with supply wagons; at Oxford the college buildings had been transformed into hospitals. Mrs Ward, 'tormented and obsessed by the spectacle of war',[1] sought escape by writing her memoirs and recreating in her mind that distant, idyllic Victorian Oxford which she had known as a young woman. In an Epilogue to *A Writer's Recollections*, composed on Christmas Eve, 1917, she wrote:

For a while these Recollections, during the hours I have been at work on them, have swept me out of the shadow of the vast and tragic struggle in which we live, into days long past on which there is still sunlight— though it be a ghostly sunlight; and above them, the sky of normal life.

But the dream and the illusion are gone. The shadow descends again. . . .
(p. 372)

Eventually she shook off this sense of numbness and wrote three propagandistic books about the war which required strenuous trips to the front lines in France. *England's Effort* (1916), *Towards the Goal* (1917), and *Fields of Victory* (1919) are unusual pieces of wartime journalism to have come from a woman in her sixties, containing not only eloquent descriptions of the ravaged French countryside but also a surprisingly perceptive understanding of the new military technology. But the books reveal at the same time Mrs Ward's inability to comprehend the brutalizing effect of modern warfare upon its participants. The War constituted a moral and intellectual crisis for Mrs Ward, because it revealed a potential for human depravity which could not be explained by her system of ideas. 'Does not the difference between us on the question of sin come very much to this—that to you the great fact in the world and in the history of man, is *sin*,— to me, *progress*?' she had asked Gladstone in 1888.[2] In the Epilogue to *Fields of Victory* one can observe her bewilderment as she wrestles unsuccessfully with this disturbing problem: 'Germany has done things in this war which shame civilization, and seem to make a mockery of all ideas of human progress. But yet!—we must still believe in them; or the sun will go out in heaven' (p. 265).

The novels written during the War years likewise displayed a new sombreness. In *Missing* (1917), for example, Mrs Ward returned to the paradise of her childhood, that stretch of the Rotha between Rydal Water and Fox How. The Westmorland scene was never more beautifully evoked by Mrs Ward, for her landscape is filled with powerful Arnoldian and Wordsworthian memories. The heroine lives in the lodging house near Rydal Mount where Dr Arnold and his family once stayed; there are walks up Loughrigg Fell; the moss-gatherer (p. 50) is a reincarnation of Wordsworth's leech-gatherer; the passing hours are marked by the striking of the bell in Rydal chapel, where the Arnolds and Wordsworths formerly worshipped together. Even the dreams of Nelly Sarratt are shaped by unconsciously recalled scenes from *The Prelude*: 'And through the night she was haunted, sleeping and waking, by the image of the solitary boat rocking gently on the moonlit lake, the water lapping its sides. She saw herself and George adrift in it—sailing into—disappearing in—that radiance of silver light' (p. 35).

There is a haunting, melancholy quality to the novel. The modern world, with all of its woes, has at last encroached upon Westmorland; even here there are signs everywhere of the War—hospitals, wounded soldiers, and, most significantly, an aeroplane that violates the eternal silence of the sky above the fells. Mrs Ward unceasingly praises the moral influence of the War upon the people of England, arguing that it was increasing solidarity between the classes and ennobling their aims. But there is a sad undercurrent beneath the surface of the story, a feeling of revulsion and disillusionment which belies the repeated expressions of optimism by the author. 'After the war!' exclaims one character—'what sort of world shall we tumble into!' (p. 102).

The greatest strength of Mrs Ward's religion was that she believed in it, and acted upon it, with a glowing enthusiasm that could be matched by few orthodox Christians. Perhaps its most conspicuous deficiency was that it was the product of a middle-class, primarily academic environment which had sheltered her from the more extreme manifestations of human cruelty and suffering. Mrs Ward's religious synthesis, impassioned and impressive as it undoubtedly was, often strikes us as being too comfortably bourgeois Victorian in its ignorance of how most people on this planet live and die. It is too much imbued with that groundless optimism about the inevitable progress of civilization which weakened so much liberal religious thinking of the last century. Though the War destroyed such illusions for most of Mrs Ward's contemporaries, she continued to reassert the old articles of faith until her death. Hence the widening gulf between her and younger readers. As William Inge observed, 'If you marry the Spirit of your generation, you will be a widow in the next.'[3]

It is also worth noticing that *Missing*, despite its wartime setting, is in its broad outlines almost identical to Mrs Ward's earliest published tale, 'A Westmoreland Story'. Nelly Sarratt, guilty of disloyalty (though not of actual sexual infidelity) to her soldier husband, must, after his death, atone for her sin by taking up nursing—just as Dorothy Morden had in 1870. That the pattern of one of Mrs Ward's latest stories should resemble so closely that of her first surely suggests the degree to which her psychological development had been arrested. Mrs Humphry Ward, so intellectually fearless and so emotionally timid, is the classic example of the Victorian psyche at war with itself.

Ironically, it was probably the very success of *Robert Elsmere* which helped to retard her personal and literary growth. No critic has ever provided a more astute or chilling summary of her career than Mrs Ward herself did in these prophetic words in *Miss Bretherton*:

Her instantaneous success—dependent as it was on considerations wholly outside those of dramatic [for 'dramatic' read 'literary'] art— had denied her all the advantages which are to be won from struggle and from laborious and gradual conquest. And more than this, it deprived her of an ideal; it had tended to make her take her own performance as the measure of the good and the possible. For, naturally, it was too much to expect that she should herself analyse truly the sources and reasons of her popularity. She must inevitably believe that some, at least, of it was due to her dramatic talent in itself. (p. 294)

And yet though *Robert Elsmere*, in a curious manner, blighted all of Mrs Ward's other novels, it is a remarkable book which belongs to a select group of the most moving religious autobiographies in English literature. For modern readers it derives its power, at least in part, from our awareness that her story of a doubting Anglican clergyman, while told from a sometimes narrowly Victorian perspective, is emblematic of that withering of the old faiths which has transformed Western culture in our century and has fundamentally altered the inner landscapes of our lives. Whatever its shortcomings, *Robert Elsmere* towers like the broken figure of Ozymandias over the Victorian spiritual wasteland, casting a long shadow upon the sands that stretch towards the twentieth century.

Appendix A
THE *ROBERT ELSMERE* NOTEBOOK

This notebook (owned by the Honnold Library, Claremont University), which is discussed in Chapter 6, has a dark blue cover and is 115 x 154 mm in size. In addition to the material transcribed below, the notebook contains lists of Westmorland dialect words, a description of a visit to Fox How in October 1885, financial accounts, and extensive notes on Biblical criticism. I have not recorded these, though the dialect words and notes on Biblical criticism are probably related to the novel. (I have, however, included some passages from *Supernatural Religion* and Renan's *Vie de Jésus* that seem to bear more directly on *Robert Elsmere*.)

The first portion of the notebook (ending 'in its austerest & simplest & yet deepest form') was probably written shortly after the experience it describes; the other notes, which are scattered at random throughout the remaining pages of the notebook, were evidently composed as the novel was in progress. I have transcribed these notes in the order in which they appear, but it should be kept in mind that they may not have been written in this exact sequence. I have retained Mrs Ward's spelling and punctuation, except that in the first section I have substituted full stops for dashes at the ends of sentences. Any necessary annotation has been placed within square brackets. Since the chapter numbers of *Robert Elsmere* were altered several times, I have annotated such references by supplying the chapter numbers of the published version.

One final minor observation: the name of Robert's wife appears here as both 'Catherine' and 'Catharine' because Mrs Ward did not finally settle upon the former spelling until October 1887.

Journey to the Lakes May 29-June 3, 1885. Drove up Long Sleddale valley June 2nd. Details noted for future use. Lower end of the valley uninteresting; green sloping sides divided by stone walls, and dotted at intervals with farm house[s]. Clear stream [the River Sprint] running down the middle, masses of white heckberry flowering along the road, & in the little enclosures of trees round the farm. One house [which becomes in *Elsmere* 'Burwood Farm', the home of the Leyburns] on the further side of the stream, on a projecting spur of land with a larch wood behind. Grey roof, grey house, except for a white washed front & white edges to the windows. Sycamores & Scotch firs sheltering the house. Level with the house & under the same roof the barns. General snug well to do air. Rough garden stretching up the fell behind.

A tiny hamlet called Little London stretching up along a tributary stream. Grey walls a few trees—must be austere indeed in winter or wet weather.

Towards the head of the valley the scenery gets wilder. Great crags on either side, between a rounded receding mountain with a great fold in it along which winds the mountain path which connects the valley with Haweswater.

Before the head is reached the carriage road crosses the river by a bridge & practically comes to an end in the hamlet of Sad Ghyll. The hamlet consists of three farm houses. High Sad Ghyll, Middle Sad Ghyll and Low Sad Ghyll [which in the novel becomes 'High Ghyll', the home of Mary Backhouse]. Behind them a beautiful piece of hazel planting stretches up the fell, broken with rocks crowned with birches [*sic*] trees.

The path to Kentmere passes behind the houses, skirts the plantation & then enters an open piece of fell. On the right a stretch of boggy ground, studded with alders & brightened in May by the pink blossoms of the Primula Farinosa, rises to some high birch crowned rocks. The road winds upwards sometimes beside a little stream adorned in a late spring with a poetical medley of flowers. In one corner a tiny waterfall & in the little green corner beside the stream primroses[,] purples, orchises, & windflowers star the ground, while on the bank opposite are fern & white patches of windflower. The path winds round & up into a heathery moorland tract out of sight of the valley, & which ultimately leads to the descent into Kentmere. [Robert and Catherine become engaged on this fell.]

The farm houses, built of grey stone, & grey roofed, some white washed. A few copper beeches make in spring bright splashes of colour in the tree groups mainly composed of sycamores & larches which protect the farms. Beyond the hamlet the road goes up into the furthest recess of the valley, overhung by crags & aiming at the sunnier & rounder hills over which lies the road of exit. The river runs beside and even in the finest weather the clouds have a tendency to come down in a long level sweep along the brow of Goat Crag.

The farm (Low Sad Ghyll)[–]a sweet faced woman with perfect simplicity of manner & a rather loud voice presiding at tea in the kitchen[.] Kitchen has a rough oak cabinet, a long deal table & a small round table drawn near the fire with a white cloth on it for meals.

Meal consists of tea home-made bread—cream, a sort of currant cake —rhubarb puffs.

Two children, rather thin faced & sharp featured, but pretty,—blue eyes, bright complexions, shy but friendly, the Westmoreland type. The woman a native of Kentmere. Which does she prefer. Cannot tell. Soom say Long Sleddale is t'best, soom stand oof for Kentmere. At Kentmere t'houses are more togither. The children have to be sent two miles to school.

Parlour of the farm, fine mahogany table with flaps brightly polished, mahogany cupboard, pretty old brass fender, a few pictures of ministers, almanacks &c—a sewing machine.

Church modern, with grave yard round it towards the middle of the valley. Small grey parsonage with garden. Clergyman busy on a low church commentary on the book of Esther.

Curious mound near upper end of valley, looks like old burial mountain surmounted by one blasted pine.

Masses of white heckberry, a few plantations, where the young wood in all the variety of its May finery[?] is interspersed with carpets of blue bells—delicate iridescent effect. Loneliness of the hill sides— over their green bare tops lies the remote valley of Bannisdale in which there is no house. Farms of course entirely pastoral. Piece of ploughed land unknown in the valley.

Names in the valley—Thornburgh—Leyburn. [These names do not appear on any of the gravestones today in Longsleddale churchyard.] Sawing mill at the entrance of the valley.

Bobbin mill higher up now disused. Small wooden bridge leading to it. Gentleman leading his horse across it thirty years ago—the horse slipped dragged the man with him over the brink, horse killed man mortally injured.

Ideas for characters—

The girl Catherine Leyburn—her father the son of a statesman[–] educated at Kendal grammar school. Then at Queen's College becomes a fellow, a school master, a house-master[−] saves money. Dr. [John] Percival [1834-1918; son of a Westmorland farmer, became President of Trinity College, Oxford (1879), headmaster of Rugby (1887), and Bishop of Hereford (1895)] type. His brother succeeds to the family property[−] becomes embarrassed, wants to sell it & emigrate. The younger brother buys it, keeps the house field & garden lets off the land & retires there with joy in his summer vacations. Some cousins yet left in the valley. Remembers days when the clergyman like Robert Walker [1709-1802; Cumberland cleric and schoolmaster of simple habits who was admired by Wordsworth] taught school in chapel with the altar for his desk. Meditative poetic character[−] its defects. Great strength of will, but lack of tact & knowledge of men. Austerity & purity of aim. Married a gentle woman with a certain restlessness & weakness about her, a habit of depending on the last speaker & taking the tone of the society about her with a good deal of eagerness, but made beautiful by the strength of her affections which gain upon her & make the whole life lovely.

Had certain accomplishments which had first attracted her husband [−] a certain gentle taste for music & drawing.

The husband dies leaves a few hundreds a year & the house. She is lost & helpless but the eldest daughter supports her—description of Catherine. Two other girls—one like Nelly [Eleanor Mary Arnold, afterwards Wodehouse and Sandhurst (1861-1934), Matthew Arnold's second daughter] —round soft amusing, gentle without deeper life, but capable of a great sympathetic interest in that of other[s]. Placid, idle, popular. Catherine has qualms about her sometimes—yet delights in her. The other, enthusiastic artistic pretty in an irregular red-haired way. The face of the district—great musician. Nothing else real to her. Both these are bored in the valley—Catherine alone is perfectly happy.

What Catherine does. Her friendship with the old clergyman—she helps him in his literary work. She teaches school. She wanders, reads Madame Guyon [French mystic (1648-1717); see *Elsmere*, ii, 137, 142], Thomas à Kempis, the Bible—Wordsworth—Carlyle—how the strong nature is fed & built up. The stores of tenderness towards the mother, the sisters the people about.

The accident on the bridge[−] Catherine's share in it. (Reminiscent of the death of Winwood Reade.) [On Reade's death, see Warren S. Smith, *The London Heretics 1870-1914* (New York, 1968), p. 25.] Her intellectual limitations[.] Prejudice made beautiful in her. Religion intertwined with her every fibre. The watch over self.

Two chief notes in her *affection*, extraordinary sensitiveness to human love, human claims human suffering—*religious passion*, in its austerest & simplest & yet deepest form.

English Dialect Society
  Series C
  Original Glossaries
Dialect of Cumberland
  Wm Dickinson
  Trübner & Co Ludgate Hill
    1878.

Dress of parson [possibly the vicar of Longsleddale church]
  Drab fustian coat—
  corduroy knee breeches—
  checked linen shirt
  blue duffle coat large buttons
  waistc[oat] of [illegible abbreviation]
  drab corduroy knee breeches—

Books wanted
  Demos— [George Gissing, *Demos: A Story of English Socialism*, 3 vols (1886).]
  Joe Payne— [1808-76; writer and lecturer on modern educational methods.]
  Darwin—
  Grant Allen— [1848-99; novelist, poet, and writer on scientific subjects.]
  Stirling [*sic*]— [John Sterling (1806-44), poet and Anglican clergyman who left the Church; presumably the book in question is Carlyle's *Life* (1851).]

Contemporary vol. 41. article on Mr. Green [R. L. Nettleship and James Bryce, 'Professor T. H. Green: In Memoriam', *Contemporary Review*, xli (May 1882), 857-81.]

Ideas for characters in vol III
  A character suggested by Macaulay's description of Lady Holland [see G. O. Trevelyan, *The Life and Letters of Lord Macaulay* (New York, 1877), i, 191 ff.; cf. *Elsmere*, i, 429]—the dinners at Holland House—say Lady Albandale—Takes up Robert—he meets Madame de Netteville there.

Notes
Macaulay sees Hume put up in a bookseller's window & advertised as
"an introduction to Macaulay." [See Trevelyan, *op. cit.*, ii, 221.]
His description of [Henry Peter] Brougham. [John W.] Croker.
[Samuel] Rogers– [See index to Trevelyan, *op. cit.*]

―――――――――

Ideas for chapters–in Vol II
Chapter on confinement [Chapter 19] should contain a paragraph
on Robert's intellectual growth. Converging pressure of science &
history. Begins to descend to first principles to approach the realisa-
tion of that choice which the majority of us go through life without
realising & wh.[ich] is perhaps never realised without renunciation.
The choice between law & exception between monism & dualism.
Conceals it from Catharine.

―――――――――

Notes of alterations in vol II
Mrs. Leyburn & Agnes not able to come back at Christmas because
of Mrs. Leyburn's health [Chapter 23].
Langham's relation to Robert at end of visit [Chapter ?15].
Description of Rose in first chapter vol II [Chapter ?14].
Langham's going to London[–] prepare it [Chapter 16].
Sharpen Squire's onslaught on Robert [Chapter ?17].
Catharine to go up to London at April to receive Rose [Chapter 23].
Rose's disappointment at not being able to stay in London. Cath-
arine's letter to Robert on the subject.
Robert to say to Catharine in Chap XVII [Chapter 28], I have seen
Grey. He sent me back to you & I have come.
? Transfer Henslowe piece originally written for Chap. XIX [Chapter
23] to Chap. XII [Chapter 30].
? Shorten Chap. X [Chapter ?20].
Expand love scene between Rose & Langham [Chapter 16].

―――――――――

La force est la servé du monde & non pas l'opinion–mais l'opinion est
celle qui use de la force–
                    Pascal–
Use in conv.[ersation] betw.[een] Flaxman & Robert. [The sentence
does not appear in the published version of the novel.]

―――――――――

England understands nothing of the truth of Strauss because she is "si lourdement raisonnable." Vie de Jesus Introd. p. XXII. [Ernest Renan, *Vie de Jésus* (Paris, 1863).]

Murray Edwardes must be brought in the New Association [i.e., the New Brotherhood of Christ] somehow [Chapter 49]. Difficulty about the chapel.

Mr. Flaxman's character—

---

p. 267 French—The Squire & Langham. [In Chapter 18 of the *Elsmere* MS. (Honnold), the Squire and Langham discuss a reception at the French Academy.]

---

points that affect Robert—
  points of testimony—
  Critical judgement—quotation from the O.[ld] T.[estament] Jewish book on the subject. Theory of quotation.
  superstitious belief
    Deutsch's article— [Samuel M. Deutsch (1837-1909), German church historian.]
  demoniac possession—angels
  "Twelve legions of angels"— ['Thinkest thou that I cannot now pray to my Father, and he shall presently give me more than twelve legions of angels?'—*Matthew* 26:53.]
  Harnack's article— [Adolf Harnack (1851-1930), liberal German church historian and theologian whom Mrs Ward later met.]
  ? First subject of conversation between S[quire] & R[obert]— [Chapter 22].
  R[obert]'s sermon—"This day is this scripture fulfilled in your ears["]—[Chapter 22; cf. *Luke* 4:21].
  The Squire's comments—You haven't made a special study of these things? [Chapter 22.]

Supernatural Religion. [Walter R. Cassels, *Supernatural Religion*, 3 vols (London, 1874-77).]
  Mentions of demons in the N.[ew] T.[estament]. Look up passages given p. 111—
  Tertullian's view of the book of Enoch, p. 103—
  The angel at the pool of Bethesda p. 113—
  Matthew XII.27—
  Miraculous beliefs in Josephus p. 119
  Tertullion p. 126
  Origen p. 129

Note for the dedication of R.E.

Shelley's Alastor. Eng. Poets IV. 372 [T. H. Ward, ed., *The English
Poets*, 4 vols (1880).]

But Thou art fled
Like some frail exhalation which the dawn
Robes in its golden beams,—Ah thou hast fled!
The brave, the gentle, & the beautiful,
The child of grace & genius [ll. 686-90]

Appendix B

SALES OF *ROBERT ELSMERE*

The following is based primarily upon unpublished correspondence between Mrs Ward and George Smith, articles in *Publishers' Weekly*, and advertisements in various periodicals.

The first British edition (Smith, Elder) of *Robert Elsmere*, consisting of 500 copies, was issued on 24 February 1888, and a second edition was required by 10 April. Editions of 500 copies each followed at intervals of approximately a fortnight throughout the spring and summer. On 26 July Smith, Elder published a crown 8vo. edition selling for 6s., with advance orders for 5,000 copies. During August 7,000 copies of this cheaper edition were sold, and between September and December sales averaged 4,000 copies per month. By 20 November 1888, 29,500 copies of the Smith, Elder editions had been sold. In December a 'Library Editon' (12s.) was also issued. It was estimated that by March 1889 between 30,000 and 40,000 copies of the various editions had been sold in Britain, with sales continuing at the rate of 700 copies a week.

The authorized American edition ($1.25) was issued on 28 July 1888 by Macmillan, but numerous pirated editions, including the following (with prices and approximate dates of publication indicated), soon dominated the market: J. W. Lovell (50¢, August), Belford, Clarke ($1.25, August), G. Munro (40¢, September), Ogilvie (50¢, December), Rand, McNally (25¢, January 1889), Ivers (25¢, January), Hurst ($1.25, January), and J. Alden (cloth 25¢, paperback 15¢, January). In the meantime Macmillan also published a paperback edition (50¢) in September and a two-volume edition ($3) in December. In November 1888 it was reported that some 100,000 copies of all editions of *Robert Elsmere* had been sold in the U.S.A.; by the following month that figure had risen to 150,000. In March 1889 the estimate was 200,000 copies.

Figures for sales in America after 1889 are scarce, but it is clear that in Britain at least Smith, Elder continued to dispose of surprisingly large numbers of copies year after year. On 26 February 1890 they issued a cheaper crown 8vo. edition (2s. 6d.), and within nine months 20,000 copies had been sold. The following year (1891) 23,000 more were purchased. Altogether 70,500 copies of various Smith, Elder editions had been sold by 1891. Beyond this point, the records of Smith, Elder sales among Mrs Ward's papers also become very incomplete, yet, to choose a mere random example, 767 copies were sold during 1896. In 1907 an even less expensive edition sold 100,000 copies within a year.

Mrs Ward estimated in 1909 that nearly a million copies of the book had been circulated in English-speaking countries. When one adds the numerous translations, the Nelson's Library edition that was in print for many decades, and a recent paperback reprint by the University of Nebraska Press, then, at a conservative guess, total sales of *Robert Elsmere* have by now probably approached a million and a quarter.

NOTES

Places of publication are given only for books published outside the U.K. Quotations from Mrs Ward's books are taken from either the Westmoreland Edition of her writings (i.e., those novels published between 1884 and 1911) or the first English editions. Except where otherwise noted, correspondence between Mrs Ward and George and Reginald Smith is in the Honnold Library; her literary notebooks are also in the Honnold; Gertrude Ward's diary is owned by Basil Ward, Esq.; correspondence between Mrs Ward and the Macmillan Company is in British Library Add. MS. 54928; and correspondence between her and members of her family is in the Library of Pusey House.

The following abbreviations have been used:

'Gladstone's Review'	Peterson, William S. 'Gladstone's Review of *Robert Elsmere*: Some Unpublished Correspondence'. *Review of English Studies*, n.s. xxi (November 1970), 442-61.
Life	Trevelyan, Janet P. *The Life of Mrs. Humphry Ward* (1923).
'Six Letters'	Peterson, William S. 'Mrs Humphry Ward on *Robert Elsmere*: Six New Letters'. *Bulletin of the New York Public Library*, lxxiv (November 1970), 587-97.
W.R.	Ward, Mary A. *A Writer's Recollections* (1918).
B.L.	British Library.
Honnold	The Honnold Library, Claremont University (California).
Moorman	Mrs Mary Moorman.

| Pusey House | The Library of Pusey House, Oxford. |
| Texas | The Stark Library, University of Texas |

A.W.	Arnold Ward (Mrs Ward's son).
G.S.	George Smith.
J.A.	Julia Arnold (Mrs Ward's mother).
M.W.	Mary A. (Mrs Humphry) Ward. (For the sake of convenience, this set of initials is also used in identifying letters written before her marriage.)
R.S.	Reginald Smith.
T.A.	Thomas Arnold the Younger (Mrs Ward's father).
T.H.W.	Thomas Humphry Ward.
W.T.A.	William T. Arnold (Mrs Ward's brother).

CHAPTER ONE

1. *Life*, 307.
2. William R. Inge, *Diary of a Dean: St. Paul's 1911-1934* (1949), 54.
3. Ellis, *Impressions and Comments*, 3rd Ser. (Boston, 1924), 115.
4. Maugham, *The Vagrant Mood* (1952), 194-5.
5. Doyle, *Memories and Adventures* (Boston, 1924), 306; 'Mrs. Humphry Ward at the Author's Club', *Queen*, cix (25 May 1901), 827.
6. Michael Holroyd, *Lytton Strachey: A Critical Biography* (1967), i, 443.
7. Charles R. Sanders, *The Strachey Family, 1588-1932: Their Writings and Literary Associations* (Durham, N.C., 1953), 292.
8. West, review of *A Writer's Recollections*, *Bookman* (London), lv (December 1918), 106-7.
9. *Letters of George Gissing to Edward Bertz, 1887-1903*, ed. Arthur C. Young (New Brunswick, N.J., 1961), 145.
10. *Letters of Arnold Bennett*, ed. James Hepburn (1968), ii, 16; Bennett, *Books and Persons* (1917), 52.
11. Phelps, 'The Novels of Mrs. Humphry Ward', *Forum*, xli (April 1909), 323-31; reprinted in his *Essays on Modern Novelists* (New York, 1914), 191-207.
12. Lawrence P. Jacks, *Life and Letters of Stopford Brooke* (1917), ii, 406.
13. E. Merrill Root, *Frank Harris* (New York, 1947), 93.
14. Mrs Ward and John Morley, 'Anthony Trollope', *Macmillan's Magazine*, xlix (November 1883), 47-56.
15. G.S. to M.W., 8/3/90.
16. *Daphne*, 235.
17. *Eleanor*, 289.
18. *Marcella*, i, 435.
19. *W.R.*, 214.

20. M.W. to T.H.W., 24/7/90.
21. M.W. to Campbell Clarke, 16/11/92 (Fales Library, New York University).
22. *Coryston Family*, 128.
23. *Delia Blanchflower*, 138.
24. Rev. of *Marius, Macmillan's Magazine*, lii (June 1885), 136.
25. M.W. to J.A., 23/4/86.
26. Bell, *Landmarks* (New York, 1929), 98.
27. Trilling, *Matthew Arnold* (New York, 1955), 287.
28. Gladstone, ' "Robert Elsmere" and the Battle of Belief', *Nineteenth Century*, xxiii (May 1888), 767.
29. Introduction to *Elsmere*, I, xiv.
30. Acton to Gladstone, 5/4/88 (B.L. Add. MS. 44094).
31. *Cousin Philip*, 82.
32. *Macmillan's Magazine*, lii (June 1885), 134.

CHAPTER TWO

1. Gladstone to Mary Drew, 17/4/88 (B.L. Add. MS. 46221).
2. M.W. to G.S., 6/10/96.
3. Notebook entitled 'Journal of My First Visit to Scotland', entry dated 23/6/67.
4. [Hutton], 'Dr. Arnold after Fifty Years', *Spectator*, lxviii (18 June 1892), 840.
5. More, 'Oxford, Women, and God', *Shelburn Essays* (1904; reprinted New York, 1967), xi, 282.
6. Jowett to A. P. Stanley, 1856, in Evelyn Abbott and Lewis Campbell, *Life and Letters of Benjamin Jowett* (1897), i, 285.
7. *Letters of Matthew Arnold*, ed. G. W. E. Russell (1895), ii, 23.
8. Arnold, 'The Sign of the Prophet Jonah', *The Christian Life* (1842), 15-16.
9. Newman to Keble, 13/6/44, in *Correspondence of John Henry Newman with John Keble and Others, 1839-1845*, ed. J. Bacchus (1917), p. 321.
10. Arnold 'Early Roman History' (1825), *Miscellaneous Works* (New York, 1845), 398. See also Merton A. Christensen, 'Thomas Arnold's Debt to German Theologians', *Modern Philology*, lv (August 1957), 14-20, and Eugene L. Williamson, Jr., *The Liberalism of Thomas Arnold* (University, Ala., 1964).
11. [Hutton], 'Robert Elsmere', *Spectator*, lxi (7 April 1888), 479.
12. Arnold to J. T. Coleridge, 18/11/35, in Arthur P. Stanley, *Life and Correspondence of Thomas Arnold, D.D.* (1842), Chap. 8. (Letters in the *Life of Arnold* will be cited by date and chapter number, as the book went through so many editions and reprints.)
13. *Principles of Church Reform*, ed. M. J. Jackson and J. Rogan (1962), 87.
14. Newman to R. F. Wilson, 18/3/33, in *Letters and Correspondence of John Henry Newman During His Life in the English Church*, ed. Anne Mozley (1890), i, 329.
15. Arnold to an old pupil, 30/10/41, in *Life of Arnold*, Chap. 10.
16. Reprinted in Arnold Whitridge, *Dr. Arnold of Rugby*, with an Introduction by Sir Michael Sadler (New York, 1928), 215-35.
17. Newman to R. H. Froude, 15/6/34, in *Letters and Correspondence of John Henry Newman*, ii, 42.
18. Charles L. Graves, *Life and Letters of Sir George Grove* (1903), 219.
19. Arthur C. Benson, *Life of Edward White Benson* (1899), ii, 721-2.
20. Arnold to J. Hearn, 17/1/42, in *Life of Arnold*, Chap. 9.
21. *Henry Crabb Robinson on Books and Their Writers*, ed. Edith J. Morley (1938), ii, 476.

22. Arnold to J. T. Coleridge, 5/4/32, in *Life of Arnold*, Chap. 6.

23. Mary Wordsworth to Jane Marshall, 27/12/[34], in *Letters of Mary Wordsworth, 1800-1855*, ed. Mary E. Burton (1958), 137.

24. Arnold to his mother, 2/8/69, in *Letters of Matthew Arnold*, ii, 21.

25. Letter dated 6/11/50, in Elizabeth Gaskell, *Life of Charlotte Brontë*, ed. C. K. Shorter, vol. vii of the Haworth Edition of the Brontë sisters' works (1900), 493.

26. *Letters of Matthew Arnold*, i, 106.

27. Arnold, *Passages in a Wandering Life* (1900), 38.

28. William Knight, *Life of William Wordsworth* (1889), iii, 225.

29. Matthew Arnold's preface to *Poems of Wordsworth* (1891), xxvi.

30. Arnold to Chevalier Bunsen, 26/5/40, in *Life of Arnold*, Chap. 9.

31. Mitford to Boner, 11/10/47, in *Mary Russell Mitford: Correspondence with Charles Boner and John Ruskin*, ed. Elizabeth Lee (1914), 77.

32. Frances J. Woodward, *The Doctor's Disciples: A Study of Four Pupils of Arnold of Rugby* (1954), 180.

33. *Henry Crabb Robinson on Books and Their Writers*, ii, 566.

34. *New Zealand Letters of Thomas Arnold the Younger*, ed. James Bertram (Wellington, 1966), 114n.

35. *W.R.*, 57.

36. Introduction to *Miss Bretherton*, 223.

37. Owned by Mr Arnold Whitridge.

38. *Complete Prose Works of Matthew Arnold*, ed. R. H. Super (Ann Arbor, Mich., 1968), vi, 142-3.

39. Leonard Huxley, *The House of Smith Elder* (1923), 191.

40. Frank Harris, *His Life and Adventures: An Autobiography*, with an Introduction by Grant Richards (1947), 296.

41. *W.R.*, 235.

42. *Complete Prose Works* (1962), iii, 279-80.

43. William T. Arnold [and Mrs Ward], 'Thomas Arnold the Younger', *Century Magazine*, lxvi (May 1903), 119.

44. T.A. to Jane Arnold, 8/8/48, in *New Zealand Letters*, 72.

45. T.A. to J. C. Shairp, 1/11/47, in *New Zealand Letters*, 210.

46. *Passages in a Wandering Life*, 153-5.

47. Arnold and Ward, 'Thomas Arnold the Younger', 127.

48. *W.R.*, 19.

49. T.A. to W. A. Greenhill, 21/5/91 (Bodleian MS. Autogr. e. 5).

50. Newman to Maria Giberne, 11/2/68, in *Letters and Diaries of John Henry Newman*, ed. C. S. Dessain and Thomas Gornall, S.J. (1973), xxiv, 34.

51. *W.R.*, 99, 136.

52. Newman to Giberne (see n. 50, above).

53. 21/4/65 (Birmingham Oratory).

54. 23/4/65, in Newman, *Letters and Diaries*, xxi, 450.

55. M.W. to J.A., [20/6/65].

56. Newman to Giberne (see n. 50, above).

57. Julian Huxley, *Memories* (1970), 17.

58. Mark Pattison's diary, entry dated 11/5/76 (Bodleian MS. Pattison 130).

59. T.A. to T.H.W., 14/10/76 (Moorman).

60. *Ibid.* See also Newman, *Letters and Diaries*, xxviii, 124n.

61. M.W. to T.A., 23/10/76.

62. Matthew Arnold to A. P. Stanley, 13/5/80, in David J. DeLaura, *Hebrew and Hellene in Victorian England: Newman, Arnold, and Pater* (Austin, Tex., 1969), 6. At the time of his second conversion to Roman Catholicism, Julia had

written an extraordinarily abusive letter to Newman; see Newman, *Letters and Diaries*, xxviii, 157n.
63. M.W. to T.H.W., 30/8/81.
64. 23/10/76.
65. M.W. to W.T.A., 24/3/97; *Life*, 151.
66. T.A. to F. J. Furnivall, 14/5/91 (Huntington Library).
67. *Life*, 174.
68. M.W. to W.T.A., 10/11/00.
69. Notebook entry dated 5/4/02.

CHAPTER THREE

1. Besant to Ross, 7/8/88, in *Robert Ross: Friend of Friends*, ed. Margery Ross (1952), 356.
2. *W.R.*, 100.
3. 17/1/55 (Moorman).
4. Clara Boyle, 'Mrs. Humphry Ward' (letter), *Manchester Guardian*, 19 June 1951, 6. See also T. C. Down, 'Schooldays with Miss Clough', *Cornhill Magazine*, 3rd Ser., xliviii (June 1920), 674-84.
5. Margaret L. Woods, 'Mrs. Humphry Ward: A Sketch from Memory', *Quarterly Review*, ccxxxiv (July 1920), 148.
6. *Milly and Olly*, 74.
7. M.W. to J.A., 4/3/60.
8. M.W. to A.W., 9/8/98.
9. Dr. Arnold to George Cornish, 6/7/39, in *Life of Arnold*, Chap. 9.
10. *Elsmere* MS., Chap. 20 (Honnold).
11. 'Mrs. Humphry Ward on Public Libraries', *The Times*, 12 Apr. 1897, 15.
12. Margaret L. Mare and Alicia C. Percival, *Victorian Best-Seller: The World of Charlotte M. Yonge* (1948), 200; Yonge to M.W., 16/12[?70] (owned by Mrs Georgina Battiscombe).
13. Maison, *The Victorian Vision: Studies in the Religious Novel* (New York, 1961), 37.
14. Notebook (Honnold).
15. Yonge to M.W., 21/9/[?70] (owned by Mrs Georgina Battiscombe).
16. R.S. to M.W., 26/7/01.
17. *A Complete Guide to the English Lakes*, 3rd edn (Windermere, n.d.) [1st edn, 1855], 55.
18. 3/8/07 (Harvard College Library).
19. Mrs Ward, 'Nathaniel Hawthorne', *Cornhill Magazine*, n.s. xvii (August 1904), 167.
20. 1/10/69, in *Life*, 25.
21. Edith C. Rickards, *Felicia Skene of Oxford: A Memoir* (1902), 133.
22. *Marriage of William Ashe*, 289.

CHAPTER FOUR

1. M.W. to G.S., 7/8/92.
2. N.d. [?1865] (Pusey House).
3. Pattison, 'A Chapter of University History' (1875), *Essays*, ed. Henry Nettleship (1889), i, 310.
4. Pattison, *Memoirs*, [ed. Emilia Pattison] (1885), 236.
5. Louise Creighton, *Life and Letters of Mandell Creighton* (1904), i, 48.
6. Sayce, *Reminiscences* (1923), 35.

7. Kingsley to A. P. Stanley, 19/2/61, in *Charles Kingsley: His Letters and Memories of His Life*, ed. Mrs Kingsley (1884), 242.

8. *W.R.*, 97.

9. John O. Johnston, *Life and Letters of Henry Parry Liddon*... (1904), 254.

10. Liddon to C. T. Redington, 2/11/82, in *ibid.*, 278.

11. *Ibid.*, 120.

12. 28/10/16 (Pusey House).

13. *W.R.*, 102.

14. Mrs Pattison to James Thursfield, 2/12/72 (Bodleian MS. Pattison 139).

15. Johnson, 'The First Beginnings, 1873-1900', *Lady Margaret Hall: A Short History*, ed. Gemma Bailey (1923), 29.

16. Sir Charles Dilke, 'Memoir', in Emilia (Pattison) Dilke, *The Book of the Spiritual Life* (New York, 1905), 22.

17. Betty Askwith, *Lady Dilke: A Biography* (1969), 50.

18. 21/1/76 (Bodleian MS. Pattison 60).

19. *W.R.*, 105.

20. Pattison's engagement diaries, 1867-79 (Bodleian MSS. Pattison 20-32).

21. Pattison, *Sermons* (1885), 59.

22. Introduction to *Elsmere*, I, xxi.

23. Lionel A. Tollemache, *Recollections of Pattison* (1885), 6.

24. Francis C. Montague, 'Some Early Letters of Mark Pattison', *Bulletin of the John Rylands Library*, xviii (1934), 160-1.

25. Pattison's diaries (Bodleian MSS. Pattison 130-4).

26. *W.R.*, 106.

27. Reprinted in Pattison, *Essays*, ii, 42-118.

28. Newman to Charles Crawley, 6/3/61, in *Letters and Diaries of John Henry Newman*, xix, 475.

29. 'Calvin at Geneva' (1858), *Essays*, ii, 3-4.

30. *Memoirs*, 317.

31. *W.R.*, 106.

32. Pattison to Gertrude Tuckwell, 25/6/81 (B.L. Add. MS. 44886).

33. Bodleian MS. Pattison 144.

34. Mrs Pattison to Rosa Tuckwell, 30/7/84 (Bodleian MS. Pattison 140).

35. *W.R.*, 106.

36. Moncure Conway, *Autobiography: Memories and Experiences* (Boston, 1904), ii, 318.

37. Jowett to Florence Nightingale, 4/12/73, in Owen Chadwick, *The Victorian Church* (1970), ii, 143.

38. Jowett to A. J. Matthews, 23/4/89 (B.L. Add. MS. 34813).

39. Introduction to *Meynell*, vii.

40. M.W. to Anna Swanwick, 6/6/95 (Bodleian Walpole d. 19).

41. Jowett notebook No. 8 (1876-8), 97 (Jowett papers, Balliol College Library).

42. Bodleian MS. Pattison 112.

43. Symonds to Charlotte Green, 3/11/86, in *Letters of John Addington Symonds*, ed. Herbert M. Schueller and Robert L. Peters (Detroit, 1969), iii, 176.

44. Pattison, *Memoirs*, 167. Cf. *Elsmere*, i, 113.

45. Green's phrase (1861), in R. L. Nettleship, 'Memoir', *Works of T. H. Green* (1888), III, xxxv.

46. *Ibid.*, xlv.

47. *Ibid.*, xxxvi.

48. M.W. to Gladstone, 17/4/88, in 'Gladstone's Review', 459; cf. *Elsmere*, ii, 109.

49. M.W. to Gladstone, 15/4/88, in 'Gladstone's Review', 457.
50. Gladstone to M.W., 16/4/88, in *ibid.*, 458.
51. Sidgwick, MS. 'Reminiscences of T.H.G.' (Green papers, Balliol College Library).
52. 6/10/72, in *Henry Scott Holland . . . Memoir and Letters*, ed. Stephen Paget (1921), 65.
53. *Works*, iii, 230-52, 253-76. Cf. *Elsmere*, i, 105-7.
54. M.W. to Gladstone, 17/4/88, in 'Gladstone's Review', 459.
55. *Ibid.*
56. MS. note by A.W., 1925 (Pusey House).
57. *W.R.*, 105.
58. *W.R.*, 112.
59. Green to Louise von Glehn (afterwards Creighton), 6/3/71 (Bodleian MS. Eng. lett. e. 48).
60. *Elsmere* MS., Chaps. 37-8 (Honnold).
61. Taine to his wife, 4/6/71, in *Life and Letters of H. Taine, 1870-1892*, trans. E. Sparvel-Bayley (1908), 58.
62. M.W. to Mrs Thomson, 5/3/[01] (Fales Library, New York University).
63. T.H.W.'s diaries (Library of University College, London).
64. Knowles to Gladstone, 2/4/88, in 'Gladstone's Review', 447; Pattison's diary, entry dated 21/9/77.
66. *Life*, 28.
67. *W.R.*, 163.
68. *Life*, 106.

CHAPTER FIVE

[*The* Macmillan's Magazine *articles quoted in this chapter are listed chronologically in the bibliography.*]
1. M.W. to T.H.W., 26/3/97.
2. M.W. to T.H.W., 3/6/90.
3. 9/12/84 (Pusey House).
4. 4/3/88 (Honnold).
5. Freeman to Edith Thompson, 25/12/88, in W. R. W. Stephens, *Life and Letters of Edward A. Freeman* (1895), ii, 390.
6. Taine to his wife, 4/6/71, in *Life and Letters of H. Taine, 1870-1892*, 58.
7. *W.R.*, 151.
8. Humphry Sandwith to Allon, 15/1/79, in *Letters to a Victorian Editor: Henry Allon, Editor of the British Quarterly Review*, ed. Albert Peel (1929), 68-9.
9. M.W. to W.T.A., 10/9/81 and 24/12/81.
10. *W.R.*, 145n.
11. 26/4/[80].
12. M.W. to Macmillan, 18/10/82.
13. Morley to M.W., 22/3/83, in *Life*, 42.
14. 28/9/83 (Pusey House).
15. M.W. to Macmillan, 6/9/83.
16. M.W. to J.A., 2/1/87.
17. M.W. to J.A., [16/10/86].
18. 4/12/99 (Brotherton Collection, University of Leeds).
19. Introduction to *Elsmere*, I, xxxv.
20. M.W. to Mandell Creighton, 13/3/88, in 'Six Letters', 591.
21. R.S. to M.W., 19/1/06.
22. *Sartor Resartus*, ed. Charles F. Harrold (New York, 1937), 236.

23. Shorthouse to Margaret Evans, 11/7/81, in Sarah Shorthouse, *Life and Letters of J. H. Shorthouse* (1905), 133.

24. *Saturday Review*, liii (9 July 1881), 50-1. The review is unsigned, but both internal evidence and Shorthouse's attribution indicate that it is Mrs Ward's. See also W. S. Peterson, 'J. H. Shorthouse and Mrs. Humphry Ward: Two New Letters', *Notes and Queries*, n.s. xviii (July 1971), 259-61.

25. 2/6/85, in *Letters of Walter Pater*, ed. Lawrence Evans (1970), 60.

26. *Guardian*, xliii (28 March 1888), 468-9; reprinted in Pater, *Essays from "The Guardian"* (1901), 55-70.

27. Renan, *The Poetry of the Celtic Races, and Other Studies*, trans. William G. Hutchison [?1896], 195-6.

28. 5/3/84.

29. 'Amiel', *Essays in Criticism*, 2nd Ser., vol. iv of Arnold's *Works*, Edition de Luxe (1903), 220-42; Edmond Scherer, 'Mark Pattison and Amiel' (letter), *The Times*, 2 June 1885, 8.

30. Mrs Ward, 'English Men and Women of the 19th Century, No. XII: Elizabeth Barrett Browning', *Atalanta*, i (September 1888), 708.

31. M.W. to William Blackwood, 21/1/98 (National Library of Scotland, MS. 4683).

32. 2/4/88, in 'Gladstone's Review', 448.

33. Mrs Ward, 'Some Thoughts on Charlotte Brontë', *Charlotte Brontë, 1816-1916: A Centenary Memorial*, ed. Butler Wood (1917), 30-1.

34. W. S. Peterson, 'Henry James on "Jane Eyre" ', *Times Literary Supplement*, 30 July 1971, 919-20.

35. 22/9/[?95] (Pusey House).

36. 11/9/90.

37. Introduction to *Grieve*, I, xxxvi.

CHAPTER SIX

1. M.W. to J.A., 23/4/86.

2. Frederick Macmillan to M.W., 17/9/88 (Honnold).

3. Morley to M.W., 26/7/84 (Texas); Morley to M.W., 8/10/84 (Pusey House).

4. N.d. [c. December 1884] (Texas).

5. *Athenaeum*, 27 Dec. 1884, 857.

6. J.A. to M.W., 14/12/84.

7. Pusey House.

8. Texas.

9. M.W. to Craik, 2/3/[85].

10. Introduction to *Tressady*, I, xiv-xv. For George Smith's inaccurate recollections of this event, see Leonard Huxley, *The House of Smith Elder* (1923), 191-2.

11. 3/3/85, in Charles L. Morgan, *The House of Macmillan* (1943), 133-4.

12. 12/1/90.

13. Reprinted in *North American Review*, cxlviii (February 1889), 161-79.

14. Wordsworth, *The One Religion* (1881), *passim*.

15. *W.R.*, 184.

16. *Elsmere* MS., Chap. 25 (Honnold).

17. Norman W. Webster, *Joseph Locke: Railway Revolutionary* (1970), 133, 137, 142.

18. Introduction to *Elsmere*, I, xxviii.

19. Taine to M.W., 1/2/89, in *Elsmere*, ii, 569.

20. Warren S. Smith, *The London Heretics, 1870-1914* (New York, 1968), 25.

21. 15/8/90 (Huntington Library).

22. M.W. to G.S., 5/10/94.
23. 26/3/88, in 'Six Letters', 592.
24. M.W. to Ethel Arnold, [12/4/87].
25. Pusey House.
26. M.W. to Mrs Alfred Austin, 12/9/[87] (Yale University Library).
27. M.W. to G.S., 17/12/87.
28. Lyttelton to M.W., 19/1/88 and 25/2/88, in Edith S. Lyttelton, *Alfred Lyttelton: An Account of His Life* (1917), 159-60.

CHAPTER SEVEN

1. Pattison, *Essays*, ed. Henry Nettleship (1889), i, 304.
2. Arnold, *Complete Prose Works*, ed. R. H. Super (Ann Arbor, Mich., 1968), vi, 3.
3. The dates are established by internal evidence. (1) In the first year of the story, Robert becomes engaged to Catherine on Friday 23 June; between 1871 and 1893 this date falls on Friday only in 1882. (2) In June of the fourth year, Robert attends a gathering at Madame de Netteville's, where Lord Rupert is 'beaming under the recent introduction of a Land Purchase Act for Ireland' (ii, 403). On 20 May 1885, Gladstone gave notice to the introduction of a Land Purchase Bill, afterwards known as the Ashbourne Act; on 15 August the bill was passed by Parliament. (The chronology suggested by Professor Clyde Ryals in his paperback edition of *Robert Elsmere* [Lincoln, Nebr., 1967] is off by one year [p. xxvi].)
4. 13/3/88, in 'Six Letters', 590.
5. Introduction to *Elsmere*, I, xliii.
6. 28/11/88, in Margot Asquith, *Autobiography* (1920), i, 120-1.
7. Arthur Sidgwick and E. Mildred Sidgwick, *Henry Sidgwick: A Memoir* (1906), 488.
8. N.d. [1888], in 'Six Letters', 597.
9. Introduction to *Elsmere*, I, xlii.
10. M.W. to Hugh R. Haweis, 8/5/88, in 'Six Letters', 596.
11. Carlyle, *The Life of John Sterling*, with an Introduction by W. Hale White (1933), 44, 110.
12. Frederic W. Maitland, *The Life and Letters of Leslie Stephen* (1906), 133-44.
13. F. Reginald Statham, 'The Real Robert Elsmere', *National Review*, xxviii (October 1896), 252-61.
14. *W.R.*, 295-6.
15. 12/9/63, in Margaret A. Crowther, *Church Embattled: Religious Controversy in Mid-Victorian England* (Hamden, Conn., 1970), 18.
16. 'Obermann Once More', l. 238.
17. Matthew Arnold, 'Stanzas from the Grande Chartreuse', l. 171.
18. Incomplete corrected proofs are in the Honnold Library.
19. Clara Lederer, 'Mary Arnold Ward and the Victorian Ideal', *Nineteenth Century Fiction*, vi (December 1951), 205.
20. Introduction to *Marcella*, I, ix.
21. See John H. Sparrow, *Mark Pattison and the Idea of a University* (1967), 19-22. Pattison's library, which is similar to that of Squire Wendover, is described in the Sotheby, Wilkinson, and Hodge sale catalogue, *Catalogue of the Valuable Library of the Late Rev. Mark Pattison, B.D.* (27 July-3 Aug. 1885).
22. M.W. to Hugh R. Haweis, 8/5/88, in 'Six Letters', 596; Introduction to *Elsmere*, I, xxii.

23. 26/3/88, in 'Six Letters', 592.

24. Thomas Arnold, 'Christian Conviction', *The Christian Life: Its Hopes, Its Fears, and Its Close* (1842), 40.

25. For a description of her, see T. H. Ward, 'Reminiscences: Brasenose, 1864-72', in *Brasenose College Quarterly Monographs* (1909), ii, Pt II, 77-8.

26. The comparison has been suggested by Betty Askwith, *Lady Dilke: A Biography* (1969), 18. In Chap. 36 of the *Elsmere* MS. (Honnold) Langham tries to envision a life with Rose at Oxford, and the picture he conjures up is nearly identical to Mrs Pattison's unhappy experiences there.

27. James to M.W., 5/7/88, in Introduction to *Elsmere*, I, xxxix.

28. James to M.W., 3/7/88, in *ibid.*, I, xxxviii.

29. Alice Green to Beatrice Potter (afterwards Webb), 9/8/89, in Robert B. McDowell, *Alice Stopford Green: A Passionate Historian* (Dublin, 1967), 56.

30. M.W. to T.A., 27/12/86.

31. Knowles to Gladstone, 2/4/88, in 'Gladstone's Review', 448.

32. M.W. to Anna Swanwick, 6/6/95 (Bodleian Walpole d. 19).

33. M.W. to Skene, 18/1/89 (Fales Library, New York University).

CHAPTER EIGHT

[*Reviews of* Robert Elsmere *and sermons about it quoted in this chapter are listed chronologically in the bibliography.*]

1. James, 'Mrs. Humphry Ward', *English Illustrated Magazine*, ix (1892), 253-4.

2. See Appendix B, 'Sales of *Robert Elsmere*'.

3. *Life*, 78.

4. Conway, *Autobiography: Memories and Experiences* (Boston, 1904), ii, 158; Jowett to Margot Tennant, 11/3/89, in Margot Asquith, *Autobiography* (1920), i, 122-3; Alexander H. G. Craufurd, *Recollections of James Martineau* (1903), 138-9; Lady Gwendolen Stephenson, *Edward Stuart Talbot, 1844-1934* (1936), 52; Davidson to John Murray III, 7/11/88, in George Paston, *At John Murray's: Records of a Literary Circle, 1843-1892*, with a Preface by the Rt. Hon. Lord Ernle (1932), 284; Shorthouse to E. S. Talbot, Low Sunday, 1888, in Sarah Shorthouse, *Life and Letters of J. H. Shorthouse* (1905), 264-5; Julian Huxley, *Memories* (1970), 153.

5. Twain in an interview with Rudyard Kipling, as recorded in Kipling, *From Sea to Sea* (1900), ii, 162; vol. xviii in *Collected Works* (Garden City, N.Y., 1941).

6. Introduction to *Elsmere*, I, xxxvi-xl.

7. Leon Edel, *Henry James: The Middle Years* (Philadelphia, 1962), 207.

8. Taine to M.W., 1/2/89, in *Elsmere*, ii, 569; M.W. to R.S., 10/11/12.

9. M.W. to T.A., 28/1/89; M.W. to G.S., 24/5/93.

10. Scherer to M.W., 22/4/88 (Texas); Introduction to *Elsmere*, I, xiii.

11. *W.R.*, 245, 246, 248; *Life*, 68; *The Works of Robert G. Ingersoll*, Dresden Edition (Dresden, 1909-11), viii, 418.

12. 'Mr. Gladstone's New Preoccupation', *Pall Mall Gazette*, 7 April 1888, 1.

13. M.W. to W.T.A., 16/12/[85].

14. *Life*, 48.

15. B.L. Add. MS. 44232.

16. Gladstone to Mary Drew, [March 1888] in John Morley, *The Life of William Ewart Gladstone* (1903), iii, 356.

17. B.L. Add. MS. 44094.

18. *Ibid.*

19. 'Gladstone's Review', 447-8.

20. *Letters of Matthew Arnold, 1848-1888*, ed. G. W. E. Russell (New York, 1895), ii, 441.

21. 'Mr. Gladstone and "Robert Elsmere"', *Pall Mall Gazette*, 6 April 1888, 10.

22. 'Gladstone's Review', 453.

23. M.W. to T.H.W., 5/4/88, in *ibid.*, 449.

24. Pusey House.

25. Her notes of the interview are printed in 'Gladstone's Review', 449-52.

26. M.W. to T.H.W., 9/4/88, in *ibid.*, 452-3.

27. Gladstone to Mary Drew, 17/4/88 (B.L. Add. MS. 46221).

28. 'Gladstone's Review', 458.

29. G.S. to M.W., 18/4/88.

30. *Life*, 73.

31. B.L. Add. MS. 44094.

32. 28/6/88, in Lawrence P. Jacks, *Life and Letters of Stopford Brooke* (1917), ii, 398.

33. Honnold.

34. Introduction to *Elsmere*, I, xxxiv-xxxv.

35. *Nineteenth Century*, xxv (March 1889), 454-80; reprinted in *Elsmere*, ii, 570-602. The phrase 'New Reformation' had been used earlier by T. H. Huxley and Frances Power Cobbe.

36. Huxley, 'Agnosticism: A Rejoinder', *Nineteenth Century*, xxv (April 1889), 482.

37. Scherer to M.W., 22/4/88 (Texas).

38. 'Six Letters', 595.

39. Wace, 'Christianity and Agnosticism', *Nineteenth Century*, xxv (May 1889), 714.

40. Jowett to Margot Tennant, 28/11/88, in Margot Asquith, *Autobiography*, i, 120.

41. M.W. to H. R. Haweis, 8/5/88, in 'Six Letters', 596.

42. *W.R.*, 247.

43. G.S. to M.W., 30/8/88.

44. Bentzon, 'La Roman de la Nouvelle Réforme en Angleterre', *Revue des Deux Mondes*, xcvi (1 Dec. 1889), 649-81 (English abstract in *Review of Reviews*, i [January 1890], 61-2); Beyschlag, 'Robert Elsmere', *Deutsch-evangelische Blätter* (Berlin), xv (January 1890), 14-34 (English abstract in J. H. W. Stuckenberg, 'A German Criticism of Robert Elsmere', *Homiletic Review*, xix [April 1890], 367-71); Van Loenen Martinet, 'Robert Elsmere', *De Gids*, iii (August 1890), 257-89 (English abstract in *Review of Reviews*, ii [August 1890], 233).

45. 'The Lounger', *Critic*, n.s. x (15 Dec. 1888), 302. The literary news columns of the *Critic* contained frequent reports of *Elsmere*'s American reception.

46. 17/5/94 (Huntington Library).

47. Ellen B. Ballou, *The Building of the House: Houghton Mifflin's Formative Years* (Boston, 1970), 366.

48. Simon Nowell-Smith, ed., *Letters to Macmillan* (1967), 215-6.

49. Madeleine B. Stern, *Imprints on History: Book Publishers and the American History* (Bloomington, Ind., 1956), 266.

50. 'The Opposition to International Copyright', *Publishers' Weekly*, xxxiv (15 Dec. 1888), 950.

51. 'What "Robert Elsmere" Has to Say to the Trade', *Publishers' Weekly*, xxxiv (3 Nov. 1888), 651-2.

52. Hamilton W. Mabie, 'The Most Popular Novel in America', *Forum*, xvi (December 1893), 509.

53. M.W. to Henrietta Arnold, 3/1/89.

54. Gladstone was asked by Mrs Hetherington to review it but declined. See his letter printed in 'Agnosticism and Christianity: Elsmerism and Paul Nugent', *Newbery House Magazine*, iii (September 1890), 261.

55. Published serially in *Our Day* during 1889.

56. Whitteker Whimsey, 'An Omitted Chapter of "Robert Elsmere" ', *New Englander*, n.s. xiv (February 1889), 103-17.

57. *Life*, 76.

58. See the *Critic* for March, April, and May 1889; 'A. M. Palmer Drops "Robert Elsmere" ', *New York Times*, 11 Feb. 1889, 5; ' "Robert Elsmere." Mr. Gillette Will Not Dramatise It Without Permission', *New York Times*, 14 Feb. 1889, 9. Reviews of the New York performance appeared in the *Herald* and the *New York Times* on 30 April 1889.

59. M.W. to A. M. Palmer, 8/2/89 (Lilly Library, Indiana University).

60. For their histories, see *Life*, 81-95, 123-42, 182-206; John Rodgers, *Mary Ward Settlement (Late Passmore Edwards Settlement): A History, 1891-1931* [?1931]; Enid Huws Jones, *Mrs Humphry Ward* (1973), 101-35.

61. Mrs Ward, 'The New "Settlement" ' (letter), *Standard* (London), 10 March 1890, 3; M.W. to G.S., 24/2/90.

CHAPTER NINE

[*Reviews of* Richard Meynell *quoted in this chapter are listed chronologically in the bibliography.*]

1. Moorman.

2. Walter Elliott, *The Life of Father Hecker* (New York, 1891); 'Hermann Schell', *Catholic Encyclopaedia*, xii, 1124; John E. B. Mayor, 'The Late Professor Reusch' (letter), *The Times*, 17 April 1900, 11. For Mrs Ward's comments on them, see M.W. to T.A., 18/4/00; M.W. to T.H.W., [19/4/99]; M.W. to Mandell Creighton, [July 1900] (Pusey House); *W.R.*, 342.

3. For an account of its development in England, see H. D. A. Major, *English Modernism: Its Origin, Methods, Aims* (Cambridge, Mass., 1927).

4. 29/9/07 (Pusey House).

5. Mrs Ward, 'The Crisis in the Church', *The Times*, 5 Sept. 1899, 5.

6. Mrs Ward, 'The New Reformation—II: A Conscience Clause for the Laity', *Nineteenth Century*, xlvi (October 1899), 654-72.

7. 9/8/98 (Pusey House). A portion of this letter is quoted in *Life*, 151-3.

8. 24/1/20 (Pusey House).

9. Honnold.

10. Brooke to M.W., 19/8/09, in Lawrence P. Jacks, *Life and Letters of Stopford Brooke* (1917), ii, 619.

11. R.S. to M.W., 26/7/10.

12. R.S. to M.W., 28/4/10.

13. *Life*, 250.

14. M.W. to Mme d'Oillamson (Honnold).

15. 27/8/[10] (Huntington Library).

16. M.W. to Louise Creighton, 14/9/10 (Pusey House).

17. Diary of Dorothy Ward, 27/3/11 (Library of University College, London); Introduction to *Meynell*, xii-xiii.

18. M.W. to T.H.W., [9/10/10]. On Hudson Shaw's strange career, see Agnes Maude Royden, *A Threefold Cord* (1947).

19. 14/9/10 (Pusey House).

20. M.W. to Louise Creighton, 6/9/11 (Pusey House).

21. 1/10/11 (Honnold).

22. Lawrence P. Jacks, ed., *Jesus or Christ?* (*Hibbert Journal* Supplement, 1909).

23. Sabatier, *Modernism*, trans. C. A. Miles (Jowett Lectures, 1908) (New York, 1908), 68. A typescript of Mrs Ward's introductory speech at the first of Sabatier's lectures is in the Pusey House Library.

24. *W.R.*, 366.

25. Introduction to *Meynell*, xii.

26. Mrs Ward, 'The Opening of Manchester College', *Manchester Guardian*, 20 Oct. 1893, 5-6.

27. 9/12/11 (Brigham Young University Library).

28. 15/11/11 (Pusey House).

29. 4/11/11 (Pusey House).

30. *Life*, 260.

31. 13/11/11 (Pusey House).

32. Library of University College, London.

33. F. N. Doubleday to R.S. (Honnold).

34. M.W. to A.W., 4/2/12.

35. 2/12/11 (Pusey House).

EPILOGUE

1. *England's Effort*, 1.

2. M.W. to Gladstone, 15/4/88, in 'Gladstone's Review', 456.

3. Inge, *Diary of a Dean: St. Paul's 1911-1934* (1949), 12.

BIBLIOGRAPHY

I. Unpublished sources

Since Mrs Ward's letters and literary papers are scattered about in scores of libraries and private collections, I will describe here only the most important groups of manuscript material that I have used in writing this book. Some of the other repositories are indicated in my notes.

The Library of Pusey House, Oxford. This, the largest and most important collection of Mrs Ward's papers in England, is comprised chiefly of correspondence between her and members of her family. It also includes letters from readers about her books, her letters to the Creightons, and other miscellaneous material.

The Honnold Library, Claremont University (Claremont, California). The Honnold owns the correspondence between Mrs Ward and Smith, Elder (as well as some of her other publishers), her literary notebooks, and the manuscripts of many of her novels, including portions of *Robert Elsmere*.

The Henry W. and Albert A. Berg Collection, the New York Public Library (Astor, Lenox, and Tilden Foundations). The Berg Collection has acquired a large group of manuscripts and proofs of *Robert Elsmere*. (Chapter 27 of the *Elsmere* manuscript is in my possession; Chapter 51 is in the Pierpont Morgan Library, New York.)

The Stark Library, University of Texas. The Stark Library possesses a substantial collection of letters to Mrs Ward.

Mrs Mary Moorman. She owns a number of Tom Arnold's letters that are presently being edited for publication by Professor James Bertram as a sequel to his *New Zealand Letters of Thomas Arnold the Younger* (1966).

Basil Ward, Esq. Mr Ward owns the diary of Gertrude Ward.

The British Library. Mrs Ward's correspondence with the Macmillan Company is Add. MS. 54928.

The Library of University College, London. The diaries of Dorothy Ward and Humphry Ward have been deposited there by Mrs Moorman.

II. Published sources (primary)

There being no adequate published bibliography of Mrs Ward's writings, I include below many titles that are not actually cited in this book. (The most complete previous bibliography is supplied by Norman W. Webster in the *Antiquarian Book Monthly Review*, 2 [August 1975], 18-21.) The lists of Mrs Ward's letters to periodicals and of her speeches are deliberately incomplete; the other lists are as complete as I can make them, though I am conscious that many unsigned items, particularly in *The Times* and the *Pall Mall Gazette*, have eluded me. From 1896 onwards, many of Mrs Ward's books were serialized simultaneously in English and American magazines. In the case of items that are unsigned or signed with initials only, I have recorded my basis for attribution; as indicated below, I am especially indebted to the first volume of *The Wellesley Index to Victorian Periodicals*, edited by Walter E. Houghton (1966), in identifying anonymous articles. Place of publication for books is London unless otherwise noted.

A. Fiction

'A Westmoreland Story', *Churchman's Companion*, 3rd Ser., ii (1870), 45-57, 121-40, 187-95.
Milly and Olly, or A Holiday among the Mountains (Macmillan, 1881).
Miss Bretherton (Macmillan, 1884).
Robert Elsmere (3 vols, Smith, Elder, 1888).
The History of David Grieve (3 vols, Smith, Elder, 1892).
Marcella (3 vols, Smith, Elder, 1894).
The Story of Bessie Costrell (Smith, Elder, 1895).
Sir George Tressady (Smith, Elder, 1896).
Helbeck of Bannisdale (Smith, Elder, 1898).
Eleanor (Smith, Elder, 1900).
Lady Rose's Daughter (Smith, Elder, 1903).
The Marriage of William Ashe (Smith, Elder, 1905).
Fenwick's Career (Smith, Elder, 1906).
The Testing of Diana Mallory (Harper, 1908).
Daphne, or Marriage à la Mode (Cassell, 1909). [American title: *Marriage à la Mode*.]
Canadian Born (Smith, Elder, 1910). [American title: *Lady Merton, Colonist*.]
The Case of Richard Meynell (Smith, Elder, 1911).
The Mating of Lydia (Smith, Elder, 1913).
The Coryston Family (Smith, Elder, 1913).
Delia Blanchflower (Ward, Lock, 1915).
Eltham House (Cassell, 1915).
A Great Success (Smith, Elder, 1916).

Lady Connie (Smith, Elder, 1916).
Missing (Collins, 1917).
The War and Elizabeth (Collins, 1918). [American title: *Elizabeth's Campaign.*]
Cousin Philip (Collins, 1919). [American title: *Helena.*]
Harvest (Collins, 1920).

B. Nonfictional books

England's Effort: Six Letters to an American Friend. With a Preface by the Earl of Rosebery. (Smith, Elder, 1916). [On the War. The 3rd edition (1916) has 'an epilogue bringing the story down to the middle of August'.]
Towards the Goal. With an Introduction by Theodore Roosevelt. (John Murray, 1917). [On the War.]
A Writer's Recollections (Collins, 1918). [Memoirs. 3rd edition (1918) has an index.]
Fields of Victory (Hutchinson, 1919). [On the War.]

C. Pamphlets

A Morning in the Bodleian (privately printed, Windermere, 1871). [Dedication: 'To Mrs. Arnold, on her birthday, from her eldest grand-daughter and her youngest grandson. Fox How, August 21st, 1871.']
Plain Facts on Infant Feeding (Oxford, [c. 1874]). [No copy located. Mentioned in *Life*, 29.]
Unbelief and Sin (privately printed, Oxford, 1881). [Unsigned. Reprinted by Mrs Ward in *North American Review*, cxlviii (February 1889), 161-79.]
The Coming Election: Letters to My Neighbours (Smith, Elder, 1910).
Letters to My Neighbours on the Present Election (Smith, Elder, 1910). [A sequel to *The Coming Election.*]

D. Articles and reviews

'The Poem of the Cid', *Macmillan's Magazine*, xxiv (October 1871), 471-86.
'Alfonso the Wise, King of Castile', *Macmillan's Magazine*, xxvi (June 1872), 126-36.
'Historical Study in Spain', *Saturday Review*, xlii (7 Oct. 1876), 449-51. [Unsigned. Attribution: Introduction to *Elsmere*, I, xvii. Review of *Cronicas de los Reyes de Castilla* (1875), ed. Don Cayetana Rosell.]
'A Medieval Spanish Writer', *Fortnightly Review*, n.s. xx (1 Dec. 1876), 809-32. [On Juan Ruiz.]
Review of *John Inglesant* (1881) by J. H. Shorthouse: *Saturday Re-*

view, lii (9 July 1881), 50-1. [Unsigned. Attribution (tentative): Sarah Shorthouse, *Life and Letters of J. H. Shorthouse* (1905), 133.]

[Co-author with T.H.W.] Review of *Life of Richard Cobden* (1881) by John Morley: *The Times*, 22 Oct. 1881, 4; 1 Nov. 1881, 3. [Unsigned. Attribution: *W.R.*, 188-9.]

'Foreign Table-Talk', *Guardian*, xxxvii (1 March 1882), 323-4 (supplement). [Signed 'M.A.W.'. Attribution: see above, p. 87.]

'Foreign Table Talk', *Guardian*, xxxvii (29 March 1882), 453-4 (supplement). [Unsigned.]

Review of *Spain* (1882) by Wentworth Webster: *Academy*, xxi (22 April 1882), 278-9.

'Foreign Table-Talk', *Guardian*, xxxvii (26 April 1882), 602-3 (supplement). [Signed 'M.A.W.'.]

'Foreign Table-Talk', *Guardian*, xxxvii (31 May 1882), 773 (supplement). [Signed 'M.A.W.'.]

Review of *Democracy: An American Novel* (1880) by Henry Adams: *Fortnightly Review*, n.s. xxxii (1 July 1882), 78-93.

'Foreign Table-Talk', *Guardian*, xxxvii (5 July 1882), 945-6 (supplement). [Signed 'M.A.W.'.]

'Foreign Table Talk', *Guardian*, xxxvii (26 July 1882), 1040-1 (supplement). [Signed 'M.A.W.'.]

'Foreign Table Talk', *Guardian*, xxxvii (30 Aug. 1882), 1198-9 (supplement). [Signed 'M.A.W.'.]

'Foreign Table-Talk', *Guardian*, xxxvii (27 Sept. 1882), 1329 (supplement). [Signed 'A.M.W.' (*sic*).]

Death of Anthony Trollope. *The Times*, 7 Dec. 1882, 9. [Unsigned. Attribution: *W.R.*, 192.]

'Spanish Novels', *The Times*, 26 Dec. 1882, 5. [Unsigned. Attribution: M.W. to T.H.W., 14/10/82 (Pusey House); *W.R.*, 192.]

Review of vol. iii of *A Dictionary of Christian Biography* (1882), ed. Henry Wace and William Smith: *The Times*, 12 Jan. 1883, 4. [Unsigned. Attribution: Wace to M.W., 12/1/83 (Pusey House).]

'A Spanish Romanticist: Gustavo Becquer', *Macmillan's Magazine*, xlvii (February 1883), 305-20.

'French Souvenirs', *Macmillan's Magazine*, xlviii (June 1883), 141-53. [Signed 'M.A.W.'. Attribution: *Wellesley Index*. Review of *Literary Souvenirs* (1883) by Maxime du Camp.]

'M. Renan's Autobiography', *Macmillan's Magazine*, xlviii (July 1883), 213-33. [Signed 'M.A.W.'. Attribution: *Wellesley Index*. Review of *Souvenirs d'Enfance et de Jeunesse* (1883) by Ernest Renan.]

'Francis Garnier', *Macmillan's Magazine*, xlviii (August 1883), 309-20. [Signed 'M.A.W.'. Attribution: *Wellesley Index*.]

'A Swiss Peasant Novelist', *Macmillan's Magazine*, xlviii (October 1883), 453-64. [Signed 'M.A.W.'. Attribution: *Wellesley Index*. On Jeremia Gotthelf (pseudonym of Albert Bitzius).]

[Co-author with John Morley.] 'Anthony Trollope', *Macmillan's Magazine*, xlix (November 1883), 47-56. [Unsigned. Attribution: *Wellesley Index*. Review of Trollope's *Autobiography* (1883).]

Review of *The Life and Times of Jesus the Messiah* (1883) by Alfred Edersheim: *The Times*, 9 Nov. 1883, 4. [Unsigned. Attribution: M.W. to T.A., 17/11/83.]

'The Literature of Introspection: Two Recent Journals' [Part I], *Macmillan's Magazine*, xlix (January 1884), 190-201. [Signed 'M.A.W.'. Attribution: *Wellesley Index*. Review of *Journal d'un Solitaire* (1884) by Xavier Thiriat.]

'The Literature of Introspection: Amiel's *Journal Intime*' [Part II], *Macmillan's Magazine*, xlix (February 1884), 268-78. [Signed 'M.A.W.'. Attribution: *Wellesley Index*. Review of *Henri-Frédéric Amiel: Fragments d'un Journal Intime* (1883).]

'A New Edition of Keats', *Macmillan's Magazine*, xlix (March 1884), 330-40. [Signed 'M.A.W.'. Attribution: *Wellesley Index*. Review of *The Poetical Works and Other Writings of John Keats* (1884), ed. Harry Buxton Forman.]

'Messonier', *Macmillan's Magazine*, l (June 1884), 92-8. [Unsigned. Attribution: *Wellesley Index*.]

'M. Renan's New Volume', *Macmillan's Magazine*, l (July 1884), 161-70. [Signed 'M.A.W.'. Attribution: *Wellesley Index*. Review of the final volume of *Histoire des Origines du Christianisme* (1863-83) by Ernest Renan.]

'Modern Spanish Literature', *Quarterly Review*, clviii (July 1884), 40-78. [Unsigned. Attribution: *Wellesley Index*. Review of seven books.]

'Recent Fiction in England and France', *Macmillan's Magazine*, l (August 1884), 250-60. [Unsigned. Attribution: *Wellesley Index*.]

Review of *Maelcho* (1884) by Emily Lawless: *The Times*, 30 Nov. 1884, 14. [Unsigned. Attribution: M.W. to A.W., 31/10/94.]

'Style and Miss Austen', *Macmillan's Magazine*, li (December 1884), 84-91. [Signed 'M.A.W.'. Attribution: *Wellesley Index*. Review of *Letters of Jane Austen* (1884), ed. Edward, Lord Brabourne.]

'Lord Tennyson's *Becket*', *Macmillan's Magazine*, li (February 1885), 287-94. [Unsigned. Attribution: *Wellesley Index*.]

Review of *Diana of the Crossways* (1885) by George Meredith: *Athenaeum*, 14 March 1885, 339-40. [Unsigned. Attribution: Arthur Symons to Churchill Osborne, 13/4/85 (Princeton University Library).]

'Modern Geneva', *Quarterly Review*, clix (April 1885), 387-423. [Unsigned. Attribution: *Wellesley Index*. Review of nine books about Geneva or by Genevese authors.]

'French Views of English Writers', *Macmillan's Magazine*, lii (May 1885), 16-25. [Signed 'M.A.W.'. Attribution: *Wellesley Index*.]

Review of *Marius the Epicurean* (1885) by Walter Pater: *Macmillan's Magazine*, lii (June 1885), 132-9. [Signed 'M.A.W.'. Attribution: *Wellesley Index*.]

'The New National Gallery at Amsterdam', *Macmillan's Magazine*, lii (September 1885), 383-91. [Unsigned. Attribution: *Wellesley Index*.]

'English Men and Women of Letters of the 19th Century, No. XII: Elizabeth Barrett Browning', *Atalanta*, i (September 1888), 708-12.

'The New Reformation: A Dialogue', *Nineteenth Century*, xxv (March 1889), 454-80. [Reply to Gladstone's review of *Robert Elsmere* in *Nineteenth Century* (May 1888).]

'A New Book on the Gospels', *Nineteenth Century*, xxvii (April 1890), 651-8. [Review of *The First Three Gospels: Their Origin and Relation* (1890) by J. Estlin Carpenter.]

Review of *Philomythus: An Antidote Against Credulity* (1891) by Edwin A. Abbott: *Nineteenth Century*, xxix (May 1891), 768-74.

Review of *Grania* (1892) by Emily Lawless: *New Review*, vi (April 1892), 399-407.

'The Apostles' Creed: A Translation and Introduction', *Nineteenth Century*, xxxiv (July 1893), 152-8. [The introduction is by Mrs Ward; the 'translation' or analysis (pp. 158-76) is by Adolf Harnack.]

Review of *Charlotte Brontë and Her Circle* (1896) by Clement K. Shorter: *The Times*, 23 Oct. 1896, 10. [Unsigned. Attribution: M.W. to G.S., 22/10/96.]

'Mrs. Garnett's Translations of Turguenev's Novels', *Manchester Guardian*, 23 Dec. 1896, 8. [Review of *The Novels of Ivan Turgenev* (1894-9), trans. Constance Garnett, 15 vols.]

'John Richard Green', *Associate* (Passmore Edwards Settlement), October 1898, 7-12.

'The New Reformation—II: A Conscience Clause for the Laity', *Nineteenth Century*, xlvi (October 1899), 654-72. [An amplification of her letter in *The Times*, 5 Sept. 1899.]

'M. Bourget's New Book', *Times Literary Supplement*, 21 Feb. 1902, 44. [Unsigned. Attribution: M.W. to A.W., 20/2/02. Review of *Monique* (1902) by Paul Bourget.]

'The Vacation School Experiment', *The Times*, 26 Aug. 1902, 9.

Arnold, William T. [and Mrs Ward]. 'Thomas Arnold the Younger',

Century Magazine, lxvi (May 1903), 115-28. [Signed by W.T.A. only. Attribution: M.W. to R. W. Gilder, 13/9/02 (Huntington Library.]

Review of *Studies in Theology* (1903) by J. Estlin Carpenter and P. H. Wicksteed: *Hibbert Journal*, ii (October 1903), 156-61.

'Nathaniel Hawthorne', *Cornhill Magazine*, n.s. xvii (August 1904), 167-71.

'The Women's Anti-Suffrage Movement', *Nineteenth Century*, lxiv (August 1908), 343-52.

'Why I Do Not Believe in Woman Suffrage', *Ladies' Home Journal*, xxv (November 1908), 15, 72.

'Woman Suffrage: A New Bill and a New Book', *The Times*, 4 June 1910, 14.

'An Experiment in Organized Playgrounds', *The Times*, 5 Sept. 1911, 11.

'Let Women Say! An Appeal to the House of Lords', *Nineteenth Century*, lxxxiii (January 1918), 47-59. [On women's suffrage.]

'Young Cripples', *Times Educational Supplement*, 9 May 1918, 195-6.

E. Introductions and prefaces to her own books

Miss Bretherton. With a Preface by the author. (2nd edn, Macmillan, 1885).

David Grieve. With a Prefatory Letter by the author. (6th edn, Smith, Elder, 1892).

Milly and Olly; or, a Holiday among the Mountains. With a Preface by the author. (2nd edn, T. Fisher Unwin, 1907).

The Case of Richard Meynell. With a Foreword by Mrs H.W. (Garden City, N.Y.: Doubleday, Page, 1911). [This foreword, which is addressed to 'those of my American readers who are not intimately acquainted with the conditions of English rural and religious life', does not appear in the English edition.]

The Writings of Mrs. Humphry Ward. With Introductions by the author. (Westmoreland Edition.) (16 vols, Smith, Elder, 1911-2). [A large-paper edition was printed by Houghton Mifflin in America from the same plates a year earlier.]

F. Prefaces, forewords, introductions, and contributions to books by others

Smith, William, and Wace, Henry, eds. *A Dictionary of Christian Biography* (4 vols, John Murray, 1877-87). [Mrs Ward contributed 209 articles on early Spanish figures to volumes ii and iii.]

Ward, Thomas Humphry, ed. *The English Poets* (5 vols, Macmillan, 1880, 1918). [Mrs Ward contributed the introductions to Sir Philip

Sidney, Fulke Greville (Lord Brooke), Sir Edward Dyer, Sir John Davies, and Emily Lawless.]

Amiel, Henri-Frédéric. *Amiel's Journal: The Journal Intime of Henri-Frédéric Amiel*, translated with an Introduction by Mrs H.W. (Macmillan, 1885).

Hausrath, Adolf. *A History of the New Testament Times . . . The Time of the Apostles*, trans. Leonard Huxley. With a Preface by Mrs H.W. (4 vols, Williams, 1895). [Mrs Ward also revised the translation (M.W. to W. A. Sanday, 3/2/20 [Bodleian Library]).]

Joubert, Joseph. *Joubert: A Selection from His Thoughts*, trans. Katherine Lyttelton. With a Preface by Mrs H.W. (Duckworth, 1898).

The Life and Works of Charlotte Brontë and Her Sisters. With Introductions to the works by Mrs H.W. and Introduction and notes to the Life by Clement K. Shorter. (Haworth Edition.) (7 vols, Smith, Elder, 1899-1900). [Six copies of the Introductions were privately reprinted in the form of a separate volume.]

Webb, Beatrice, ed. *The Case for the Factory Acts*. With a Preface by Mrs H.W. (Grant Richards, 1901).

Jülicher, Adolf. *An Introduction to the New Testament*, trans. Janet P. Ward (afterwards Trevelyan). With a Prefatory Note by Mrs H.W. (Smith, Elder, 1904). [Mrs Ward also assisted in the translating (*Life*, 172-3).]

Arnold, William T. *Studies of Roman Imperialism*, ed. Edward Fiddes. With a Memoir of the author by Mrs H.W. and C. E. Montague. (Manchester, Manchester University Press, 1906).

Cena, Giovanni. *The Forewarners: A Novel*, trans. Olivia A. Rossetti. With a Preface by Mrs H.W. (Smith, Elder, 1908).

Bibby, M. E., *et al. The Pudding Lady: A New Departure in Social Work*. With a Letter from Mrs H.W. (Stead's Publishing House, 1912).

Palmer, William T. *Odd Yarns of English Lakeland: Narratives of Romance, Mystery and Superstition Told by the Dalesfolk*. With a Preface by Mrs H.W. (Skeffington, 1914).

Caine, Hall, ed. *King Albert's Book: A Tribute to the Belgian King and People from Representative Men and Women Throughout the World* (Hodder and Stoughton, 1915). [Mrs Ward contributed an untitled essay.]

Wood, Butler, ed. *Charlotte Brontë, 1816-1916: A Centenary Memorial*. With a Foreword by Mrs H.W. (T. Fisher Unwin, 1917).

Trevelyan, Janet P. *Evening Play Centres for Children: The Story of Their Origin and Growth*. With a Preface by Mrs H.W. (Methuen, 1920).

G. Letters to Periodicals

'Mr. Wordsworth's Bampton Lectures', *Guardian*, xxxvi (8 June 1881), 811. [Signed 'The Author of "Unbelief and Sin" '.]

'Miss Bretherton', *Athenaeum*, 27 Dec. 1884, 857. [On Mary Anderson and *Miss Bretherton*.]

'The New "Settlement" ', *Standard*, 10 Mar. 1890, 3. [On the relationship between *Robert Elsmere* and the University Hall settlement.]

'An Explanation', *Athenaeum*, 14 May 1892, 633. [On *David Grieve*.]

'The Opening of Manchester College', *Manchester Guardian*, 20 Oct. 1893, 5-6.

'A Letter from Mrs. Humphry Ward', *Critic*, n.s. xxiii (26 Jan. 1895), 66. [Declining an invitation to visit America.]

'Mrs. Ward's New Novel', *Spectator*, lxxx (25 June 1898), 906. [On *Helbeck of Bannisdale*.]

'The Crisis in the Church', *The Times*, 5 Sept. 1899, 5.

'The Academic Committtee', *The Times*, 27 Mar. 1911, 15. [On the Academic Committee of the Society of Authors and of the Royal Society of Literature.]

'The Academic Committee', *The Times*, 31 Mar. 1911, 11.

'Mr. Passmore Edwards', *The Times*, 8 May 1911, 3. [Tribute.]

'Eminent Victorians', *Times Literary Supplement*, 11 July 1918, 325. [On Lytton Strachey's treatment of Dr Arnold and A. H. Clough in *Eminent Victorians* (1918).]

'Church Patronage: An Anecdote', *Times Literary Supplement*, 31 Oct. 1918, 525. [Corrects an anecdote in *W.R.*]

'Church Membership', *The Times*, 19 Dec. 1919, 8. [On the Enabling Bill.]

H. Lectures

University Hall: Opening Address (Smith, Elder, 1891). [Address delivered 29 Nov. 1890.]

'New Forms of Christian Education', *New World*, i (June 1892), 329-48. [Footnote: 'This paper was delivered as an address to the University Hall Guild, a body connected with the University Hall Settlement in Gordon Square. It has been revised and enlarged for publication, but I have not thought well to interfere with the main lines of its original form.' Reprinted as a pamphlet (Smith, Elder, 1892).]

The Future of University Hall (Smith, Elder, 1892). [Introductory note: 'The following paper was delivered as an address to Meetings held at Manchester, Liverpool and Leeds, in November 1892. It has since been revised and corrected, but I have not thought well to interfere with its original form.']

Unitarians and the Future (Essex Hall Lecture, 1894) (P. Green, 1894). [An address delivered at a meeting of the British and Foreign Unitarian Association, 19 June 1894.]

'Mrs. Humphry Ward on Public Libraries', *The Times*, 12 April 1897, 15. [Summary of an address delivered at the opening of the Edmonton public free library, 10 April.]

Social Ideals (Williams, 1897). [An address delivered at the Passmore Edwards Settlement, 10 Oct. 1897. No copy located.]

'Mrs. Humphry Ward at the Authors' Club', *Queen*, cix (25 May 1901), 827. [Address on 'novels with a purpose' delivered at the Authors' Club, 20 May.]

'James Martineau', *Critic*, n.s. xl (September 1903), 217-20. [Internal evidence suggests that this was an address delivered at the Passmore Edwards Settlement.]

'Wuthering Heights', *Brontë Society Transactions*, ii (1905), 227-32. [Abstract of a paper read at the Annual Meeting of the Brontë Society in Batley, 14 Jan. 1905. Substantially the same as the Introduction to the Haworth Edition *Wuthering Heights* (see above).]

'Passmore Edwards' Settlement', *The Times*, 23 March 1906, 10. [Summary of an address on Matthew Arnold and Benjamin Jowett delivered at the Settlement, 22 March.]

'M. Sabatier on Modernism', *The Times*, 26 Feb. 1908, 7. [Summary of her introductory remarks at a lecture by Paul Sabatier, 25 February.]

'Mrs. Humphry Ward', *Outlook*, lxxxviii (18 April 1908), 849-50. [Brief summary of an address on 'The Peasant in Literature' delivered in New York. The address was written *c.* 1897 and delivered by Mrs Ward on various occasions for more than a decade. MS. notes for the address are in the Honnold Library.]

'Thomas Hardy'. [A lecture delivered in Paris in 1909. Incomplete corrected proofs (29 pp.) in the Honnold Library, with the following printer's stamp: *Spottiswoode & Co. Ltd., 11 March 1910*. (Spottiswoode was Smith, Elder's printer.) Mrs Ward considered publishing it but evidently did not do so.]

'Some Thoughts on Charlotte Brontë', in *Charlotte Brontë, 1816-1916: A Centenary Memorial*, ed. Butler Wood (T. Fisher Unwin, 1917). [An address delivered at the meeting of the Brontë Society in Bradford, 30 March 1917.]

'England and Italy', *Contemporary Review*, cxii (August 1917), 160-2. [An address delivered at the First Annual Meeting of the British-Italian League, 9 July.]

I. Plays

Robert Elsmere. An unauthorized adaptation of the novel; by William Gillette and others. Hollis Street Theatre, Boston, Mass., 13 April 1889; Union Square Theatre, New York, 29 April 1889.

Eleanor. Adaptation of the novel; by Mrs Ward and Julian Sturgis.
Court Theatre, London, 30 Oct. 1902; Court Theatre, 29 June 1905
(revised). Published (Smith, Elder, 1903).

Agatha. By Mrs Ward and Louis N. Parker. St James's Theatre, London,
7 March 1905. Privately printed (Smith, Elder, 1903).

The Marriage of William Ashe. Adaptation of the novel; by Margaret
Mayo. Garrick Theatre, New York, 21 Nov. 1905; Terry's Theatre,
London, 22 April 1908.

J. Films

Missing. Paramount, 1918. Five reels. Director: James Young. Scenario:
J. Stuart Blackton.

Lady Rose's Daughter. Paramount-Artcraft, 1920. Five reels. Director:
Hugh Ford. Scenario: Burns Mantle.

The Marriage of William Ashe. Metro Pictures Corporation, 1921. Six
reels. Director: Edward Sloman. Scenario: Ruth Ann Baldwin. From
Margaret Mayo's dramatization of the novel.

K. Poetry

'Charlotte and Emily Brontë', *Cornhill Magazine*, n.s. viii (March 1900),
289. [Signed 'M.A.W.'. Attribution: *Life*, 166.]

III. Published sources (secondary)

The major sources in this category are indicated in my notes; I have
therefore listed only a few titles below, chiefly those dealing directly
with Mrs Ward.

Arnold, Thomas, Jr. *New Zealand Letters of Thomas Arnold the
Younger,* ed. James Bertram (Wellington, N.Z., 1966).

Colby, Vineta. *The Singular Anomaly: Women Novelists of the Nineteenth Century* (New York, 1970).

Culler, A. Dwight. *Imaginative Reason: The Poetry of Matthew Arnold*
(New Haven, Conn., 1966).

Down, T. C. 'Schooldays with Miss Clough', *Cornhill Magazine*, 3rd
Ser., xlviii (June 1920), 674-84.

Gwynn, Stephen L. *Mrs. Humphry Ward* (Writers of the Day; 1917).

Huws Jones, Enid. *Mrs Humphry Ward* (1973).

J., R. W. 'In Memoriam: Thomas Humphry Ward', *Brazen Nose*, iv
(November 1926), 207-8.

'Mrs. Humphry Ward', *Times Literary Supplement*, 15 June 1951, 372.

Peterson, William S. 'Gladstone's Review of *Robert Elsmere*: Some Unpublished Correspondence', *Review of English Studies*, n.s. xxi (November 1970), 442-61.

————. 'Mrs Humphry Ward on *Robert Elsmere*: Six New Letters', *Bulletin of the New York Public Library*, lxxiv (November 1970), 587-97.

Ryals, Clyde de L. Introduction to *Robert Elsmere* (Lincoln, Nebr.,
    1967).
Trevelyan, Janet P. *Life of Mrs. Humphry Ward* (1923).
Trevor, Meriol. *The Arnolds: Thomas Arnold and His Family* (New
    York, 1973).
Trilling, Lionel. *Matthew Arnold* (New York, 1955).
Willey, Basil. 'How *Robert Elsmere* Struck Some Contemporaries',
    Essays and Studies, x (1957), 53-68.
Williams, Kenneth E. 'Faith, Intention, and Fulfillment: The Religious
    Novels of Mrs. Humphry Ward' (Ph.D. thesis, Temple University,
    1969).
Woods, Margaret L. 'Mrs. Humphry Ward: A Sketch from Memory',
    Quarterly Review, ccxxxiv (July 1920), 147-60.

IV. Reviews and sermons

These lists, though by no means exhaustive, represent the most important critical responses to *Robert Elsmere* and *The Case of Richard Meynell* in Britain and America. The items are arranged chronologically.

A. Reviews of 'Robert Elsmere'

'New Novels', *Scotsman*, 5 March 1888, 3.
'Robert Elsmere', *Morning Post* (London), 5 March 1888, 3.
'The Woman of Feeling', *British Weekly*, iii (9 March 1888), 345.
Sharp, William. 'New Novels', *Academy*, xxxiii (17 March 1888), 183-4.
'Robert Elsmere', *Manchester Guardian*, 21 March 1888, 6.
'Novels', *Saturday Review*, lxv (24 March 1888), 356.
Pater, Walter. 'Robert Elsmere', *Guardian*, xliii (28 March 1888), 468-9.
    Reprinted in Pater, *Essays from "The Guardian"* (1901), 55-70.
'Novels of the Week', *Athenaeum*, 31 March 1888, 395.
'Notes on Novels', *Dublin Review*, 3rd Ser., xix (April 1888), 427-8.
'Our Library List', *Murray's Magazine*, iii (April 1888), 576.
'A Romance of the New Religion', *Pall Mall Gazette*, 5 April 1888, 2-3.
[Hutton, R. H.] 'Robert Elsmere', *Spectator*, lxi (7 April 1888), 479-
    80. Reprinted in Hutton, *Criticisms on Contemporary Thought and
    Thinkers* (1894), ii, 263-9.
'Robert Elsmere', *The Times*, 7 April 1888, 5.
'Novels', *Illustrated London News*, xcii (28 April 1888), 465.
Gladstone, William E. ' "Robert Elsmere" and the Battle of Belief',
    Nineteenth Century, 23 (May 1888), 766-88. Reprinted in Glad-
    stone, *Later Gleanings* (New York, 1897), 77-117.
'Literature', *Liverpool Daily Post*, 10 May 1888, 7.
M., S. 'Robert Elsmere', *Time*, vii (June 1888), 723-9.

Lang, Andrew. 'Theological Romances', *Contemporary Review*, liii (June 1888), 814-24.

Adams, H. C. 'Robert Elsmere', *Churchman*, n.s. ii (June 1888), 544-53.

'Robert Elsmere', *Congregational Review*, ii (June 1888), 497-509.

'Recent Novels', *Nation* (New York), xlvi (7 June 1888), 471.

[Cowell, Herbert.] '*Robert Elsmere* and Modern Oxford', *Blackwood's Magazine*, cxliv (July 1888), 1-20.

'The Theology of *Robert Elsmere*', *London Quarterly Review*, lxx (July 1888), 345-58.

'Elsmere's Unbelief', *New York Daily Tribune*, 29 July 1888, 10.

'A Theist for Its Hero', *New York Times*, 5 Aug. 1888, 10.

'Robert Elsmere', *Literary World* (Boston), xix (18 Aug. 1888), 268-9.

'Talk about New Books', *Catholic World*, xlvii (September 1888), 847-50.

'Editorial: "Robert Elsmere" ', *Andover Review* (Boston), x (September 1888), 297-306.

Magnus, Julian. 'Robert Elsmere', *Epoch* (New York), iv (21 Sept. 1888), 118-9.

[Wace, Henry.] '*Robert Elsmere* and Christianity', *Quarterly Review*, clxvii (October 1888), 273-302.

'Recent Fiction', *Independent* (New York), xl (18 Oct. 1888), 1344-5.

'Editor's Study', *Harper's New Monthly Magazine*, lxxvii (November 1888), 964.

Payne, William M. 'Recent Fiction', *Dial* (Chicago), ix (November 1888), 160.

'Theology in Fiction', *Atlantic Monthly*, lxii (November 1888), 699-706.

Davidson, Randall. 'The Religious Novel', *Contemporary Review*, liv (November 1888), 674-82.

Bixby, James T. ' "Robert Elsmere" and Its Critics', *Unitarian Review* (Boston), xxx (November 1888), 419-38.

Sempers, Charles T. 'Robert Elsemere' [*sic*], *Harvard Monthly*, vii (December 1888), 113-21.

Albert, Charles S. 'Robert Elsmere', *Lutheran Quarterly*, n.s. xix (January 1889), 83-91.

Stevens, Henry D. 'Robert Elsmere', *Unitarian* (Boston), iv (January 1889), 17-9.

Hale, Edward Everett, *et al.* 'Robert Elsmere's Mental Struggles', *North American Review*, cxlviii (January 1889), 97-116.

Lyman, Albert J. ' "Robert Elsmere" Once More', *Homiletic Review* (New York), xvii (February 1889), 122-32.

Van Antwerp, W. H. 'Robert Elsmere', *Church Review* (New Haven, Conn.), liii (April 1889), 16-26.

de Concilio, J. ' "Robert Elsmere" as a Controversial Novel', *American Catholic Quarterly Review*, xliv (April 1889), 268-82.

Tyrrell, Robert Y. *'Robert Elsmere* as a Symptom', *Fortnightly Review*, n.s. xlv (May 1889), 727-31.

Bentzon, Th. 'La Roman de la Nouvelle Réforme en Angleterre', *Revue des Deux Mondes* (Paris), xcvi (1 Dec. 1889), 649-81. English abstract in *Review of Reviews*, i (January 1890), 61-2.

Beyschlag, Willibald. 'Robert Elsmere', *Deutsch-evangelische Blätter* (Berlin), xv (January 1890), 14-34. English abstract in J. H. W. Stuckenberg, 'A German Criticism of Robert Elsmere', *Homiletic Review*, xix (April 1890), 367-71.

Van Loenen, Martinet J. 'Robert Elsmere', *De Gids* (Amsterdam), iii (August 1890), 257-89. English abstract in *Review of Reviews*, ii (August 1890), 233.

Urquhart, J. 'Robert Elsmere', *King's Own*, ii (March 1891), 321-5.

J[ames], H[enry]. 'Mrs. Humphry Ward', *English Illustrated Magazine*, ix (1892), 399-401. Reprinted in James, *Essays in London and Elsewhere* (New York, 1893), 253-8.

B. Sermons on 'Robert Elsmere'

Chapman, William S. *The Critical Method and the History of Testimony as Discoursed in "Robert Elsmere"* (Melbourne, 1888) [no copy located].

Wendte, Charles W. *The Story of "Robert Elsmere" and Its Lessons* (privately printed, San Francisco, [?1888]).

Hughes, Hugh Price. *Social Christianity: Sermons* (1889). [' "Robert Elsmere" and Mr. Gladstone's Criticisms of the Book', 95-105. Sermon delivered in London, 6 May 1888.]

'Mr. [Hugh R.] Haweis on "Robert Elsmere" ', *Christian World*, 31 May 1888, 432. [Sermon delivered in Marylebone, 27 May.]

'An Ethical Culturist on "Robert Elsmere" ', *Unitarian*, iii (November 1888), 489-90. [Sermon delivered by Stanton Coit in London, 23 Sept. See also Coit, 'Robert Elsmere', *Ethical Record*, i (January 1889), 139-50.]

'An Attack on a Novel: the Rev. Mr. [Frank] Gunsaulus Assails "Robert Elsmere" ', *Chicago Tribune*, 22 Oct. 1888, 1. [Sermon delivered in Chicago, 21 Oct.]

' "Robert Elsmere" Reviewed', *Inter Ocean* (Chicago), 29 Oct. 1888, 6. [Sermon delivered by the Revd J. H. Barrows in Chicago, 28 Oct.]

Gordon, George A. *"Robert Elsmere"* (Church Committee, Old South Church, Boston, 1888). [Sermon delivered in Boston, 16 Nov. 1888.]

Armstrong, Richard A. *Pulpit Studies from "Robert Elsmere"* (2nd edn, Liverpool, 1888). [Preface dated 21 Nov. 1888.]

Goddard, John. ' "Robert Elsmere," or, the Division of the Saviour's Garments', *Helper* (Philadelphia), ii (19 Dec. 1888), 3-18.

Armstrong, George D. *A Half Hour with Robert Elsmere* (privately printed, Norfolk, Va., 1889).

Clarke, George. *"Robert Elsmere": A Lecture* (2nd edn, Hobart, Tasmania, 1889).

"Robert Elsmere": A Reply to the Rev. George Clarke's Lecture (Hobart, Tasmania, 1889).

Elsmere Elsewhere; or, Shifts and Makeshifts, Logical and Theological ('by a Disciple of James Freeman Clarke, D.D.') (Boston, 1889).

'Rev. Dr. Thomas on "Robert Elsmere" ', *Unitarian* (Boston), iv (January 1889), 19-20.

'Rev. A. G. Jennings on "Robert Elsmere" ', *Unitarian*, iv (January 1889), 20-1.

'Rev. John W. Chadwick on "Robert Elsmere" ', *Unitarian*, iv (January 1889), 21.

MacColl, John A. *"Robert Elsmere": A Lecture* (privately printed, St Albans, Vt, 1889). [Lecture delivered in St Albans, 22 Jan. 1889.]

Gilbert, C. R. *Robert Elsmere v. Christianity* (York, 1889). [Paper read before the York Clerical Brotherhood, 26 March 1889.]

Hughes-Games, Joshua. *The Bible and Some Current Sceptical Thought, with Special Reference to "Robert Elsmere" and "Lux Mundi"* (Liverpool, 1890). [Paper read before the Yorkshire Evangelical Union, 5 June 1890.]

C. Reviews of 'The Case of Richard Meynell'

'Mrs. Humphry Ward's Latest Novel', *Times Literary Supplement*, 26 Oct. 1911, 412.

'A New "Robert Elsmere" ', *Daily News* (London), 26 Oct. 1911, 3.

'Mrs. Humphry Ward's New Novel', *Westminster Gazette*, 26 Oct. 1911, 1-2.

de Sélincourt, Basil. 'Mrs. Humphry Ward's New Novel', *Manchester Guardian*, 26 Oct. 1911, 4.

'A "Robert Elsmere" Sequel', *Christian World*, 26 Oct. 1911, 13.

'Mrs. Humphry Ward's New Novel', *Athenaeum*, 28 Oct. 1911, 516.

'Mrs. Humphry Ward', *Pall Mall Gazette*, 30 Oct. 1911, 4.

'Mrs. Humphry Ward's New Novel', *Guardian*, 3 Nov. 1911, 1489-90.

W., N. H. 'Religious Controversy and the Novel', *T. P.'s Weekly*, xviii (3 Nov. 1911), 557.

'Mrs. Humphry Ward's New Novel', *Record*, 10 Nov. 1911, 1054.

'Novels', *Saturday Review*, cxii (11 Nov. 1911), 617.

'The Case of Richard Meynell', *Spectator*, cvii (11 Nov. 1911), 785-6.

'Mrs. Humphrey [*sic*] Ward's New Story', *Church Times*, 17 Nov. 1911, 672-3.

'The Case of Richard Meynell', *Academy*, lxxxi (18 Nov. 1911), 635.
'Mrs. Humphry Ward's New Novel', *Bookman* (London), xli (December 1911), 166.
'Current Fiction', *Nation* (New York), xciii (21 Dec. 1911), 604-5.
McComb, Samuel. 'Mrs Humphry Ward's "The Case of Richard Meynell" ', *Bookman* (New York), xxxiv (January 1912), 544-6.
'Some Recent Books', *Dublin Review*, cl (April 1912), 419-21.

INDEX

Abbott, Evelyn, 225
Acton, Lord (Sir John E. E. Dalberg),
  14, 164-5, 168, 225
Albandale, Lady, 217
Alden, Henry, 176
Allon, Henry, 229
Amiel, Henri-Frédéric, 50, 90, 97,
  99-101, 151
Anderson, Mary, 108-9
Anglo-Catholicism, 63-4, 66, 72, 98,
  154, 160, 188
Arnold, Eleanor (afterwards Wode-
  house and Sandhurst), 115, 216
Arnold, Ethel, 121, 205, 231
Arnold, Frances, 27, 44, 103, 165
Arnold, Henrietta, 177, 234
Arnold, Jane (afterwards Forster),
  30, 119, 226
Arnold, Julia (née Sorrell), 36-40, 42,
  118, 120, 126-30, 165-7, 184,
  225-6, 229-30
Arnold, Mary (afterwards Twining),
  30, 46
Arnold, Matthew, 3, 13, 17-8, 20, 22,
  26-35, 40, 42-3, 73, 78-9, 81, 83-
  4, 88, 90-1, 100-1, 110, 112-3,
  128, 132, 136-7, 141, 145, 148,
  151, 155, 165, 170, 179-80, 196,
  199, 207, 216, 226, 231
Arnold, Dr Thomas, 2, 17-31, 35, 37,
  46, 49, 69, 137, 149, 190, 202,
  209, 225, 227, 232
Arnold, Mrs Thomas, 28, 44-5, 50,
  226
Arnold, Thomas, Jr, 27-8, 30, 34-42,
  80, 109, 117, 126, 136, 164, 226-
  7, 232, 234, 237
Arnold, William D., 27, 29

Arnold, William T., 106, 109, 117,
  128, 226-7, 229, 232
Askwith, Betty, 228, 232
Austen, Jane, 102, 115, 142-3, 161
Austin, Mrs Alfred, 231

Bacon, Benjamin, 205
Balestier, Wolcott, 176
Ballou, Ellen B., 233
Battiscombe, Georgina, 227
Becquer, Gustavo, 89
Bell, Lady Florence, 13, 225
Bennett, Arnold, 3-4
Benson, Arthur C., 225
Benson, Edward W., 25
Berg Collection, New York Public Li-
  brary, 122, 237
Bentzon, Th., 175, 233
Bertram, James, 226
Besant, Walter, 43, 153, 227
Beyschlag, Willibald, 175, 233
Biblical criticism, 15, 21-2, 31, 43,
  63, 71, 75-6, 84, 85, 91-4, 118,
  131-3, 155, 166, 169, 195, 200-1,
  213, 219
Bixby, James T., 179
Blackwood, William, 102, 230
Bodleian Library, 70, 81-2, 86, 112,
  147
Boner, Charles, 226
Bonhoeffer, Dietrich, 15
Book of Common Prayer, 28, 188,
  201
Borough Farm, 117, 120, 127
Boyle, Clara, 227
Bradlaugh, Charles, 131
Broad Churchmanship, 153-4, 174,
  188

Brontë, Charlotte, 102-5, 107, 111, 186
Brontë, Emily, 103-4, 140-1
Brooke, Stopford, 4, 88, 136, 168, 193, 234
Browning, Elizabeth Barrett, 102
Browning, Robert, 35, 90, 196
Brunetière, Ferdinand, 162
Bulwer-Lytton, Edward, 47-9
Bunsen, C. K. J., Baron von, 226
Bunyan, John 24
Burke, Edmund, 6
Burne-Jones, Edward, 162
Burns, Robert, 102
Burton, H. D., 181
Bywater, Ingram, 67

Cambridge, 62-3, 131
Campbell, Lewis, 225
Capel, Thomas J., 39
Carlyle, Thomas, 3, 14, 16, 80-1, 96-7, 119, 135, 137, 192, 216-7, 231
Casaubon, Isaac, 71
Cassels, Walter R., 219
Chabot, E., 182
Christensen, Merton A., 225
Church of England, 22-3, 26, 32-4, 38-9, 69, 73-5, 97, 131-2, 188-90, 192-7, 201-3, 205-6
Clarke, Campbell, 225
Clough, Anne, 45
Clough, Arthur Hugh, 20, 35, 119, 151, 158
Cobbe, Frances P., 33, 121, 233
Coit, Dr Stanton, 174
Colenso, Bishop John W., 197
Coleridge, Sir J. T., 49, 225-6
Coleridge, Samuel T., 20
Comte, Auguste, 66, 82-3, 147, 154
Conway, Moncure, 160, 228, 232
Cooper, Thomas, 153
Copyright law, 176, 178
Corelli, Marie, 181
Cornish, George, 227
Cowell, Herbert, 172-3
Craddock, Mrs E. H., 151
Craik, George, 88, 110-1, 230
Cranbrook, Revd James, 136
Craufurd, Alexander H. G., 232
Crawley, Charles, 228
Creeds, 79, 188-9, 195, 200-1
Creighton, Louise, 65, 83, 106, 188, 194-5, 227, 229, 234

Creighton, Mandell, 62, 83, 85-6, 109, 132, 135, 189, 229, 234
Cropper, Mary, 189-90
Cropper family, 114
Crowther, Margaret A., 231
Cunliffe, Mrs, 49, 61, 115
Curtius, Ernst, 67

Dante Alighieri, 150
Darwin, Charles, 148, 217
Davidson, Randall, 160, 169, 173, 232
Deland, Margaret, 175
DeLaura, David J., 226
Denison, Edward, 153
Deutsch, Samuel M., 219
Dickens, Charles, 8, 18, 46
Dilke, Sir Charles, 228
Dissenting sects, 22
Dodgson, Charles, 83
d'Oillamson, Mme, 234
Doubleday, F. N., 193, 204, 235
Down, T. C., 227
Doyle, Sir Arthur Conan, 2, 224
Drew, Mary, 225, 232-3

Ecce Homo, 81
Edel, Leon, 232
Edwardian period, 2
Eliot, George, 3, 4, 102-3, 107, 115, 142, 157, 162, 170-1, 203
Eliot, T. S., 130, 152
Elliot, Walter, 234
Ellis, Havelock, 1, 224
Emerson, Ralph W., 35
Essays and Reviews (1860), 62, 69-70, 72, 75, 197, 203
Eucharist, 23, 79, 187, 189-90, 202
Evans, Margaret, 230

Ferrier, Susan, 143
Fields, Annie, 176, 194
Forster, William E., 6, 39, 119
Fox How, 19, 26-8, 36-7, 44-6, 54, 56, 118-9, 209, 213
Freeman, E. A., 86, 229
Froude, James A., 12-3, 16, 132, 141
Froude, Richard Hurrell, 24, 198, 225
Furnivall, Frederick J., 227

Garnier, Francis, 89
Gaskell, Elizabeth, 103, 107, 111,

139, 226
Giberne, Maria, 226
Gilbert, Revd C. R., 174
Gillette, William, 182
Gissing, George, 3, 153, 216
Gladstone, William E., 14, 17, 78, 90,
   92, 103, 138, 145, 163-9, 173,
   178, 200, 209, 225, 228-9, 231-5
Goethe, Johann W. von, 141
Gosse, Edmund, 91
Graves, Charles L., 225
Green, Alice (Mrs J. R.), 153, 232
Green, Charlotte (Mrs T. H.), 136,
   203, 228
Green, John Richard, 81, 86, 135,
   153, 229
Green, Thomas Hill, 43, 73, 76-9, 94,
   98, 100, 112, 130, 133-4, 136,
   166, 217, 229
Greenhill, W. A., 226
Grove, George, 24, 88
Guardian, 87, 99, 161, 170
Gunsaulus, Revd Frank, 180
Guyon, Mme, 142, 216

Hale, Edward Everett, 179
Hampden, R. D., 24, 197
Hardy, Thomas, 101, 141
Harper Brothers, 176
Harnack, Adolf, 219
Harris, Frank, 4, 226
Harrison, Frederic, 168, 203
Haweis, Revd Hugh R., 174, 231,
   233
Hawthorne, Nathaniel, 55, 81
Hearn, J., 225
Hecker, Isaac, 186
Hegelianism, 76, 94, 147
Hepburn, James, 224
Hertz, Mrs William, 72
Hetherington, Helena, 181, 234
Holland, H. S., 78
Holmes, Oliver Wendell, 162
Holroyd, Michael, 224
Honnold Library, 44, 122, 213, 223,
   237
Hort, F. J. A., 63
Houghton, Walter E., 238
Howe, Julia Ward, 179
Howells, William D., 55
Hughes, Hugh Price, 174
Hume, David, 180, 218
Hutton, R. H., 20, 22, 172, 225

Huws Jones, Enid, 2, 234
Huxley, Julian, 160, 226, 232
Huxley, Leonard, 226, 230
Huxley, T. H., 80, 153, 162, 169,
   196, 233

Inge, William, 1-2, 210, 224, 235
Ingersoll, Robert G., 162, 180
Irving, Washington, 48

Jacks, Lawrence P., 224, 233-5
James, Henry, 9, 11, 105, 109, 152,
   159, 161-2, 167, 195, 232
James, William, 194
Jesus, 20-1, 78, 84, 91, 93-5, 148-9,
   155, 172, 176, 189, 196-7, 201
Johnson, Arthur, 83
Johnson, Bertha (Mrs Arthur), 66,
   83-4, 228
Johnston, John O., 228
Jowett, Benjamin, 20, 30, 33, 65, 73-
   6, 79, 81, 84, 86, 100, 112, 133,
   144, 154, 160, 168, 173, 190,
   225, 228, 232-3

Keble, John, 225
Keim, Theodor, 91
Kempis, Thomas à, 216
Kenyon, John, 29
Kingsley, Charles, 16, 30, 62, 134-5,
   228
Kipling, Rudyard, 232
Knight, William 226
Knowles, James, 83, 92, 103, 153,
   164-5, 229, 232

Lake, W. C., 28
Lamb, Charles, 47
Lang, Andrew, 162, 174
Lederer, Clara, 231
Liddon, H. P., 62-5, 67, 228
Lightfoot, J. B., 63
Lippincott, 176
Locke, Joseph, 114
London's East End, 135, 152-4
Longsleddale, 114-6, 137, 194, 199,
   214-7
Lovell, John W., 176-7, 221
Lovett, William, 153
Luther, Martin, 201-2
Lyman, Revd Albert J., 179
Lyttelton, Alfred, 130, 231
Lyttelton, Arthur, 200

Lyttelton, Edith S., 231
Lyttelton, Laura (Mrs Alfred), 130, 133

Mabie, Hamilton W., 233
Macaulay, Rose, 34
Macaulay, Thomas B., 116, 217-8
Macmillan, Alexander, 89
Macmillan, Frederick, 230
Macmillan Company, 88, 90, 108, 110-1, 145, 176-7, 221, 223, 229, 237
Macmillan's Magazine, 86, 88-91, 96, 98-101, 105, 107-8, 110, 229
Maison, Margaret, 49, 52, 227
Maitland, Frederic W., 231
Major, H. D. A., 234
Manchester Guardian, 110, 128, 165, 170-1, 201, 204
Mare, Margaret L., 227
Marshall, Jane, 226
Martineau, Harriet, 54
Martineau, James, 154, 160
Martinet, J. Van Loenen, 175, 233
Matthews, A. J., 228
Maugham, Somerset, 2, 224
May, Miss, 38
Mayor, John E. B., 234
Mill, John Stuart, 86, 196
Mitford, Mary Russell, 226
Modernism, 32, 162, 187-8, 192-8, 201, 206
Mommsen, Theodor, 162
Montague, Francis C., 228
Montefiore, Claude, 194
Moorman, Mary, 223, 237
More, Paul E., 20, 225
Morgan, Charles L., 230
Morley, John, 89-90, 108, 110, 113, 115, 117, 154, 157, 224, 229-30, 232
Morris, Mowbray, 90
Mudie's Library, 170, 176
Murray, John, III, 232
Murray's Magazine, 90

Nettleship, R. L., 217, 228
New Zealand, 27, 35-6
Newman, John Henry, 14, 21, 23-5, 34, 36-8, 40, 62, 64, 68-9, 97-8, 144, 151, 166, 198, 202, 225-7
Nightingale, Florence, 195, 228
Nowell-Smith, Simon, 233

Oakley, Frederick, 39
Oratory, (Birmingham), 37-8
Oxford, 7, 19, 34-6, 38-40, 44, 52, 56, 60-84, 110, 112, 129-31, 133, 144, 165-6, 172, 208, 232
Oxford Movement, 23, 62, 68

Pall Mall Gazette, 87, 89, 163, 165, 171-2, 238
Palmer, A. M., 234
Parker, Dr Joseph, 181
Passmore Edwards Settlement, 183, 197
Paston, George, 232
Pater, Walter, 10-1, 16, 59, 83, 89, 91, 96, 98-9, 109, 128, 133, 161, 170, 230
Pattison, Emilia F. (Mrs Mark; afterwards Dilke), 65-7, 72, 151, 228, 232
Pattison, Mark, 60, 62, 65-76, 81-4, 90, 101, 113, 131, 141, 144-5, 154, 155, 166, 226-8, 231
Payne, Joseph, 153, 217
Percival, Alicia C., 27
Percival, Dr John, 116, 216
Peterson, William S., 223, 230
Phelps, William Lyon, 4, 224
Pius IX, 38
Porter, Jane, 47
Positivism, 80
Potter, Beatrice (afterwards Webb), 232
Pound, Ezra, 3
Pusey, Edward B., 64, 67
Pusey House Library, 223-4, 237

Ranke, Leopold von, 67
Rashdall, Revd Hastings, 203
Reade, Winwood, 116, 123, 216
Redington, C. T., 228
Renan, Ernest, 67, 100-1, 135, 180, 196, 213, 219, 230
Reusch, Franz, 186
Rickards, Edith C., 227
Robert Elsmere: as concealed autobiography, 15-6, 96, 113, 121, 133-5, 147, 173; as roman à clef, 109, 116, 132-6, 174; chronology, 132-3, 231; clerical response, 174, 180, 250-1; critical analysis, 131-58; dramatized version, 182-3, 234; fictional sequels and re-

plies, 181-2; geographical symbolism, 137-41; 'New Brotherhood
of Christ', 33-4, 138-9, 154-5,
173, 183, 188, 219; notebook,
115-6, 122, 213-20; pirated editions, 176-7, 221; problem of testimony, 93, 123-4, 148; radical
aspects, 154-6; reception, 86, 92,
131, 159-84, 233, 248-51; representative character, 13-4, 146-7,
180; sales, 159, 176-7, 221-2;
themes repeated in Mrs Ward's
other novels, 185-206; translations, 159, 175; writing and revising, 108-30
    Characters: Agnes, 115, 216,
218; Catherine, 115-7, 123, 126,
133, 137-43, 150-2, 157, 162,
180, 192, 198, 214-6, 218; Elsmere, 112, 115-7, 119, 123-6,
132-58 passim, 161-2, 172, 180,
188, 218-9; Grey, 77-8, 115, 133-
4; 149, 218; Langham, 53, 81,
101, 110, 115, 124-5, 133, 151,
218-9, 232; Madame de Netteville, 121, 124-5, 152, 156-7, 217,
231; Rose, 110, 115, 122, 124-6,
133, 138-9, 151-2, 161-2, 180,
199, 216, 218, 232; Wendover,
76, 81, 104, 115, 123-4, 126,
133, 137, 144-8, 151, 157, 162,
171, 180, 218-9, 231
Robinson, Henry Crabb, 26, 30
Robinson, Bishop John A. T., 15
Rodgers, John, 234
Roman Catholic Church, 24, 36-42,
68, 71, 95, 162, 175, 186-7, 197
Root, E. Merrill, 224
Ross, Robert, 227
Rousseau, Jean-Jacques, 90, 96, 147
Royden, Maude, 234
Rugby School, 20, 25, 27-8
Ruskin, John, 55, 57, 81, 111, 137
Russell, Lord Arthur, 129, 163
Russell, George W. E., 165, 225
Ryals, Clyde de L., 231

Sabatier, Paul, 197, 235
St John, Ambrose, 38
St Paul, 78, 170, 193
St Theresa, 100
Sainte-Beuve, C. A., 89
Sand, George, 35, 161

Sanders, Charles R., 224
Sandwith, Humphry, 229
Saturday Review, 86, 98, 170
Sayce, A. H., 62, 227
Scaliger, Joseph, 71-2
Schell, Hermann, 186
Scherer, Edmond, 109, 128, 162,
171, 230, 232-3
Scott, C. P., 110
Scott, Sir Walter, 46-8, 139
Senancour, E. P. de, 97, 151
Shairp, J. C., 226
Shakespeare, William, 141
Sharp, William, 171
Shaw, George Bernard, 4
Shaw, Revd Hudson, 195, 234
Shelley, Percy B., 220
Shorter, C. K., 134, 226
Shorthouse, J. H., 96, 98, 160, 163-
4, 230, 232
Shorthouse, Sarah, 230, 232
Sidgwick, Arthur, 231
Sidgwick, E. Mildred, 231
Sidgwick, Henry, 78, 133, 229
Skene, Felicia, 56, 82, 156, 232
Smiles, Samuel, 5
Smith, George, 30, 32, 91, 102, 104,
110-1, 118, 120, 122-3, 127-30,
159, 168, 170, 176, 178, 181,
183, 186, 190, 223-4, 230-1,
233
Smith, Goldwin, 6
Smith, Reginald, 190, 193, 204, 223,
229, 234-5
Smith, Warren S., 216, 230
Smith, Elder, and Company, 56, 110-
1, 120, 190, 193, 221-2, 237
Sparrow, John H., 231
Stanley, Arthur P., 20, 34, 83, 112,
225-6, 228
Statham, F. Reginald, 231
Stephen, Leslie, 135
Stephenson, Lady Gwendolen, 232
Sterling, John, 132, 135, 217
Stern, Madeleine B., 233
Stevenson, Robert Louis, 91
Stocks, 7, 11, 204, 207-8
Strachey, Lytton, 2
Strauss, David F., 218
Stubbs, William, 86
Stuckenberg, J. H. W., 233
Swanwick, Anna, 228, 232
Symonds, John Addington, 228

Taine, Hippolyte, 82, 86, 115, 162, 229-30, 232
Tait, Archibald, 136
Talbot, E. S., 160, 163, 203, 232
Talbot, Mrs E. S., 165-6
Tauchnitz, Christian B. von, 175
Temple, Frederick, 69
Tennant, Margot (afterwards Asquith), 133, 231-3
Tennyson, Alfred, 8-14, 16, 89, 102, 105, 145, 152, 156-7
Thackeray, William M., 107, 111
Thirty-nine Articles, 20
Thompson, Edith, 229
Thompson, Revd James M., 197, 203
Thursfield, James, 83, 228
Times, The, 4, 6, 59, 84, 87, 91, 170, 172, 188, 204, 238
Tollemache, Lionel A., 228
Tolstoy, Leo, 4, 91, 102, 106
Townsend Meredith, 124, 147, 171
Toynbee, Arnold, 188
Toynbee Hall, 154
Trevelyan, George O., 217-8
Trevelyan, Janet P. (née Ward), 223
Trilling, Lionel, 13, 225
Trollope, Anthony, 2, 4, 8
Tuckwell, Gertrude, 228
Tuckwell, Rosa, 228
Turgenev, Ivan, 102
Twain, Mark, 161, 232
Tyrrell, George, 197
Tyrrell, Robert Y., 174, 194

Unitarianism, 136, 154, 189, 201
University Hall settlement, 93, 183

Van Diemen's Land, 27, 35-7
Victorian period, 2, 6, 11-3, 119, 133, 136, 147, 211-2
Voltaire, 94, 181
Voysey, Charles, 73, 197, 203

Wace, Henry, 92, 173, 233
Walker, John, 216
Walrond, Theodore, 35
Ward, Arnold, 7, 17, 71, 191, 194, 229, 235
Ward, Basil, 223, 237
Ward, Dorothy, 166, 194, 204, 234, 237
Ward, Gertrude, 114, 117-8, 120, 153, 237

Ward, Mary A. (Mrs Humphry): and the Arnold family, 17-42; antisuffrage activities, 7-8, 91, 194; at Oxford, 61-84; bibliography of writings, 238-47; conservatism, 6-8, 199-200; critical writings, 85-107; financial problems, 191-2, 198, 208; funeral, 1; illnesses, 118-9; juvenile fiction, 43-60, 145, 211; literary reputation, 1-5; moral attitudes, 5-6, 34, 46-7, 59-60, 99, 105-7, 124, 151-2, 199-200; on French values, 105-7; on liturgical reform, 188, 193, 201; on miracles, 93-4, 154; on modern psychology, 200-1, on novels and novelists, 46-7, 101-7; on spiritual autobiography, 95-101; on the intellect, 51-2, 81-2, 145-6; on women, 7-8, 49-51, 57-9, 199; Puritanism, 55, 152; religious fiction, 13; religious writings, 92-5, 188-9; Spanish scholarship, 48, 81, 86, 88-90, 92-3, 148, 173; theological views, 21-2, 40-2, 112-4, 136-8, 154-6, 164-5, 169, 188-90, 201-2, 206, 209-11

Works: Amiel's Journal, 90, 99, 102, 114, 117-8, 130, 163; Canadian Born, 1; The Case of Richard Meynell, 13, 74-5, 183, 190-206, 251-2; Daphne, 192, 194; Delia Blanchflower, 8; The Dictionary of Christian Biography, 84, 92-3, 134, 148, 173; Eleanor, 13, 104, 186-8; Eltham House, 81, 190; England's Effort, 209; Fenwick's Career, 10, 106; Fields of Victory, 209; Haworth Brontë edition, 89, 91, 104-5; Helbeck of Bannisdale, 11, 13, 41-2, 71-2, 85, 104, 149, 186; The History of David Grieve, 5, 13, 104, 106-7, 153, 185-6, 191; Lady Connie, 59-61, 64, 67, 73; Lady Rose's Daughter, 47, 54, 58, 204; Marcella, 9-10, 18, 30, 47, 58-9, 134, 188, 191, 204; The Marriage of William Ashe, 6, 47, 207; The Mating of Lydia, 10; Milly and Olly, 19, 44-5, 108; Miss Bretherton, 32, 44, 85, 90, 108-10, 114, 179, 211; Missing,

209-11; *A Morning in the Bodleian*, 70, 82; 'The New Reformation', 92, 169, 189; *Robert Elsmere* (*see* separate entry); *Sir George Tressady*, 106, 191, 193; *The Story of Bessie Costrell*, 3; *The Testing of Diana Mallory*, 148; *Towards the Goal*, 106, 209; *Unbelief and Sin*, 112-4, 124, 134, 158, 169; *The War and Elizabeth*, 10; 'A Westmoreland Story', 56-7, 211; *A Writer's Recollections*, 17, 43, 63, 65, 80, 102, 115, 121, 145, 185, 208; *Writings* (Westmoreland Edition), 43, 223
Ward, Thomas Humphry, 40, 82-4, 87-8, 117, 119, 129, 165-6, 168, 175, 205, 208, 220, 225-7, 229, 232-4, 237
Warner, Charles Dudley, 102
Webster, Norman W., 230, 238
Wells, H. G., 3
Wendte, Charles W., 180
Wesley, Charles, 24
West, Rebecca, 3, 224
Westcott, B. F., 63

Westmorland, 26-7, 186, 209-10, 213-6
White, Joseph Blanco, 132
Whitridge, Arnold, 225-6
Wilde, Oscar, 31
Williamson, Eugene L., Jr., 225
Wilson, R. F., 225
Wood, Mrs Henry, 49
Woods, Margaret L., 227
Woodward, Francis J., 226
Wordsworth, Dora, 28
Wordsworth, Revd John, 112, 145, 198, 230
Wordsworth, William, 26, 28-9, 96, 115, 137-8; 141, 195, 209-10, 216
Wordsworth, Mrs William, 26, 28-9, 45, 226
Wyfold, Lord, 80

Yonge, Charlotte Mary, 3, 49-50, 52-6, 58-60, 66, 76, 82, 133, 227
Young, Arthur C., 224

Zola, Émile, 106